WOMEN'S DIARIES
OF THE
WESTWARD JOURNEY

Over:
Travel by covered wagon remained a primary means of pioneer travel long after the days of the overland journey.

LILLIAN SCHLISSEL

WOMEN'S DIARIES

OF THE

WESTWARD

JOURNEY

PREFACE BY CARL N. DEGLER

Gerda Lerner
Supervising Editor

Expanded and with a new Introduction by the Author

SCHOCKEN BOOKS · NEW YORK

Library of Congress Cataloging in Publication Data
Main entry under title:
Women's diaries of the westward journey.
(Studies in the life of women)
Bibliography: p.
Includes index.
1. Overland Journeys to the Pacific–Sources.
2. Women–West (U.S.)–History–19th century–Sources.
3. West (U.S.)–History–1848–1950–Sources.
1. Schlissel, Lillian. II. Series.
F593.W65   978′.02   80-54143
                                 AACR2

Studies in the Life of Women
General Editor Gerda Lerner

Design by Lynn Braswell

ISBN: 0-8052-1004-0
Manufactured in the United States of America

79B86

to my mother,
Mae Fischer,
and to my children
Rebecca
and Daniel,
who will have
roads of their own to travel

CONTENTS

THE DIARIES

PHOTOGRAPHS

viii

ON PHOTOGRAPHY

*The invention of photography
exerted a profound influence on
American society. By 1845,
daguerrotypy had become a
popular enterprise, with studios in
almost every major city. Quite
apart from the pure wonder of the
image, Americans who moved
about restlessly felt a profound
need to carry along some souvenir
of loved ones they had left behind.
The son who had gone off to the
gold rush, the daughter who had
married and gone to live in a
distant territory, the child who
had died before it learned to
walk—such portraits were the
priceless possessions of all classes
of Americans.*

*Nowhere more than on the
frontier were photographs so
passionately prized. Pleas for
family pictures filled the letters of
those who found themselves in
Oregon and California. As soon as
photographers could be found,
emigrants had formal pictures
taken to send back home. Candid
pictures were rare; studio
photographs were more common,
and many of the photographs of
women in this book were taken
years after the overland journey.
These women were posing for their
own families and for kinfolk back
home, showing how they had
prospered in the western lands.*

I write on my lap with the wind rocking the wagon.

—Algeline Ashley

PREFACE

Almost twenty years ago the late historian David Potter pointed out that one of the most influential interpretations of the American experience was based upon a fallacy. He was referring to Frederick Jackson Turner's famous hypothesis that the frontier was the key influence in the making of the character of the American people. Turner's argument was that because the United States evolved in a region of unsettled land, the conquest of that open land made Americans, among other things, individualistic, active, believers in progress, and democratic. Yet, as Potter observed, the Americans who acquired these traits in the course of cutting down forests, plowing up the tough prairie sod, fighting the Indians, and founding new governments constituted only half of the population. Women engaged in none of these activities. The frontier and the West in general, Potter implied, must have been a quite different experience for women than it was for men.

Lillian Schlissel, in her fascinating evocation of the westering experience of American women, has brought Potter's observation to life by telling us the stories of flesh-and-blood women on the Overland Trail. Although she believes that the two sexes saw the overland trek with different eyes, her method in this book has not been simply to draw conclusions or to drive home her argument. Rather, the great value of the book is that it permits the reader to experience through the writings of more than a hundred women what it was like to make that trip across the continent to Oregon or California between 1840 and 1870. Although pioneering is often seen as a masculine activity, the overland journey was a family matter. Women were essential to the success of the enterprise as they later were to the settlement of the coastal areas toward which they travelled. For women, this book shows, not only performed their womanly tasks on the trail, but also took over men's work when necessity arose.

One of the several important conclusions that emerges from these carefully organized and forcefully told stories of actual women's lives is that even though women were often drawn into performing tasks far removed from their usual domestic duties, in the end they clung almost possessively to their traditional roles. More than that, they created and maintained to the extent that they could under the circumstances those networks of support that they had known in their more traditional—and stationary—homes. Although other historians in writing about the overland experience of women and men have emphasized the similarity in the outlook of the two sexes, the life histories described in this book provide a basis for the opposite conclusion. As Schlissel points out, if the adventure of the overland journey often came at an opportune time in a young man's search for success in an America that extolled it, for a woman that same experience came at the most inconvenient time in her life cycle. Virtually all of the women who made the trek were married, and of such an age as to be vulnerable to pregnancy and during a historical period when contraception devices were at best unreliable and at worst unknown or considered immoral. About 20 percent of the women Schlissel discusses were pregnant or gave birth in the course of the move West. Some even became pregnant during the trip despite the painful lack of privacy for people to whom the taboos of sex and other bodily functions were completely controlling. Some women, for instance, could not even mention in their private diaries that they were pregnant. They merely noted the arrival of a baby! (And as Schlissel points out, none of the accounts provided the slightest clue as to how women managed to relieve themselves privately while traveling for weeks across the treeless, flat plains in the constant and close company of men.)

The differences between men's views and women's views of the overland passage extended beyond the differences in their physiology. Whereas men usually emphasized the danger from the Indians and told of their fights with the native peoples, the women, who admittedly often started out fearful of the Indians, usually ended up finding them friendly in manner and often helpful in deed. Women, it seemed, had no need to emphasize Indian ferocity.

Professor Schlissel has arranged the personal histories of these women so as to give the reader a sense of the movement of people from Independence, Missouri—whence the wagon trains usually started—to the West

Coast. Within that framework she has also suggested how the character of that epic movement altered as more and more people undertook it. The earliest overlanders had to rely upon inadequate information, poorly marked trails and only occasional sources of supply and places for repair along the route. But as the number of people making the trip neared two hundred thousand, the markings became clearer and more frequent, and the services along the way greatly improved. By the time of the Civil War, as one account tells us, some wealthy families were making the once arduous and hazardous journey in style: riding in a stagecoach, accompanied by a full-time male cook with a real stove, and with the money and opportunity to stop off at night at a farmhouse and sleep in a bed.

Professor Schlissel is always careful to tell us when an experience was typical or rare, yet she also manages to recapture the flavor of the broad diversity of people and events that makes the overland migration for us today a source of amazement. For example, there are accounts of black as well as white women on the trail, and two revealing accounts of single women. Rebecca Ketchum of Ithaca, New York, decided she wanted to go to Oregon to become a teacher. So she traveled by stagecoach, unaccompanied by anyone, from Ithaca to Independence, when she joined a group for the remainder of the way to Oregon. Although a woman, but probably because she was single, she spent most of the trip on horseback with the men; the wives apparently did not consider her worthy of riding in the wagon with mothers and children. Ketchum's account also illustrates at least one nineteenth-century woman's clear sense of her own worth. When Ketchum accidentally discovered that she was paying more than others for her place in the wagon train, she refused to do washing any more, since the men—who had paid less than she—were not expected to wash.

Curiously enough, despite the large number of children on the trail, they do not figure very prominently in these accounts. There are, to be sure, examples of children falling out of the wagons, some of whom are almost immediately run over, or of children dying at childbirth or from disease. Some of the most moving stories of hardship and misfortune, it is true, concern children, particularly those who are suddenly orphaned by the rigors of the trail. Yet children, one concludes, were the lesser of the women's worries when their energies, time, and dispositions were under more immediate pressures.

For us today, living in the physically comfortable late twentieth century, the drama and the dangers inherent in the overland journey and the spirit displayed by the women who participated in it are often difficult to feel in our guts. Yet the monotony and meagerness of the overlanders' diet, the discomfort of sleeping in a downpour from which there was usually no escape, the debilitating fatigue brought on by the humid heat of the western plains in summer, and the heavy work involved in moving all day, stopping overnight, and moving again at dawn, come through with powerful immediacy in these firsthand accounts. Through it all, one begins to sense the determination, the faith, and the loyalty that carried these women through. For, in the end, the sharpest difference between men and women on the Trail was that the great majority of the women did not want to make the trip in the first place. No clearer measure of the power of nineteenth-century patriarchy need be sought. We do not know, of course, how many wives refused to leave their settled homes to create one on the move and in the West, and by doing so prevented their husbands from going. But we do know that of those women who agreed to head into the New Country, few did so with enthusiasm. Yet, most of these women survived—many more men died on the trail than women, despite the dangers of childbirth. But they also managed to sustain their families during the ordeal and then went on to create homes in the West. In the accounts by these women we experience their determination and strength, as well as their submission. In the process we gain a clearer idea of what has gone into the making of American women, and what women have contributed to the making of America. Lillian Schlissel has given us the opportunity to appreciate in our hearts as well as in our heads what it was like to be a woman on the Overland Trail. As we read these pages we will laugh, or perhaps cry, but certainly we will exclaim at their achievements and their failures, at their affirmations of life, and at their stubborn resistance to failure and death.

CARL N. DEGLER

INTRODUCTION
TO THE REVISED EDITION

Since *Women's Diaries* was published ten years ago, the women's lives and their words have found resonance with contemporary readers who discovered women of their own families or found themselves moved by the power of the women's words.

The clear voices have always seemed the most compelling magic of the narratives. On rereading, I think more place might have been given to the lighter voices, to girls in the brief years between eight and sixteen for whom that monumental crossing was a lark. Young girls looked for beaux; they shared secrets with other girls, and sometimes they discovered themselves brides at the journey's end. They were young people whose words lighten some of the awesome drama that marked so much of the overland migration.

Susan Parrish, who started her overland journey in 1850 when she was seventeen, remembered: "We were a happy carefree lot of young people, and the dangers and hardships found no resting place on our shoulders. It was a continuous picnic and excitement was plentiful. . . . In the evenings, we gathered about the campfires and played games or told stories." She saved her old violin, and recalled that she used to play dances called "Money Musk" and "Zip Coon" as the "young folks danced in the light of the campfire and the lard burning lanterns." Young people exploded with energy. "We ran races or made swings. There was plenty of frolic and where there were young people gathered together, there is always plenty of love making." There were darker stories in her diary, but the early notes were of youth and good times.

Nancy Snow Bogart, who would be a married woman at sixteen, made the overland crossing when she was only eight. She remembered "We just had the time of our lives." And Barsina Rogers, who was thirteen in 1867 when her family traveled across the southern route into Arizona Territory, practiced her penmanship on the wagon as it inched across the desert.

Rebecca Nutting Woodson, whose account is added to this book, went West when she was fifteen. Her narrative of the crossing was written fifty-nine years later in 1909, but her words are full of the sense of adventure in westering.

LILLIAN SCHLISSEL
New York, 1992

INTRODUCTION

This book began with a fascination for the diaries of the overland women, with the detail of their lives and the dramatic dimensions of their everyday existence. These were ordinary women who were caught up in a momentous event of history. Between 1840 and 1870, a quarter of a million Americans crossed the continental United States, some twenty-four hundred miles of it, in one of the great migrations of modern times. They went West to claim free land in the Oregon and California Territories, and they went West to strike it rich by mining gold and silver. Men and women knew they were engaged in nothing less than extending American possession of the continent from ocean to ocean. No other event of the century except the Civil War evoked so many personal accounts as the overland passage. Young people and even children kept diaries and felt that their lives, briefly, had become part of history. The mundane events of each day—the accidents and the mishaps and the small victories—had grown significant. In the case of women, suddenly, because of their diaries, their daily lives became accessible, where so much of the life of nineteenth-century women has disappeared from view.

The westward movement was a major transplanting of young families. All the kinfolk who could be gathered assembled to make that hazardous passage together. Women were part of the journey because their fathers, husbands, and brothers had determined to go. They went West because there was no way for them *not* to go once the decision was made.

The emigrants came from Missouri, Illinois, Iowa, and Indiana, and some all the way from New York and New Hampshire. Most of them had moved to "free land" at least once before, and their parents and grandparents before them had similarly made several removals during their lifetime. These were a class of "peasant proprietors." They had owned land before and would own land again. They were young and consumed with boundless confidence, believing the better life tomorrow could be won by the hard work of today. Emblematic of their determination was Barsina French, who fastidiously copied penmanship and grammatical exercises into her diary as the oxen led her parents' wagon across the empty plains.

The journey started in the towns along the Missouri River between St. Joseph and Council Bluffs. These settlements came to be known as the "jumping-off places." In the winter months emigrants gathered to join wagon parties and to wait for the arrival of kin. It was an audacious journey through territory that was virtually unknown. Guidebooks promised that the adventure would take no more than three to four months time—a mere summer's vacation. But the guidebooks were wrong. Often there was no one in a wagon train who really knew what the roads would bring, or if there were any roads at all. Starting when the mud of the roads began to harden in mid-April, the emigrants would discover that the overland passage took every ounce of ingenuity and tenacity they possessed. For many, it would mean six to eight months of grueling travel, in a wagon with no springs, under a canvas that heated up to 110° by midday, through drenching rains and summer storms. It would mean swimming cattle across rivers and living for months at a time in tents.

Over eight hundred diaries and day journals kept by those who made the overland journey have been published or catalogued in archives, and many more are still in family collections. As a general category, the nineteenth-century diary is something like a family history, a souvenir meant to be shared like a Bible, handed down through generations, to be viewed not as an individual's story but as the history of a family's growth and course through time. Overland diaries were a special kind of diary, often meant to be published in county newspapers or sent to relatives intending to make the same journey the following season. Many of them are filled with information about the route, the watering places, the places where one could feed the cattle and oxen, and the quality of the grasses along the way. Such diaries seldom contain expression of intimate feelings, but there are occasions when emotions flash out, beyond control and sharp.

The story of the Overland Trail has been told many times, and emigrant diaries have been used before in these histories. Merrill Mattes, in his study *The Great Platte River Road*, drew upon some six hundred diaries as he described the Trail from the Missouri to the South Pass of the Rockies.[1] And other historians, among them John Faragher, Howard Lamar, Julie

Roy Jeffrey, and John Unruh, have used such diaries as the bases for revisions of different aspects of the West's history.[2] No study, though, has been woven entirely out of the stuff of the women's writing in order to assess whether our picture of this single event of history, the overland experience, is in significant manner altered by the perception of the women.

Working with personal papers—letters and diaries—presents the historian with special problems. As documents, these items are the accounts of singularities. They record the particular moment and the personal response. Therefore it is necessary to determine whether they are merely idiosyncratic and anomalous, or whether they form part of a larger configuration that contains and explains disparate events. Only when the patterns emerge with regularity can one believe the responses are representative.[3]

This narrative is made of the diaries, reminiscences, and letters of 103 women, a random sample among the thousands of women who went West. These are the diaries of white women, many of them daughters of second and third generation American families. Some attempt is made to include the experiences of black women, many of whom went West as slaves. White or black, these women neither directed events nor affected the course of the journey. They were ordinary women in ordinary families, and the question is whether, as their story unfolds, the historical event takes on new dimension.

What I have looked for in reading these diaries were places where the women seemed to see something different than their men saw. What I asked was whether the overland experience, studied so many times before, would be revealed in a new aspect through the writings of women, and whether such perspective as the women bring might prove to be historically valuable.

The first step was to reconstruct from the diaries in fine detail the daily lives of the women, to separate out of the diaries those writings that pertained to the "woman's sphere." In the course of describing the daily life of the women, I came to see the design of the emigrant family and something of the dimensions of its emotional balances and work roles. For while it is true that family history cannot be reconstructed from women's writings alone, nevertheless the women were the shapers of the family, and it is they who provide us with primary access to the internal dynamics of households.

Certain dimensions emerged simply and easily. For example, marriage was the social norm accepted by both men and women, although within the structure of marriage men were considerably more free. Great numbers of men went West, leaving their wives and children at home; women, in contrast, almost always traveled within a family structure.

Most marriages seemed companionable. They were entered into in recognition that farming and particularly the work of making a farm out of a frontier was work that required a large family if it were to succeed. Dynamics within the family, what historian John Faragher has termed the "political economy of sex," was determined by the work of each partner, but the balance of power always followed upon the strong prescriptions of patriarchy.[4] Men were the heads of households, and while frontier women were often called upon to perform "men's work," those additional chores did not yield them any extra perquisites.

On the Overland Trail, women strove to be equal to the demands of the day. They asked no special help or treatment. They responded to the spectacular beauty of the land, and they took keen interest in the economies of the road, recording the costs of ferriage and food supplies. They were as knowledgeable as men about the qualities of grasses for the animals. They understood what was expected of them and endeavored to do their share of the work of each day.

The women on the Overland Trail did the domestic chores: they prepared the meals and washed the clothes and cared for the children. But they also drove the ox teams and collected pieces of dung they called "buffalo chips" to fuel their fires when there was no wood. And when there were no buffalo chips, they walked in clouds of dust behind the wagons, collecting weeds. They searched for wild berries and managed to roll some dough on a wagon seat and bake a pie over hot rocks in order to lift meals out of the tedium of beans and coffee.

For women traveling with small children, the overland experience could be nerve-wracking. Children fell out of the wagons. They got lost among the hundreds of families and oxen and sheep. Children suffered all the usual childhood ills—measles, fevers, toothaches, diarrhea. But on the Trail, children who were drenched by days of heavy rains or burned by hot sun could be especially irritable and hard to care for. Free from supervision, older children were full of excitement and mischief. Their mothers worried constantly that Indians would steal them.

For women who were pregnant, the overland crossing could be a nightmare. One never knew for certain where labor might begin: in Indian territory, or in the mountains, or in drenching rain. One might be alone, with no women to help, and only fear at hand. The birth might be simple, or it might be complicated and tortuous. Among rural Americans of the nineteenth century, pregnancy and impending birth were not reasons to defer the decision to move, not when free land lay at the journey's end.

It has been suggested by historian Howard Lamar and psychiatrist Daniel Levinson that the overland passage played a vital role in the life cycle of men, corresponding to "breaking away," improving, or bettering oneself, the stages that mark a man's life.[5] If experiences attain mythic dimension because some pattern in all the endless variety reverberates against the fixed frame of human needs and yearnings, if the westward migration became an expression of testing and reaching for men, then it surely must have been an "anti-mythic" journey for women. It came when the physical demands of their lives drained their energies into other directions.[6] The severity of the dislocation of the journey can be gauged in the knowledge that about one of every five overland women was seized by some stage of pregnancy, and virtually every married woman traveled with small children. When women wrote of the decision to leave their homes, it was almost always with anguish, a note conspicuously absent from the diaries of men.

The diaries of men and women carry certain predictable characteristics, with men writing of "fight, conflict and competition and . . . hunting," and women writing of their concerns with "family and relational values."[7] But it is not true, as some have concluded, that the diaries of men and of women are essentially alike.[8] Although many women, along with the men, wrote of the splendors of the landscape and the rigors of the road, although many overland diaries seem tediously interchangeable, there are not only important distinctions, but distinctions so profound as to raise the question whether women did not ultimately perceive the westward trek differently. Traveling side by side, sitting in the very same wagons, crossing the continent in response to the call for free land, women did not always see the venture in the clear light of the expectation of success. There were often shadows in their minds, areas of dark reservation and opposition. The diaries of women differ from the accounts of the men in both simple and in subtle ways. In the diaries of the women for example, the Indians are described as helpful guides and purveyors of services far more often than they are described as enemies. Although the women universally feared the Indians, they nevertheless tell, with some amusement, that their farmer-husbands were not always good buffalo hunters, coming back to the wagon parties empty-handed and later trading shirts with the Indians for salmon and dried buffalo meat. The women, in the naturalness of their telling, offer a new perception of the relations between the emigrants and the Indians. Having no special stake in asserting their bravery, having no special need to affirm their prowess, the women correct the historical record as they write of the daily exchanges by which the Indians were part of life of the road. [9]

New configurations continue to appear when one reads the women's diaries closely. One of the commonplaces of rural life was the absence of men for periods that varied from weeks to months and years. Many of the men who traveled the Oregon Trail alone had left behind them their wives and their children, and they might be gone for two years or more. During these periods women were expected to serve as head of the household as well as of the farm or of any commercial enterprise—a mill or a store—that the family owned. On the Overland Trail, when a woman was widowed, she was expected to continue with her children and to file her claim alone. No widow ever placed her wagon and her family under the protection of another family. The expectation was that women would direct the family enterprise independently when need arose. There are indices that in the partiarchal values of rural communities there were interfaces where women were more independent—and independent in more ways—than has been commonly assumed.

In another aspect the women's diaries differ from the diaries written by men. As ritual caretakers of the sick and the dying, the women saw the real enemies of the road as disease and accident. It is in womens' diaries that we are reminded that the heaviest emigration of the Overland Trail was accomplished during years of cholera epidemic. As travelers hurried across the continent to the "rag towns" of California and Nevada in order to pan the clear streams for gold, cholera swept over the Trail.

Nowhere in the world could it have been more bleak to be stricken than on an open and unmarked road, to be left by the side of the Trail either to recover or to die. The women write of the deaths and the burials. They tell of typhoid, mountain fever, measles, dysentery and drownings. The women knew that disease and accident killed more emigrants than did Indians. The women, whose job it was to care for the dying, carefully noted the cost of the westward movement in human life. Whereas men recorded the death in aggregate numbers, the women knew death as personal catastrophe and noted the particulars of each grave site, whether it was newly dug or old, whether of a young person or an adult, whether it had been disturbed by wolves or by Indians. The women were the actuaries of the road, tallying the miles with the lives that were lost. One must suspect, finally, that many women judged the heroic adventure of their men as some kind of outrageous folly thrust upon them by obedience to patriarchal ritual.

In their accommodation to the life of the road, the women tried to weave a fabric of accustomed design, a semblance of their usual domestic circle.

Out of the disorder of traveling, the women created and held on to some order and routine. Against all odds, they managed to feed their families, do the wash, and care for the scattering children. They strove to calm the quarreling men, to keep a diary record of passing friends and families, to note who took the children when parents died on the road, to note carefully the names on the grave markers. The women even managed to bear new life on the crest of the journey's upheaval.

In the end, a woman who came through the journey felt she had won her own victory. The test of the journey was whether or not she had been equal to the task of holding her family together against the sheer physical forces that threatened to spin them to the four winds of chance. It was against the continual threat of dissolution that the women had striven. If ever there was a time when men and women turned their psychic energies toward opposite visions, the overland journey was that time. Sitting side by side on a wagon seat, a man and a woman felt different needs as they stared at the endless road that led into the New Country.

Overland women recorded their pride in having preserved the integrity of family life intact in the names they gave to the children born on the Trail. Gertrude Columbia was born on the shores of the surging Columbia River. Alice Nevada drew first breath in the rocky lands of the Sierra Nevada. Gila Parrish was born somewhere along the Gila River in Arizona. Two children lived, and one child died. The New Country, the women knew in a profound way, was a bittersweet promise that took its own toll of hope and of optimism.

In the very commonplace of their observations, the women bring us a new vision of the overland experience; they bring it closer to our own lives. They do not write of trailblazing or of adventure but of those facets of living that are unchanging. In reading their diaries we come closer to understanding how historical drama translates into human experience. Through the eyes of the women we begin to see history as the stuff of daily struggle.

NOTES

1. Merrill J. Mattes, *The Great Platte River Road*, Vol. 25, Publications of Nebraska State Historical Society, 1969.

2. John M. Faragher, *Women and Men on the Overland Trail* (New Haven, Yale University Press, 1979). Howard R. Lamar, "Rites of Passage: Young Men and Their Families in the Overland Trail Experience, 1843–69," *Soul-Butter and Hog Wash and Other Essays on the American West*, Charles Redd Monographs in Western History, No. 8 (Provo, Utah, Brigham Young University Press, 1978). Julie Roy Jeffrey, *Frontier Women: The Trans-Mississippi West, 1840–1880* (New York, Hill & Wang, 1979). John Unruh, *The Plains Across: The Overland Emigrants and the Trans-Mississippi West, 1840–60* (Chicago, University of Illinois Press, 1979). See also such works as Dale M. Morgan, ed., *Overland in 1846: Diaries and Letters of the California-Oregon Trail*, 2 vols. (Georgetown, California, Talisman Press, 1963); Irene D. Paden, *The Wake of the Prairie Schooner* (New York, Macmillan, 1943); and George R. Stewart, *The California Trail: An Epic with Many Heroes* (New York, McGraw-Hill, 1962).

3. See Gertrude Ackerman, "Family Papers and the Westward Movement." *Minnesota History* (1939):314–316; Alice Felt Tyler, "The Westward Movement as Reflected in Family Papers," *Minnesota History* (1943):111–124; Gordon W. Allport, *The Use of Personal Documents in Psychological Science* (New York, The Social Science Research Council, 1942); Louis Gottschalk, Clyde Kluckhohn, and Robert Angell, *The Use of Personal Documents in History, Anthropology and Sociology* (Washington, D.C., Social Science Research Council, 1945).

4. John M. Faragher, "Women and Men on the Farming Frontier of Illinois: The Political Economy of Sex," unpublished essay.

5. "For young men [the Overland Trail] was a dramatic rite of passage to mastery and adulthood" Howard R. Lamar, "Rites of Passage," p. 51. Also see Daniel J. Levinson, "The Mid-Life Transition: A Period in Adult Psychosocial Development," *Psychiatry* 40 (1977): 100.

6. For a valuable discussion of the concepts of life-cycle and historical time, see Tamara K. Hareven, "Family Time and Historical Time," *Daedalus*, 106 (1977), 57–70.

16

7. Faragher, *Women and Men on the Overland Trail*, p. 14.

8. Faragher compared twenty-two men's and twenty-eight women's diaries according to a list of fifty-three selected value-topics, and concluded that "the diaries indicate, first and foremost that these mid-nineteenth century men and women were part of a common culture, that they were, indeed, *more alike than different* [emphasis added]. *Ibid.*, p. 15 and Appendix II, Table AII-3, pp. 202–203. In contrast, this study finds that the value topics of the women significantly *differ* from those that prevail in the diaries of men.

9. The picture of the relationship between Indian and emigrant as described by the women in their diaries is substantiated by John Unruh in his excellent study *The Plains Across*.

FAMILIES IN TRANSIT I
1841-1850

The "New Country" to Americans in 1840 was the land of the Oregon and California Territories. California, that far-off Mexican province, was said to be an earthly paradise where the sun always shone and fruit grew wild. Trappers of the Hudson's Bay Company in Oregon reported an unending supply of furs, rich river banks for fishing, and valley land for farming. The claim of the Indians to the lands they had lived on for over a thousand years was universally nullified by the assertion that they had neither tilled the land nor built upon it. Americans saw only "free land," and they were drawn toward it as if by a magnet. They believed in the destiny that decreed the nation's sweep across the entire continent.

The Pacific Northwest Territory, particularly the Willamette Valley, a triangle formed by the Columbia River and the 46th parallel, was an area too rich to be ignored. England's interests were represented by the Hudson's Bay Company and a thousand Englishmen firmly entrenched on small farms that dotted the Puget Sound valley. Americans dominated shipping. So many Yankee ships plied the coastal waters that the Indians came to call any sailor a "Boston."[1]

In 1831, a Massachusetts schoolteacher incorporated the "American Society for Encouraging the Settlement of the Oregon Territory." His ambition was to "repeat with appropriate variations the history of the Puritan colony of Massachusetts Bay."[2] But the real spur to emigration into Oregon was the prolonged depression that swept the country in 1837. By the year's end, banks across the nation had closed, and by 1839 wages fell 30 to 50 percent. Twenty thousand unemployed laborers demonstrated in Philadelphia, and in New York two hundred thousand people were

wondering how they would survive the winter.[3] Horace Greeley told the
unemployed to "go West," but the Midwest was as hard-hit as New York. In
the Mississippi valley, prices fell lower and lower. Wheat was ten cents a
bushel, and corn could be given away. Steamboats on the Mississippi and
the Missouri rivers were burning grain for fuel.[4] As farmers surveyed the
debacle, they could find fewer and fewer reasons not to escape to better
lands.[5]

And there was another factor. In a fashion that men and women of the
twentieth century will never fully understand, farmers of the Mississippi
valley and the Plains states had begun to feel "crowded."[6] One farmer said
that the reason he had to emigrate from western Illinois was that "people
were settling right under his nose," although his nearest neighbor was
twelve miles away. He moved to Missouri, but that did not satisfy, and soon
he abandoned a half-finished clearing and packed his family and household
goods onto a wagon and made his way to Oregon where there was only the
Pacific Ocean beside him.[7]

What a farm family wanted most was a government policy that would
permit a farmer to "squat" on a piece of land, that is, to build a house and
clear the trees, and then after the region had been surveyed, to purchase
his land at the minimum auction price without being outbid by the
speculator. In 1842 the first "Preemption Bill" was passed. It protected the
farmer who had made improvements. It also whetted his appetite for free
land. If a farmer improved new land, "homesteaded," was he not performing a national service and benefiting the national economy by bringing the
wilderness under cultivation?[8]

By 1839 at least ten "Oregon Societies" were formed in the towns of the
Mississippi valley with members pledged to make the westward trek.[9]
Journals of traders and trappers, accounts of missionaries, descriptions of
travelers, government reports, letters of new settlers, guidebooks—all
excited the imagination and promised panacea for both agricultural and
personal problems. A traveler who had gone to the Oregon Territory in 1834
wrote: "The soil . . . is rich beyond comparison. . . . The epidemic of the
[Midwest] country, fever and ague, is scarcely known here. . . . the willa-
met valley is a terrestrial paradise."[10] By the spring of 1843 a major
emigration was in full swing.

The exodus to Oregon was a family affair, although not every member of
the family was equally enthusiastic. This story is typical:

One Saturday morning father said that he was going . . . to hear Mr.
Burnett talk about Oregon. . . . Mr. Burnett hauled a box out on to the

Emigrants in 1866 corralled in Echo Canyon, Nebraska.

sidewalk, took his stand upon it, and began to tell us about the land flowing with milk and honey on the shores of the Pacific . . . he told of the great crops of wheat which it was possible to raise in Oregon, and pictured in glowing terms the richness of the soil and the attractions of the climate, and then with a little twinkle in his eye he said "and they do say, gentlemen, they do say, that out in Oregon the pigs are running about under the great acorn trees, round and fat, and already cooked, with knives and forks sticking in them so that you can cut off a slice whenever you are hungry." . . . Father was so moved by what he heard . . . that he decided to join the company that was going west to Oregon. . . . father . . . was the first to sign his name. . . . [11]

Another frontiersman, Peter Burnett, told his family: "Out in Oregon I can get me a square mile of land. And a quarter section for each of you all. Dad burn me, I am done with this country, Winters it's frost and snow to freeze a body; summers the overflow from Old Muddy drowns half my acres; taxes take the yield of them that's left. What say, Maw, it's God's country." Mothers were hesitant. The new country was two thousand miles away, far from schools and churches, far from kin. But a husband's enthusiasm and optimism swept all doubts away. "Whoo-pee! Let's go, Maw, out yan where the Injuns be."[12]

Soon, there was a road with a thousand people traveling on it, six thousand animals, wagon trains curving along the horizon sometimes five miles long, the new canvas coverings gleaming in the bright sun, the campfires shining at night on both shores of the Missouri and the Platte rivers. The overland migration had begun.

Whether one's sights were set upon the lands of Oregon or of California, all journeys began at one of the many little towns called the "jumping-off places" along the Missouri River. Small towns clustered around Independence, St. Joseph and Council Bluffs. Emigrants would begin arriving at the end of March to wait for the days in early April when the snows had sufficiently melted for the journey to begin. Sometimes they wintered in these towns, preparing their wagons, gathering their supplies, waiting for kinfolk from other states.

Building a wagon and provisioning for the trip were major undertakings. The overland wagon had to be built of seasoned hardwood to withstand extremes of temperature; an ordinary farm wagon was not strong enough to stand up to two thousand miles of hard traveling. The classic prairie schooner was not the big-wheeled, boat-curved Conestoga wagon,* but a smaller, lighter wagon with straight lines top and bottom. Typically, emigrants used a farm wagon with a flat bed about ten feet wide with sides two feet high. Benjamin Bonney recalled that his father worked for months to build a wagon sturdy enough to withstand river crossings and mountain travel. A wagon meant for the overland journey could be loaded with up to twenty-five hundred pounds and required four to six yoke of oxen to pull it. The wagon and the animals might cost four hundred dollars, the largest single expense of the expedition. The wagon was built to be amphibious. A tar bucket hung from the side of each wagon, and the slats were caulked for river crossings. The covering of the wagons was a double thickness of canvas as rainproof as oiled linen, or muslin, or sailcloth could be made to be. Wagon tongues, spokes, axles, and wheels were liable to break, and most emigrants traveled with spare parts slung under the wagon beds.

*The Conestoga wagon was designed by Pennsylvania Dutch craftsmen and was used early in the eighteenth century. Its front and rear panels were slanted and were thought to resemble a frigate.

Grease buckets, water barrels and heavy rope were essential equipment. As wagons deteriorated from overloading or breakage, repairs were made.

Foodstuffs were assembled at the start of the journey. The *Emigrants Guide to Oregon and California*, in 1845, recommended that each emigrant supply himself with 200 pounds of flour, 150 pounds of bacon, 10 pounds of coffee, 20 pounds of sugar, and 10 pounds of salt.[13] Additional supplies included chipped beef, rice, tea, dried beans, dried fruit, saleratus (baking soda), vinegar, pickles, mustard, and tallow. The basic kitchenware was a kettle, fry pan, coffee pot, tin plates, cups, knives, and forks.

Provisions for the journey could cost from three to six hundred dollars, depending on how much the family brought from home. In addition, each family needed a supply of powder, lead, and shot. It needed rifles, too, for an additional sixty or seventy dollars. Thus the basic outfitting cost was between five hundred and one thousand dollars, and emigrants starting east of the Missouri River incurred additional expenses in getting to the jumping-off places from homes in Ohio and western Pennsylvania. Then there was always the need for cash to have on hand through the course of the journey itself: to replace stores that were used up; to pay for the charges of the ferrymen at river crossings; to buy replacements for wagons that had broken or oxen that had gone lame; to buy food through the first winter in the new lands.[14]

Financing the journey along the Overland Trail required liquidating property holdings and selling household goods and farms. It took John and Cornelia Sharp and their seven children four years to save enough money to outfit for the overland journey, and even then John had to borrow $500 from his brother-in-law.[15]

Approximately three hundred fifty thousand men, women and children emigrated to the Pacific Territories. The annual tallies are imposing: see table following page.

Starting on the Missouri River, wagons would continue until the Missouri joined the Platte. Like the Mississippi, that river was a continental waterway, muddy, and stretching a thousand miles. It resembled no other river: "My first impression on beholding the Platte River was, that as it looked so wide and so muddy . . . that it was . . . perfectly impassable. Judge my surprise when I learned that it was only three or four feet deep."[17] The river was sometimes described as "moving sand," and those who did not find it beautiful said it was "hard to ford, destitute of fish, too dirty to bathe in, and too thick to drink."[18] But it was not necessary that the Platte be beautiful; it served the emigrants as a clear road. Following it, emigrants could go across "broad yellow Nebraska," and more than halfway through

WESTWARD MIGRATION[16]					
YEAR	ESTIMATE	YEAR	ESTIMATE	YEAR	ESTIMATE
1841	100	1850	55,000	1859	30,000
1842	200	1851	10,000	1860	15,000
1843	1,000	1852	50,000	1861	5,000
1844	2,000	1853	20,000	1862	5,000
1845	5,000	1854	10,000	1963	10,000
1846	1,000	1855	5,000	1864	20,000
1847	2,000	1856	5,000	1865	25,000
1848	4,000	1857	5,000	1866	25,000
1849	30,000	1858	10,000		
				Total	350,000

Wyoming. For two decades, the Platte formed a two-lane highway with travelers along both of its shores. The road on the northern bank was called the Mormon Trail or the Nebraska City Road or California Road. Interstate 80 today follows the Platte from Omaha to Cheyenne, and one can cover 600 miles in a day, reaching California in three days time. The emigrant in the covered wagon was lucky if he started in April and reached California by October. Many did not end their journeys until November or December.

The overland journey was twenty-four hundred miles long from the Missouri River. The first stops along the road were at Fort Kearney and Scotts Bluff in Nebraska Territory. Emigrants could stop for water, rest and provisions. When the travelers reached Fort Laramie in Wyoming, they had traveled about six hundred and thirty-five miles. It was summer. The days were hot and the nights cool as the road climbed to higher altitudes. Inevitably there were hailstorms and virtually no diary omits mention of a fierce pelting with ice the size of snowballs. The road then traveled through Sioux territory and although the emigrants were anxious, they most likely met with no Indians at all save those who wished to barter or be paid for guiding them across the rivers.

Emigrants to Oregon and California continued together past such landmarks as Independence Rock, Soda Springs, Court House Rock. Mountain men and trappers had inscribed their names on Independence Rock, and the emigrants continued the custom, carving or painting or marking them in axle grease. As the migration grew heavier, letters were posted on the rock, and notices and road directions for later-comers. Slowly, the road led by easy grades up the eight-thousand-foot summit of the Rocky

Mountains to the South Pass, which seemed more like a broad plain than part of the Rockies. Only the westward flow of the river waters told the emigrants that they had crossed the Pacific watershed.

From the South Pass to Fort Bridger, and from Fort Bridger to Fort Hall was the second major leg of the journey, another five hundred and thirty-five miles. Altogether, the emigrants by then had traveled twelve hundred miles from Independence, Missouri. And they were only halfway to their destination.

For the men, ordinary work of the journey included driving the wagons and swimming the cattle across innumerable river crossings. There were always tires to be reset, wheels to be taken off and soaked overnight, others to be greased, broken locks to be tightened up, whiplashes to be spliced and cut. Adrietta Hixon remembered that "One man finally said to father: 'We are doing nigger's work.' "

Ordinary work for the women meant cooking in wind and rain, and using weeds or buffalo chips to make their fires. If river waters were high, then everything inside the wagons—sometimes all two thousand pounds of supplies and possessions—might have to be unloaded, placed on rafts, and repacked again on the other side. Every bit of ingenuity and physical stamina the women could muster was needed.

After leaving Fort Hall, the emigrants separated, with those who were going to Oregon traveling north, following the Snake River to Fort Boise in Idaho territory, and then west to the Columbia River and the Willamette Valley. Those bound for Sutter's Fort and the Sacramento Valley in California traveled south until they came to the Humboldt River in northeastern Nevada, past two hundred miles of startling rock formations and desertlike land thinly patched with dry grass, sagebrush and prickly pear. The only animals to be seen were jackrabbits, coyotes, and rattlesnakes.

For both groups, the hardest part of the journey was at hand. This was the time when the temptation to try a new "cutoff" in order to shorten the tortuous process was overwhelming. Word of a new road, sometimes only a piece of paper nailed on a tree, was enough to split parties that had traveled amicably for a thousand miles. Some routes proved disastrous. Some of the guidebooks carried misinformation. A rumor, a secondhand account of a way to cut short the arduous journey by so much as ten miles was enough to set some wagons one way, some wagons another. The westward emigration is a history of false starts and near disasters.

Arguments broke out among the men. Tension and anxiety led to short tempers, and the women watched fearfully.[19] Sooner or later foul weather and mishap befell every party in turn, and the summer days drew into

An emigrant train pulls into Manhattan, Kansas, in 1860, to purchase supplies before setting out across the plains.

August and September. A mistaken road, a broken axle, a disabled draft animal, a lost child, a lay-over to recover from a illness, a serious accident, an Indian skirmish, a rainstorm—anything might happen on the open road. Food supplies were doled out with care; emigrants perpetually worried about finding adequate grass and water for their oxen. Once mountain passes were closed by snow, once food was gone, once the animals were exhausted, a party might have to leave everything behind and pack their belongings onto mules in a desparate effort to reach the journey's end.

The last part of the journey came when nerves were taut and fatigue had invaded the bodies of every man, woman, and child. Californians found that the Humboldt River ends in the Nevada sands, a miserable stream, "without a source, without an outlet, and indeed, without any visible reason for its existence." At the Humboldt Sink the California-bound travelers faced fifty miles of desert and the vicious heat of the desert sun. Oxen died of exhaustion if they had not yet been poisoned by the water. Elizabeth Goltra wrote in her diary on August 11, 1853; "This morning some of our cattle are sick and we hardly know what is the matter, [but] . . . many have died around us during the night and this morning. It is the prevailing opinion that swimming the river so choken up with dust causes irritation of the lungs as they bleed very freely at the nose and mouth just before they die."

Once past the desert, the emigrant faced a seventy-mile journey up the eastern slopes of the Sierra Nevada. The wagons had to be hoisted up with ropes and chains, winches and pulleys, and then let down again in the same way. There was another hundred miles through the twisting slopes of the mountains until the travelers saw the green color of the Sacramento valley.

Emigrants to Oregon found their road lay along the steep ledges of the Snake River. On reaching Fort Boise, they followed on the edge of a desert region until they came to the forbidding wall of the Blue Mountains. There they had to lift the wagons up the mountains with ropes and pulleys, blocking the rear wheels with rocks as they inched their way up, and then using those same devices, and sheer muscle, to hold onto the wagons to keep them from smashing to pieces on the way down. Helen Marnie Stewart wrote: "The hills ware dreadful steep locking both wheels and coming down slow got down safe oh dear me the desert is very hard on the poor animals going without grass or water for one night and day."

After two hundred miles, the travelers reached the Dalles, an "evil branch of the Columbia River." The cliff walls of the river were too high to cross. Most of the emigrants ferried the final hundred miles down the Columbia into the Willamette Valley, but some, who could not afford the ferry, loaded their possessions into canoes and hired Indians to paddle them across the swirling river. For women who were pregnant or who carried small children, that fearful canoe ride seemed the most unbearable part of all their travel. Some emigrants tied their possessions onto pack mules, and others just left everything behind them and walked the last miles into Oregon territory. It was "not a trip for the fainthearted; perhaps it was only for the foolhardy."[20]

Most of the emigrants shared certain characteristics as a group: they were men and women who had already made one or more moves before in a restless search for better lands. They were children of parents who themselves had moved to new lands. If ever a people could be said to have been "prepared" for the adventure of the Overland Trail, it would have to be these men and women. They possessed the assortment of skills needed to make the journey and to start again. They had owned land before, had cleared land before, and were prepared to clear and own land again. And they were young. Most of the population that moved across half the continent were between sixteen and thirty-five years of age.[21]

In only one essential was this a new kind of enterprise. This destination was twenty-four hundred miles away. Previous advances toward the West had been accomplished by a progression of settlements that were more or less contiguous. An emigrant might start in New Hampshire or in Massachusetts and move on to western Pennsylvania or Ohio. The land he crossed was dotted by other settlements, and his own homesite, once he chose it, was within reach of neighbors. But the Overland Trail stretched wider than the Atlantic Ocean and not even the Atlantic put forward such a variety of tests in crossing: deserts, mountains, Indians, and illness.

Women understood the decision to cross the continent as a man's decision.[22] Diaries are eloquent records that leave-taking was a painful and agonizing time. Mary A. Jones tells that:

> In the winter of 18 and 46 our neighbor got hold of Fremont's *History of California* and began talking of moving to the New Country & brought the book to my husband to read, & he was carried away with the idea too. I said *O let us not go* Our neighbors, some of them old men & women, with large families, but it made no difference. They must go. . . . We sold our home and what we could not take with us and what we could not sell . . . we gave away & on the 7th day of May 1846 we joined the camp for California.

And Margaret Hereford Wilson (the grandmother of General George S. Patton) in 1850 wrote to her mother: "Dr. Wilson has determined to go to California. I am going with him, as there is no other alternative. . . . Oh, my dear Mother . . . I thought that I felt bad when I wrote you . . . from Independence, but it was nothing like this." Time did not abate the reluctance women felt in leaving. Abby E. Fulkerath, writing almost twenty years later, echoed the same feelings: "Agreeable to the wish of my husband, I left all my relatives in Ohio . . . & started on this long & . . . perilous journey. . . . it proved a hard task to leave them but still harder to leave my children buried in . . . graveyards."

The overland journey wrenched women from the domestic circle that had encased much of their lives in stable communities. Agnes Stewart felt that she had been rudely torn from her friend: "O Martha my heart yearns for thee my only friend. . . . O my friend thou art dear to me yet my heart turns to thee I will never forget thee . . . the earliest friend. . . . I know I

This large wagon party paused to rest at the South Pass of the Rocky Mountains and to have their picture taken. The juncture marked the crossing of the Continental Divide and signaled that the most difficult portion of the journey was about to begin.

Margaret Hereford Wilson.

can never enjoy the blessed privilege of communing with thee yet look for the loss of one I will never see on earth. . . . I cannot bear it."

On the Trail, Agnes spent the greater part of her days with her sister Elizabeth, even though her sister had been newly married. But the dislocation she felt persisted: "O I feel lonesome today sometimes I can govern myself but not always but I schooled in pretty well considering all things." The phrase is a nice one—"schooled in." It meant that one drew in the reins of emotion and hid from the world those ways in which one was vulnerable. Emigrant women tried not to reveal their emotions. But to her diary, Agnes confided: "O Martha, what I would give to see you now. . . . I miss you more than I can find words to express I do not wish to forget you but your memory is painful to me I will see you again I will if I am ever able I will go back."

Women, as Agnes saw them, belonged to a group of beings elevated in emotional calibre, finer in all ways in their sensibilities. Men were arrogant and given to quarreling. They were the brutish partners to whom women eventually were wed. They moved in a separate world, one which Agnes disdained. Younger men were constantly brawling: "As usual Fred came to blows Tom is impudent Fred overbearing and arrogant. . . ." Six years later, however, after they had reached Oregon, Agnes would bow to the inevitable and marry the impudent Tom.[23]

The decision to leave superceded all the personal reasons that might keep a family at home. The illness of a family member, even when the journey meant weeks of exposure and hardship, was not reason enough to delay departure. Mrs. M. S. Hockensmith recalled: "I had never been in good health and there were diverse opinions as to whether I would improve or fail under the stress of the trip." The advanced age of a parent, a wife's pregnancy, none of these was reason enough to delay.

Family needs faded before the magnetism of the "Oregon fever" or "gold fever." Once men felt the pull of those powerful lures, they were bound to tie their lives and the lives of their family to the kite strings of history before it blew away and left them behind. Nothing would keep them from setting forth on the journey.[24]

Women, for their part, responded to a powerful necessity to keep the family intact. Jane Cazneau was writing about fighting off Indians, but her attitude was shared by many women who determined to make the best of a husband's decision to go to Oregon:

It was well enough for single men to run away from Indians, but when people had stock and children . . . the shortest way was for the mother to sit down by the fire and run bullets for her old man to give to the

Indians. There is a heap less trouble in it, and less scare too, than to be scattering off, and letting the hogs and cattle scatter off, every time the Indians come about.

Women like Jane believed that come what may, it was better to keep the family together than to let husband, hogs, and cattle "scatter off" in different directions. Some women clung to their conviction that preserving the family was their Christian obligation. Others, like Margaret Wilson, felt there was simply no alternative.

Whenever possible, families moved west within a kinship network. It seemed to matter very little whether one traveled in matrilinear or patrilinear families. Once the decision was made, families drew together from neighboring counties and states so that the extended family with all its households might be transplanted. On the Trail, families were the natural unit of social order. Single men attached themselves to family groups, engaging to serve as extra hands rather than outfitting a wagon alone. Wherever there was a woman, there was the nucleus of a home.[25]

In the spring of 1841 a small group of wagons carrying thirty-five men, five women, and ten children started from a town called Sapling Grove, about twenty miles west of Independence, Missouri. Three of the women were married, one was a widow, and one was a girl of marriageable age traveling with kin. The party did not get under way until May 12, already late in the season. Together, their combined ignorance of what was ahead of them was at least as vast as the journey itself. One man told them he had seen a map showing a great lake with two rivers running out of it clear to the Pacific Ocean. All they need do was find the lake and follow the rivers to the sea, and there lay California. No one had a compass. They just turned their teams west and followed the Platte River. They had no trouble reaching Fort Laramie, and then the South Pass of the Rocky Mountains. But by July 23, seven men decided they had enough westering and turned back to Missouri. On July 30, the remaining emigrants celebrated the wedding of the widow who very pragmatically decided to marry one of the men in the company. The emigrants had covered twelve hundred miles.

At Fort Hall some of the emigrants continued north on the more prudent road to Oregon. Some kept on toward California. Among these was Nancy Kelsey and her baby. Married at fifteen, Nancy is reported to have said; "I can better endure the hardships of the journey than the anxieties for an absent husband." The party had no guide and so little information when they determined to go to California that they were forced, as one of them put it, to "smell" their way west. They knew there was supposed to be a river, called Mary's River, or Ogden's River, or the Humboldt River, but where would they find it? By August 22, food was low. The animals were tired, and by August 26 the emigrants were completely lost. They kept moving west, abandoning one wagon and slaughtering their own oxen for food. On September 7, the ragged group again divided, two wagons going south with some Indians, six wagons remaining in camp. The next day they reunited, dismissed the Indians and continued looking for a river. Through much of September they blundered on until mid-month when they abandoned all the wagons and tied their belongings onto their oxen. They found Mary's River, but they could not find the road that would lead from there to the Truckee River. They were, by then, not traveling west as they thought, but south. On October 22, they killed their last ox, and found themselves trapped in the almost impassable canyons of the Sierra Nevada. Mule meat became a delicacy, but each killing of a mule reduced another emigrant to walking. They shot jackrabbit and coyote when they could. Nancy walked and carried her year-old baby in her arms. The emigrants tried boiling acorns, but no one could eat them. On October 30 they finally came into the San Joaquin Valley.

We have no diary of Nancy Kelsey's journey. We know her through the accounts of the men and through an interview she gave a newspaper many years later.[26] Her experience, were it to have been shared with her sister emigrants during her own time, might have forewarned them of what lay ahead. It might, just might, have deterred some of them from the terrible adventure.

Nancy Dickerson Welch was another woman in the vanguard of the overland migration. Nancy's parents had been born in Virginia and Pennsylvania, and her grandfather had fought in the revolutionary war. Her mother, widowed with nine children, took them herself from Ohio to Iowa where she remarried. Nancy cared for her brothers and sisters until she was twenty-one, and then married James Welch, who was from Kentucky.

In 1843, Nancy and James Welch and their year-old son went from Iowa to Missouri, where in the winter of 1843–44 Nancy's second son was born. In the spring they started again, their only guidebook the "notices" posted on trees by emigrants of previous years. It proved to be a rainy season, rain drenching the wagon tops, the young mother, and her two infants. The road was muddy. On reaching the Deschutes River in Oregon, they loaded everything they had onto rafts. Nancy held her two babies as they were piloted across that raging river by the Indians. It was a cold, wet December.

When James Welch finally arrived in Oregon, he bought 320 acres of

Nancy Kelsey.

Nancy Welch.

land. Nancy remembered that hers was the first wooden house to be built. Her husband also built a lumber mill, but in 1849 he set out after gold. Nancy recalled that she was often left alone with her children (who eventually numbered eleven) to stand off the Indians.

The spare accounts of the journeys of Nancy Kelsey and Nancy Welch tell us that neither pregnancy nor the care of very young infants were judged by emigrant families as sufficient cause to defer travel. Childbearing did not in any degree alter the determination to emigrate. The decision to make the journey rested with the men, and farm men of the early nineteenth century were not inclined to excuse women from their daily responsibilities to prepare for the occasion of childbirth. Women were expected to be strong enough to serve the common needs of the day, and strong enough to meet the uncommon demands as well. The society of emigrants yielded little comfort to frailty or timidity—or, for that matter, to motherhood.

One of the earliest reminiscences of the overland crossing is that of Martha Ann Morrison who came West in 1844, when she was a girl of thirteen. "At 13 and 14 we were considered young ladies, however, in this country." The lot of the women is remembered in her notes with unadorned simplicity:

> The men had a great deal of anxiety and all the care of their families, but still the mothers had the families directly in their hands and were with them all the time, especially during sickness.
>
> Some of the women I saw on the road went through a great deal of suffering and trial. I remember distinctly one girl in particular about my own age that died and was buried on the road. Her mother had a great deal of trouble and suffering. It strikes me as I think of it now that Mothers on the road had to undergo more trial and suffering than anybody else.

The division of work on the Overland Trail provided that "the women always did the cooking." But in addition, a special lifestyle began to develop through the months of the Overland Trail in which the women did much more. Martha Morrison recalled that "the women helped pitch the tents, helped unload, and helped yoking up the cattle. Some of the women did nearly all of the yoking; many times the men were off. One time my father was away hunting cattle that had been driven off by the Indians, and that left Mother and the children to attend to everything. . . ." The work of packing and unpacking was formidable and never-ending. It had to be done at major river crossings, after heavy rains, and when wagons got stuck in the mud. Esther Hanna wrote:

I am now sitting in our carriage in the middle of a slough. Our mules all fell down attempting to get through. I have never witnessed anything like it We have put 14 yoke of oxen to the wagons to get them out. . . . Our provisions got wet and they had to be unpacked to air and then packed again.

Cooking out of doors, driving the oxen, collecting buffalo chips and weeds, helping to pitch the tent, washing on river banks, all these and more began to suggest to many women that the journey had reduced them to work that was only fit for "hired hands."

The children, though they were called upon to share the heavy jobs, kept good heart and good cheer.[27] Years later, Martha realized that:

We did not know the dangers we were going through. The idea of my Father was to get on the coast: no other place suited him, and he went right ahead until he got there; we settled on the Clatsop Plains close to the mouth of the Columbia River. We did not get there until the middle of January or first of February. We went down the river Deschutes in an open canoe, including all the children; and when we got down there was no way to get to the place where my Father had determined to locate us, but to wade through the tremendous swamps. I knew some of the young men that were along laughed at us girls, my oldest sister and me, for holding up what dresses we had to keep from miring; but we did not think it was funny. We finally waded through and got all our goods. Mother was a very fleshy woman, and it was a terrible job for her to get through.

It is impossible to read this diary and not feel the determination of Martha's father, for whom only the Pacific signaled the end of his journey. It is impossible to read the diary and not feel the stolid steps of that "very fleshy woman," his wife, fording the swamps as she came into Oregon.

For young people, the Overland Trail was the greatest of all adventures. Like the young men who would come to see the Civil War as one of the grand evocations of the century, Martha and others felt the overland migration to be a momentous calling of history. Within a year and a half of her arrival in Oregon, Martha Morrison would marry, when she was fifteen.

By 1845, the "Oregon Fever" was in full sway. Travelers who had gone out in the spring of 1843 sent word back of rich farm land and mild climate. "Soil of the valley is rich beyond comparison. . . . Rain rarely falls, even in the winter season; but the dews are sufficiently heavy to compensate for its absence."[28] No consideration could induce them to return to their former homes. On May 6, 1843, the *Niles National Register* reprinted an article from its sister journal the *Ohio Statesman:*

Martha Morrison Minto, husband John, son.

The Oregon fever is raging in almost every part of the Union. Companies are forming in the east, and in several parts of Ohio, which added to those of Illinois, Iowa, and Missouri, will make a pretty formidable army, the largest portion will probably join companies at Fort Independence, Missouri, and proceed together across the mountains. It would be reasonable to suppose that there will be at least five thousand Americans west of the Rocky Mountains next autumn.[29]

In spite of the glowing reports, major portions of the route West were unknown and unexplored. In a given wagon train there might be no one who knew whether a new trail or "cut-off" led into an impassable canyon, or if it might lengthen the journey until provisions ran out. A traveler might carry word that rivers were swollen or turbulent; a story might be passed on from a ferryman at a river crossing—any of these was enough to re-route an entire wagon train.

Lucy Hall Bennett was thirteen when her family joined the emigration to Oregon. At Fort Hall:

We came across Steve Meek, told us of a better road to [The] Williamette Valley. Part of our train refused to take this cut-off and went by the old immigrant road, but a good many of us followed Meek on what has since been called Meek's Cut Off. . . . The road we took had been traveled by the Hudson Bay Fur traders, and while it might have been alright for pack horses, it was certainly not adapted to immigrants traveling by ox train. The water was bad, so full of alkali you could hardly drink it. There was little grass and before long our cattle all had sore feet from traveling over the hard sharp rocks. After several of our party died, the men discovered that Meek really knew nothing about the road.

Ignorance did nothing to daunt the spirits of the travelers. Mrs. W. W. Buck told that her family met a man coming from Oregon:

Of course, we were all anxious to hear about the country we were bound for, and our captain said Doctor White, tell us about Oregon. He jumped upon the wagon tongue and all our eyes and ears were open to catch every word. He said: "Friends, you are traveling to the garden of Eden, a land flowing with milk and honey. And just let me tell you, the clover grows wild all over Oregon, and when you wade through it, it reaches your chin." We believed every word, and for days, I thought that not only our men, but our poor tired oxen, stepped lighter for having met Dr. White.

Nevertheless, the journey did not take four months, as the guidebooks promised, but eight months, and the emigrants counted themselves lucky to arrive in Oregon in late November.

Sometimes the route to the land of milk and honey was a bitter one.

Catherine Sager's father was a restless man who emigrated from Ohio to Missouri in 1838, and then in 1844 decided to move his family to Oregon. Catherine remembered that, "not being accustomed to riding in a covered wagon, the motion made us all sick, and the uncomfortableness of the situation was increased from the fact that it had set into rain, which made it impossible to roll back the cover and let in the fresh air. It also caused a damp and musty smell that was very nauseating. It took several weeks of travel to overcome this 'sea sickness.' " Their sickly feeling takes on added meaning as Catherine goes on to tell that, "on the 22nd of May we were surprised by the arrival of another little sister." Being pregnant in a damp wagon that continually rocked was a dismal fate for any woman, and for Catherine's mother the days following the infant's birth were singularly unpleasant. "Water ran through the tent, and the bedclothes were saturated with water. . . ." Bad luck plagued the family. "Soon . . . we came to a place in the road which had quite an embankment on one side; and notwithstanding Father's best efforts to prevent it, the team ran on to this and overturned the wagon, nearly killing mother. . . . A tent was set up and Mother was carried into it, where for a long time she lay insensible. The wagon was righted up, the things loaded in, and Mother having recovered we drove on." The accident would not be the journey's last:

> On the first day of August we halted to noon in a beautiful grove on the bank of the Platte River. . . . The children had become so accustomed to getting in and out of the wagon as to lose all fear, and would get out on to the tongue and leap clear of the wheel without putting Father to the trouble of stopping the team. On the afternoon of this day, in performing this feat, the hem of my dress caught on an axle-handle, precipitating me under the wheels both of which passed over me, badly crushing the left leg, before Father could stop the oxen. Seeing me clear of the wheels he picked me up and carrying me in his arms ran to stop the team, which had become unmanageable from fright. A glance at my limb dangling in the air as he ran, revealed to him the extent of the injury I had received, and in a broken voice he exclaimed, "My dear child, your leg is broken all to pieces!"

Accidents continued until the journey became a nightmare. A buffalo stampede outside of Fort Laramie, on the edge of what the emigrants called the Great American Desert, led Henry Sager to try to turn the great beasts from his wagon, and in that effort he lost his life.[30]

> It soon became apparent to all that he must die. He himself was fully aware that he was passing away and he could not be reconciled to the thought of leaving his large and helpless family. . . . Looking upon me as I lay helpless by his side, he said, "Poor child! What will become of

Catherine Sager Pringle.

you?" Soon after camping Capt. Shaw came to see him and found him weeping bitterly. . . . His wife was feeble in health, the children small, and one likely to be a cripple for a long time, with no relatives in the country and a long journey still before them. He begged the Captain in piteous tones to take charge of them and see them safely through.

After her husband's death, Mrs. Sager roused herself to shepherd her children to Oregon. She hired a young man to drive their teams, but he soon proved that neither chivalry nor loyalty were unimpeachable virtues among the overlanders. He took the family's rifle but "instead of hunting he hastened forward to overtake the company ahead of ours, in which was his lady love." Luck seemed to mock the family at every turn.

Weakened after childbirth, Mrs. Sager was soon overcome by "camp fever." "The nights and mornings were bitter cold . . . [she] was afflicted with the sore mouth that was the forerunner of the fatal . . . fever." They were in Utah territory. "She soon became delirious. . . . Her babe was cared for by the women of the train. The kind-hearted women were also in the habit of coming in when the train stopped at night to wash the dust from her face and other wise make her comfortable." When she died, a grave was dug at the side of the road. In just twenty-six days, the seven Sager children were orphans; the eldest was fourteen and the youngest only a few weeks old.

The children traveled on with the wagon train until they reached the missionary settlement of Marcus and Narcissa Whitman in southeastern Oregon. The Whitmans were Presbyterian missionaries who had established the mission in 1836.

Narcissa Whitman had lost her only child, a daughter, in an accidental drowning. She had clung to the child for four days before giving her up to be buried. When she saw the Sager children, "it was the baby she wanted most of all." In October 1844, six barefooted and bareheaded children were left at the mission, and one infant with them. For the next three years, the children lived with the Whitmans and had begun to believe their lives were securely placed when in 1847 the mission was attacked by Cayuse Indians. Marcus and Narcissa Whitman and twelve others in the mission were murdered, among them both brothers of Catherine Sager. To have been placed, on the empty breadth of the Oregon frontier, on the very site of an Indian attack seems to have been an extraordinary destiny.[31]

The lives of the Sager children provide overwhelming proof of what the emigrant generation knew at heart—that life was unstable and that death was an intrusive and frequent guest in the family. Snakebites, drownings, Indian skirmishes, stampedes, falls, fights—the frontier provided pitfalls enough for men. Maternal and infant mortality took their toll among women and children. And soon cholera would sweep over the route, attacking young and old indiscriminately. Children of the frontier knew from their earliest years that the family was not a stable unit. They recognized, early on, that the thread of life was a slender one. They saw their own families take in the children of friends and relatives overcome by sickness and death, and recognized that the same would be their lot if chance decreed. If one considers the children of Henry Sager, one must suspect that they developed personality traits not unlike children of war generations. They knew life to be harsh and they knew that there was no promise that tomorrow would resemble today. One learned to survive. One learned to build upon the ruins of each day the necessary sinew to last until tomorrow. Somehow, Catherine Sager survived. In the New Country she managed to live to maturity, to marry and to raise her own family, and even to remember her painful past.

A brighter story is told by Miriam A. Thompson Tuller. Born in Illinois, she married Arthur Thompson when she was eighteen, and in the spring following their wedding the young couple joined the migration to Oregon. She recalls that her husband was "fired with patriotism," and "I was possessed with a spirit of adventure and a desire to see what was new and strange." A young wife with no children to encumber her, strong and eager to see what life would offer, Miriam Thompson brought youth and optimism to the westward journey. She and her husband set out on May 11, 1845, part of a train of 480 wagons. The starting party was so large that the company divided and then divided again. "We were unable to make much headway with so large a company, so agreed to divide. Then we were in a company of eighty wagons and that was far too many; so we kept separating, some times twenty wagons and often only four or five—that was more convenient—and we had become indifferent to fear."[32] The buffalo "were solid masses as far as the eye could reach, and we had fresh meat galore." At Fort Hall, the travelers met a man who "gave us the consoling information that the Indians would kill us before we got to Oregon. . . ." But the emigrants were of stout heart—in Miriam's words, "indifferent to fear," and the diary notes that the Indians "proved better than represented." In fact, during a raging sandstorm "some Indians were there with their canoes who were more than willing to take us over for some calico shirts. The wagons were unloaded and taken apart and after many loads, we were safely over." Missionaries along the road sold beef and potatoes. The travelers had unbounded confidence: "we felt quite sure we could go almost anywhere."

By October, however, confidence alone was not enough. The mountains had become treacherous and the men decided to send the women and children ahead on horseback and mules. "I was mounted on a Cayuse [Indian] pony . . . left husband and camp—everything—but a few clothes and a little provision to try to reach some place before the rains set in." The little party of women and guides climbed Mount Hood. "The coming down was worse [than the going up]. The zigzag trail a foot or more deep with sand. There it rained very hard all night. We had no tent or shelter of any kind. The fourth night we met three men from Oregon City, coming to meet those emigrants in the mountains with some provisions, as they heard we were in distress. The rescue missions that came out from the settlements in Oregon and California saved thousands of emigrants who found the Sierras too much punishment after the long route they had covered.

Miriam Tuller's diary contains one vignette that etches clearly the nature of the Trail and its troubles for women with children:

We reached Oregon City the sixth day of camp, but when I saw a woman on a very poor horse with a little child in her lap and one strapped on behind her and two or three tied on another horse, I felt thankful and imagined I was only having a picnic.

The final diary entry provides a dark interface to the boundless optimism of the first pages:

In the fall of 1848, when gold was discovered in California my husband went, as did many others, to seek gold, but never returned. He was murdered by the Indians. . . . There were four in the camp and none left to tell the tale. . . . July, 1850, I was married to Jeremiah G. Tuller.

Family life on the frontier—as that frontier passed from the Appalachians to the Sierras—was continually broken. Indians, illness, and accidents beset every family in turn. Remembering the days on the Trail, Nancy Hembree Snow Bogart wrote:

I've often been asked if we did not suffer with fear in those days but I've said no we did not have sense enough to realize our danger we just had the time of our lives but since I've grown older and could realize the danger and the feelings of the mothers, I often wonder how they really lived through it all and retained their reason.

[Crossing the Deschutes River,] the women took their places in the boats, feeling they were facing death . . . the frail craft would get caught in a whirlpool and the water dashing over and drenching them through and through. The men would then plunge in the cold stream

and draw the half drowned women and children ashore, build fires and partly dry them, and the bedding, and start on again. The women preferring to try it afoot, but *that* was no pleasure trip, carrying a small child in arms whilst another one or two clung to their skirts whilst they climbed over fallen trees and rocks. . . .

There were both deaths and births on the way, the dead were laid away in packing boxes, but could not be covered so deep but the prowling savage would exhume them to get the clothes they were buried in, then leave the body for the hungry wolfe, that left bones to be gathered up and reintered by the next company that passed along. *All* those things sorely taxed their powers of endurance.

Marriages on the frontier were often made before a girl was half through her adolescent years, and some diaries record a casualness in the manner in which such decisions were reached. Mrs. John Kirkwood recounts that her brother Jasper decided to get married on Christmas Day, but was unable to find a minister or justice of the peace to marry him:

The night before Xmas, John Kirkwood . . . the path finder, stayed at our house over night. I had met him before and when he heard the discussion about my brother's Jasper's wedding, he suggested that he and I also get married. I was nearly fifteen years old and I thought it was high time that I got married so I consented. Jack Kirkwood volunteered to go to Bethel and get Rev. Glen Burnett. . . . He came back with Elder Burnett early in the afternoon. Shortly after he arrived, my brother Jasper and his girl, Mary Ring, who had just come from Missouri, stood up and were married. Immediately after the ceremony had been performed, Jack and I stepped out and Elder Burnett married us. No one knew that we were going to be married and they were all very much surprised. I remember that we had a mighty fine wedding dinner and a big celebration. One of the things I remember best about the wedding dinner was a pie my mother had made from dried tomatoes. You need not turn your nose up at it either for it was mighty good.

Marriages arose out of a sense of mutual congeniality and the conviction that a man and a woman together were necessary to do the work of living on the frontier. Both young men and young women were free to follow their inclinations, and weddings were made expeditously. The young couple was expected to set off on their own, sometimes with a "chivaree" or communal celebration, and sometimes with only a tomato pie.

Martha Morrison Minto, who had married at fifteen, soon found herself facing some major problems. "When my second child was born my husband and I were alone, three miles from any woman or doctor; my oldest child [was] 18 months old—my husband had to do the washing." Martha was embarrassed to tell that her young husband undertook chores

Nancy H. Snow Bogart.

that were known to be "women's work," but she also suggests that he assisted her in the delivery of the baby. Life began early and in good earnest for those who lived on the frontier.

The emigrants starting out in the spring of '46 believed there was a clear route ahead of them. In contrast to those who had journeyed in 1843, 1844, and 1845, these travelers felt the way had been cleared. Lansford W. Hastings, author of *The Emigrants Guide*, was there that season, imposingly self-confident and assured. Respectable men—clergymen, lawyers, physicians—and even the young Francis Parkman out of Harvard College were among the years' travelers. But among the emigrants, too, was the Donner party, ignorant of the savage days that lay before them. How could the men and women, sitting high on new wagons, with their names proudly painted on the wagon sides, enjoying holiday spirits, know that neither the guidebooks or the guides were reliable? How could they know that ten thousand men and women who had gone ahead of them were not yet enough to tame that wild road?

It did not take very long for it to become apparent that there was considerable uncertainty about the route, and talk of cutoffs and shortcuts filled the air at each layover. Trails that had served riders on horseback proved impassable to heavily laden wagons pulled by oxen. There were the Wasatch Mountains that lay between Wyoming and Utah, and the Blue Mountains that rose up in Oregon, and the Sierra Nevada—that ugly ridge of rock in California. The only way to come over them was to hoist the wagons with chains and pulleys and ropes and improvised winches. If a chain snapped, the emigrants would watch helplessly as their wagons hurtled over the mountainside.

On this year's journey, Samuel Young's wife gave birth on the rocky cliffs of the Sierra Nevada just days before one of their wagons was wrecked when a chain broke. When the husband built a small carriage to carry his wife and her newborn and harnessed it to eighteen yoke of oxen to pull it up the steep slopes, his wife could not rid her mind of the picture of the careening wagon and begged to be allowed to walk. With her infant, she walked over the mountain cliffs rather than risk the fate of the falling wagon.[33]

In 1846 William Smith and his family were part of the thousands who went West. Smith was a descendant of the John Smith who sailed from France to Boston in 1625. The family had moved West, generation by generation until in 1839, Smith and his wife and five children moved from Iowa to Missouri. Seven years later, they "hoisted the Sails of there Prairie Schooner and started for the grate North West to Parts unknown." Their wagon train was three hundred wagons strong at the start, but soon it had split into smaller groups. By midsummer it was apparent that the journey begun in such high hopes was in trouble. Bad luck and illness combined to make their progress dangerously slow. "Sickness entered the camp and worst of all they lost their way. . . . they conciled together What to do and they desided there was nothing to do but to strugel on." Stricken with typhoid, and lost, the travelers made a dangerous mistake. They "struck a camp there & they Were in Camp fir six weeks waiting for the sick to die or get well Enough to Travil it was Sourten to die for there was no Hopes of geten Well there." There was "nothing to Eat onley the Emergrant cattle."

Even the men were "so Hart Sick and disscouraged they said there was no use in trying they never could get throw that canyon it was impossible." William Smith tried to encourage the men in the party and declared that he himself intended to "take his little Spring Wagon to holl the littel children and doughter Louisa who had mountin feavre as might say starvation [she had] nothing to eate She was 16 years old." Just at that point, Smith suffered a heart attack, and the men he tried to cheer made his coffin out of the "little Spring Wagon." William Smith was buried in "Cowcrick Canyon." His wife was left with nine children, among them a dying daughter, a crippled six-year-old and the youngest child scarcely two.

Ellen Smith "put her sadle on the White ox and Put the three little Boys on the ox, packed the bed close all around them and the other oxens was packed with the bed close and cooking utencils and the rest Walked and drove the oxens with these loads." Mother and children pushed on, but the rough road and the exposure weakened sixteen-year-old Louisa. When the girl became too ill to ride, the family packed pillows and blankets on an ox, making a kind of bed for her, but she felt herself dying, and "told her Mother she wanted . . . a Grave six feet deep for she did nat want the wolves to dig her up and eat her."

One of the overriding anxieties of the overlanders was the thought that a grave—their own or a loved one's—might be dug open by wolves or by Indians. Again and again that fear stalked them, no matter how stoical or disciplined they might be. The Smith party stopped, and Ellen Smith selected a "prity little Hill and the men went to work diggin with such Poar tools to dig with thay dug down about 4 feet when her Mother went to see if it was dug six feet as Louisa had Reguested she told them it would nat do it had to (be) dug two feet deeper they said it was deeper Enough she told them if they would nat do it deag it deeper she would so she got down in the Grave and begin to dig, herself." The frantic mother, who had already buried her husband, was determined that her daughter's grave would be deep enough to escape the wolves. The sight of the mother digging the grave was too much for the men to bear. "Unc[l]e Henry Smith told her to get out and he would see that it was dug as deep as she wanted it to be." Louisa told her Mother "to Pile a lot of Racks on her Grave after they had covered it up."

After Louisa's death, Ellen Smith trudged on by foot. The smaller boys were tied to the oxen; they had become so cold they could not be trusted to sit in the saddle. The provisions were exhausted. The children "would go out in the woods and smoke the Woud mice out of the Logs and Rost and Eat them."

Just when all hope had been given up, a great cry was heard through the camp as two young men who had gone on ahead were sighted coming through on "government mules" from the army post at Salem, Oregon. There was a pack train with them, and provisions and the stragglers were saved. Ellen Smith and her children arrived in Salem two days before Christmas, 1846. She took up her claim of 640 acres, and she and her eight children cleared the land and built a house. Angelina Smith, who had been nine when the family made its tortuous journey, married at fifteen and bore four children of her own in Oregon. Interestingly, her own family was only half as large as her emigrant mother's.

The strains of the journey can be traced in the faces of this family as they rest at midday.

Sarah and Henry Helmick, married in April 1845, made the overland journey as a wedding trip. On the morning following their marriage ceremony, they set out across the plains. They were young and inexperienced, and at one of the first river crossings their raft was swept downstream with all of their possessions on board. The bride and groom sat down beside the river bank, huddled against the winds, and waited until two Indian squaws found them and sent word to a nearby settlement. The young couple spent the winter on the prairie, and with intrepid determination, set out again for Oregon the following spring.

Children on the Overland Trail were subject to a form of benign neglect as adults carried more than their normal share of care and work. Accidents involving children became one of the hallmarks of the road. Children fell out of wagons; they lagged behind when the wagon trains started up and were lost in the confusion of the hundreds of wagons and families.[34] Mothers worried over the antics of small children who had no care for their own safety. Margaret S. Frink, part of the rush to the gold fields of California, wrote of a time when her family thought they had lost her son. The boy had found a horse, and the excitement of having a horse to ride led to some spirited gallops through the wagons lined up in camp. But at the point of starting up, the boy was nowhere to be seen. The mother was frantic, fearing the Indians would capture the horse and the boy. "To increase my agony a company of packers [told of passing five hundred Indians]. I suffered the agony almost of death in a few minutes. I besought [them] to turn back and help us look for our lost boy, but they had not time. . . . The thought of leaving the boy, never to hear him again! But just at dark, Aaron came in sight having the lost boy with him. My joy turned to tears."

There were the obvious accidents, but there were also the more subtle dangers that went with inadequate supervision. Lucy Henderson Deady recalled the following:

> Mother had brought some medicine along. She hung the bag containing the medicine from a nail on the side-board of the wagon. . . . My little sister, Salita Jane wanted to tast it, but I told her she couldn't have it. She didn't say anything but as soon as we had gone she got the bottle and drank it all. Presently she came to the campfire where Mother was cooking supper and said she felt awfully sleepy. Mother told her to run away and not bother her, so she went to where the beds were spread and lay down. When Mother called her for supper she didn't come. Mother saw she was asleep, so didn't disturb her. When Mother tried to awake her later she couldn't arouse her. Lettie had drunk the whole bottle of laudanum. It was too late to save her life.

Before we had started father had made some boards of black walnut that fitted along the side of the wagon. They were so grooved so they would fit together and we used them for a table. . . . Father took these walnut boards and made a coffin for Salita and we buried her there by the roadside in the desert. . . .

Three days after my little sister Lettie drank the laudanum and died we stopped for a few hours, and my sister Olivia was born. We were so late that the men of the party decided we could not tarry a day, so we had to press on. The going was terribly rough. We were the first party to take the southern cut-off and there was no road. The men walked beside the wagons and tried to ease the wheels down into the rough places, but in spite of this it was a very rough ride for my mother and her new born babe.

After a great hardship . . . we finally made our way through . . . to Oregon it was late in the year and the winter rains had started. We had been eight months on the road instead of five, we were out of food, and our cattle were nearly worn out. . . . My mother's brother came out and met us. We left the wagons and with mother on one horse holding her 6 week old baby in her lap, and with one of the little children sitting behind her and with the rest of us riding behind the different men, we started north . . . There were five of us children. . . . We lived on boiled wheat and boiled peas that winter. My mother got sick, so my Aunt Susan came to live with us and take care of her.

Within the space of three days, Mrs. Henderson saw one child buried and another born. There was no time to mourn and no time to grieve; the journey was relentless. For women of childbearing age—for the silent women like Lucy's mother—the hardships must have been nerve-shattering.

But Lucy's diary is another matter. "I was fifteen . . . and in those days the young men wondering why a girl was not married if she was still single when she was sixteen. That summer Judge Deady . . . came by . . . We all rode horseback. . . . We met occasionally at weddings and other social doings," and soon they married. The more diaries of women that one reads, the more one is driven to the conclusion that the overland journey and the frontier experience were primarily for the very young.

The journey was hardest of all for women who were pregnant, and for those who traveled with very small children. Mary A. Jones, traveling with her husband and children to California in 1846, had become pregnant during the first month of their travel. For her, all the ordinary problems of the road, the heat, mosquitoes, lack of water, and the necessity of having to walk beside the wagons long afternoons in order to save the oxen, the routine stooping over a cooking pot out of doors, all of these conditions were intensified and complicated by her pregnancy. She was in her seventh

Mrs. Sarah Helmick.

month when they arrived in November; a daughter was born to her in January.

The experience must have dimmed her view of the West, for her diary ends with this story: In the spring months following the birth of the baby, her husband went out to find a homesite for his family. When he came back, he insisted that she come with him to look at the place he had found. "We camped that night. . . . my husband stopped the team and said, 'Mary, did you ever see anything so beautiful?' There was nothing in sight but nature. Nothing . . . except a little mud and stick hut. . . ." Mary found nothing grand, nothing wonderful, nothing to suggest what her husband so clearly saw. She and other women did not find the new country a land of resplendent possibilities. They heard their children crying, and longed for their old homes.

But the families kept coming. In 1847, two thousand migrating people went West. As much as the emigrants feared them, the Indians proved not to be a deterring factor, and in fact they were not dangerous, although they made more or less a regular practice of stealing provisions. Horses and cows were particularly vulnerable, and journals tell of the Indians' uncanny skill in stealing livestock virtually from under the eyes of the animals' keepers. One diarist told how an Indian succeeded in stealing a blanket from a sleeping man. But more common are the accounts of Indians who sold or bartered provisions to the emigrants along the route. Indians learned that the pioneers had need of meat and fish as the journey lengthened. The women's diaries tell graphically that while the men could feel the merits of topsoil with their fingers, and knew the qualities of the different grasses as forage, and which herbs and berries could be eaten, they were often poor hunters and fishermen. Sometimes the wagon trains employed extra hands to hunt buffalo and other game for food; but when no hunter traveled with them, the farmers came back from the hunt empty-handed, and were glad enough to meet with Indians who sold or bartered salmon or buffalo for calico or cash. In fact, it was often the women who did the bartering.

Lucinda Cox Brown traveled with her husband, her father and his children, her uncle and his family. She left behind in Illinois her twin sister Malinda. They had been married in a double wedding ceremony when they were both seventeen, the twin sisters marrying two brothers. Lucinda and Elias Brown, along with their extended family, began the journey in high enthusiasm. They were young and strong; the new world was theirs to win. But Lucinda Brown's diary becomes another example of how often the overland journey began in optimism and ended in despair. They had just

Lucy Henderson Deady.

reached the Platte River, which meant the journey was hardly at its halfway mark, when Elias took a severe chill and died. He was a young man. Whether the chill had come from the many river crossings or whether it was typhoid cannot be read from the diary. Lucinda was suddenly widowed, left with three small children. Eight months and sixteen days from the time they left Wilmington, Illinois, the wagon train reached Salem, Oregon. The emigrants were alive, but stripped of everything except the clothes they wore.

During the first winter in Oregon, Lucinda supported herself by making caps and clothing. In the summer she made her bonnets out of plaited wheat straw and trimmed them with ribbons. She managed, somehow, to save enough money to move onto a claim of her own in 1849, and two years later she married Hiram Allen, with whom she had four more children. This woman who wove hats of braided wheat and decorated them with ribbons was survived by eight children, twenty-two grandchildren, and ten great-grand-children. A friend remembered her as a woman who "cheerfully accepted her lot."

One of the starkest stories among the overland diaries is that of Elizabeth Smith Geer. She and her husband and their seven children came from Indiana to Oregon Territory in 1847. There had been flute music and fiddling and dancing in the early months of summer, but by summer's end, the wagon party was in trouble. A diary entry dated September 15 signals some of the stress the women felt:

This morning one company moved on except one family. The woman got mad and would not budge, nor let the children go. He had his cattle hitched on for three hours and coaxing her to go, but she would not stir. I told my husband the circumstance, and he and Adam Polk and Mr. Kimball went and took each one a young one and crammed them in the wagon and her husband drove off and left her sitting. She got up, took the back track and traveled out of sight. Cut across, overtook her husband. Meantime he sent his boy back to camp after a horse that he had left and when she came up to her husband, says, "Did you meet John?" "Yes" was the reply, "and I picked up a stone and knocked out his brains." Her husband went back to ascertain the truth, and while he was gone, she set one of his wagons on fire, which was loaded with store goods. The cover burnt off, and some valuable articles. He saw flames and came running and put it out, and then mustered spunk enough to give her a good flogging.

Elizabeth was of sterner stuff than the woman she wrote about, but the road would soon test even her mettle.

The family came to the Deschutes River in Oregon territory at the end of

October. Many a diary verifies that the emigrants were particularly helpless at that river crossing. The river was high, rapid, and dangerous. "The water came clear to the top of the wagon beds. My children and I, with as many more women and children as could stow themselves into a canoe, were taken over by two Indians, which cost a good many shirts. . . . Anybody in preparing to come to this country should make up some calico shirts to trade to the Indians in cases of necessity. You will have to hire them to pilot you across rivers. Against we got here, my folks were stripped of shirts, trousers, jackets and 'wammusses' [a warm work jacket made of sturdy knitted or woven fabric]."

It continued to rain into November. The bad weather wore away the stamina of strong men, and her friend's husband died. By mid-November Elizabeth's husband was sick too. "It rains and snows. . . . I froze or chilled my feet so that I cannot wear a shoe, so I have to go around in the cold water barefooted." And on another day she wrote:

> It rains and snows. We start this morning around the falls with our wagons. . . . I carry my babe and lead, or rather carry, another through snow, mud and water, almost to my knees. It is the worst road. . . . I went ahead with my children and I was afraid to look behind me for fear of seeing the wagons turn over into the mud. . . . My children gave out with cold and fatigue and could not travel, and the boys had to unhitch the oxen and bring them and carry the children on to camp. I was so cold and numb I could not tell by feeling that I had any feet at all. . . . there was not one dry thread on one of us—not even my babe. . . . I have not told you half we suffered. I am not adequate to the task.

By Thanksgiving the family reached Portland and Elizabeth "found a small, leaky concern with two families already in it. I got some of the men to carry my husband up through the rain and lay him in it." It seemed that it would never stop raining. Entry after entry tells of rain and dampness. "I have not undressed to lie down for six weeks. Besides all our sickness, I had a cross little babe to take care of. Indeed, I cannot tell you half."

In the leaky shed, Elizabeth sat up "night after night, with my poor, sick husband, all alone and expecting him every day to die." In February she wrote: "We buried my earthly companion. Now I know what none but widows know; that is, how comfortless is that of a widow's life, especially when left in a strange land, without money or friends, and the care of seven children." Clutching at the hope that a new community would bring them better tidings, Elizabeth packed up her family and started out for a new home at month's end. "Having no one to assist us, we had to leave one wagon. . . . we traveled all the way up hill . . . on an intolerably bad road. We all had to walk. Sometimes I had to place my babe on the ground and help to keep the wagon from turning over. When we got to the top of the mountain, we descended through mud up to the wagon hubs and over logs two feet through and log bridges torn in pieces in the mud. Sometimes I would be behind, out of sight of the wagons, carrying and tugging my little ones along."

For a year Elizabeth and her children managed to keep themselves alive in the New Country. Three of the older boys left for the gold mines, and she was left with the four youngest. "I became poor as a snake, yet I was in good health. . . . I could run a half mile without stopping to breathe. Well, I thought perhaps I had better try my fortune again; so on the 24th of June, 1849, I was married to a Mr. Joseph Geer, a man 14 years older than myself, though young enough for me. He is the father of ten children. . . . He is a Yankee." Yankee husbands enjoyed the highest of reputations among the pioneer women, being universally judged the most considerate and gentle. And so was Elizabeth's new mate. "He is as kind to me as I can ask. Indeed, he sometimes provokes me for trying to humor me so much." Although her boys "made out poorly at the mines," Elizabeth built a good life with her second husband. A sprightly letter from him is appended to her diary:

Butteville, Sept. 9, 1850.

Dear Ladies:

As Mrs. Geer has introduced me to you as her old Yankee husband, I will say a few words, in the hope of becoming more acquainted hereafter. She so often speaks of you, that you seem like old neighbors. She has neglected to tell you that she was once the wife of Cornelius Smith. She has told you how poor she became while a widow, but has not said one word about how fat she has become since she has been living with her Yankee husband. This is probably reserved for the next epistle, so I will say nothing about it.

Of her I will only say she makes me a first-rate wife, industrious, and kind almost to a fault to me, however, that I can cheerfully overlook, you know.

We are not rich, but independent, and live agreeably together, which is enough. We are located on the west bank of the Williamette River, about 20 miles above Oregon City about 40 yards from the water—a very pleasant situation. Intend putting out a large orchard as soon as I can prepare the ground; have about ten thousand apple trees, and about 200 pear trees on hand. Trees for sale of the best kinds of fruit. Apple trees worth a dollar, and pears $1.50 apiece. I have not room to give you a description of this, the best country in the world, so I will not attempt it; but if you will answer this I will give you a more particular account next time. I will give you a brief account of myself. I left my native home, Windham, Conn. Sept. 10, 1818, for Ohio; lived in Ohio till Sept. 9, 1840 when I left for Illinois. Left Illinois April 4, 1847 for Oregon; arrived here Oct. 18, 1847. Buried my first wife Dec. 6, 1847.

Now I wish you or some of your folks to write to us and let us know about the neighbors, as Mrs. Geer is very anxious to hear from you all.

Direct to Joseph C. Geer, Sen., Butteville, Marion County, Oregon Territory.

My best respects to Mr. Ames, and if there is a good Universalist preacher there, tell him he would meet with a cordial welcome here, as there is not one in this Territory.

I must close for want of room.

Yours respectfully,
Joseph C. Geer, Sen.

Mrs. P. Foster and Mrs. C. Ames.

In the same summer, a newly married couple, James and Caroline Findley, traveled over the same route. The Trail was their honeymoon. The Findleys traced their ancestry back to 1760, when the family came from Belfast, Ireland. One ancestor fought in the Revolution. Caroline and James were young and strong and ready for a great adventure. But Caroline Findley's diary, like Lucinda Brown's, bears witness to the fact that neither youth nor good will were sufficient to withstand the dangers of the Overland Trail. Young James, barely twenty, caught "mountain fever," probably typhoid, and died at the journey's end, on December 23, 1847, two days before Christmas.

Three months later Caroline wrote that she gave birth to her first child, Sarah, at Fort Vancouver, Oregon. The notation of the child's birth is the only indication in all the diary that Caroline Findley was pregnant. Her pregnancy, however, gives a new dimension to her account of the journey. The emigrants had been reduced to boarding rafts in the month of December in order to get across the turbulent Dalles River: Caroline would have been in the sixth month. In December her husband was dying; in cold December she buried him in the Pioneer Cemetery at the Fort. Two days before Christmas, she moved back to her parent's wagon, and lived with them until her child was born in March. In view of Caroline's own pregnancy, her account of another woman in her wagon train is of great interest: "a terrific storm arose Keen flashes of lighting rent the air." The rain was so heavy, it flooded the wagons. "Within a tent, during the storm, were nurses *wading* around a bedside placed upon chairs ministering to a mother and new-born babe." Being delivered on two chairs set in a wagon leaking rain, with the floor deep in water—what did that mother feel? Perhaps she was content that she had the circle of "nurses" about her to bring her through, grateful merely that she was not alone. What did Caroline feel as she noted the occasion in her own diary?

There is scarcely a diary written during the 1840s which does not record the death of a father or husband or child or wife along the way. There is hardly a record that does not note human loss by sickness or accident. If it is true that the nineteenth century knew death as a close companion, then it is also true that the Overland Trail intensified that experience. Accident and illness were continual shadows upon the pioneers' lives. But for the women, those shadows were intensified by the twin circumstances of pregnancy and birth.

When gold was discovered at Sutter's mill near Sacramento, California, in 1848, a new kind of emigration began. Single men, arriving at the towns of the Missouri River with their possessions packed on mules, followed the siren call of the gold strikes. Sometimes the Forty-niners were married men who left their families behind in order to travel unencumbered. Five thousand emigrants and their families had crossed the Trail before 1848: thirty thousand came in 1849, and fifty-five thousand in 1850. The discovery of gold threw the nation—and the world—into a state of high excitement. The Overland Trail became an international highway. The vision of riches that could be had by dipping one's hand into a sparkling mountain stream was pure intoxication. Cornishmen and Austrians, Italians and Irishmen came to work in the mines. Chinese, Mexicans, and Latin Americans joined in the great rush for gold and silver. But nature seemed to conjure against such wild enthusiasms, as winds and heavy rains soon soaked the route and the shabbily constructed mining camps. Inexperienced both at pioneering and at mining, men suffered through the winter of 1850 in dismal hovels. Lonesome and wet, cold and sick, they lived in tents and blankets. Local newspapers carried flamboyant stories of golden nuggets, but many letters home told of lonesomeness and bad luck.[35]

The secret enemy of the gold-seekers was cholera. It had appeared initially in the United States in 1832–34, dissipated, and then burst forth again in the winter of 1848–49. From 1849 until 1854, there was no period when the dreaded disease did not appear somewhere in the country. Like revolution, cholera had swept through Europe. In July 1847, it was in Astrakhan, a year later, in Berlin; early in October of 1848 it appeared in London. When the packet *New York* settled into its berth in New York on December 1, 1848, it was placed in quarantine, but seven immigrants on the ship had already died below deck. The disease was uncontainable. By

May, five thousand in New York City had died, and the disease rushed westward. Carried by rats on the ships that came from Asia and from Europe, the disease spread to the ports of New Orleans, and from there by river steamer to St. Louis and up the Missouri River. Cholera followed the migrants across the Plains. It ravaged the Mississippi Valley; by May of 1849 it appeared as far west as Wisconsin. Milwaukee built special bathhouses for newly arriving immigrants, and other town councils voted to distribute chloride of lime to the poor, who were believed most susceptible. "It was in the infant cities of the West, with no adequate water supply, primitive sanitation, and crowded with a transient population, that the disease was most severe. St. Louis lost a tenth of her population. Cincinnatti suffered almost as severly. Sandusky even more severely than St. Louis."[36] Half of the three hundred and fifty persons in the United States Eighth Regiment Camp at Lavacca, Texas, died. In the Rio Grande valley, an army surgeon estimated that two thousand out of twenty thousand were cholera victims.[37]

Did the emigrants know what awaited them? Is it possible that word of lonely death had not yet reached the travelers as they waited at the Mississippi River? The diaries indicate that they did indeed know what lay ahead. Jane D. Kellogg wrote, in early June of 1852, before they had traveled far: "There was an epidemic of cholera all along the Platte River. Think it was caused from drinking water from the holes dug by campers. . . . All along the road up the Platte River was a grave yard; most any time of day you could see people burying their dead; some places five or six graves in a row, with board head signs with their names carved on them. It was a sad sight; no one can realize it unless they had seen it." On reaching Oregon, Kellogg wrote: "One family I can't forget; the mother was sick, had to be helped up the bank of [the Cascade River] and her little child was dead and laid out on the bank."

There can be no doubt that some overlanders believed they were fleeing from cholera when they started on their journeys. Health, as well as gold, became reasons given for migration. The truth was that the gold-seekers and emigrants carried the disease across the continent. "The route westward was soon marked with wooden crosses and stone cairns. Nowhere could the disease have been more frightening than on the trails, where men died without physicians, without ministers, and without friends."[38] "The road from Independence to Fort Laramie is a grave-yard."[39] One emigrant put the number of burials at fifteen hundred to two thousand. Another put the number at five thousand.[40] Some large wagon trains lost two-thirds of their number, and it was not uncommon to find children orphaned or entire families wiped out. It is probably impossible to arrive at an accurate or even reasonable estimate of the number who died on the Trail during the peak years of the epidemic. Abraham Sortore wrote that along the Platte River he was "scarcely out of sight of grave diggers."[41] On the south side of the Platte River, Ezra Meeker wrote that it looked like a battlefield. "The dead lay sometimes in rows of fifties or more. . . . Crowds of people were continually hurrying past us in their desperate haste to escape the dreadful epidemic."[42]

The most fearful aspect of the disease was its speed, for often the victim was dead within hours. Sometimes the emigrants took the precaution of burning the clothing of the victim and also burning the wagon. At other times, the wagon was abandoned and the emigrants fled as quickly as they could. Margaret Frink, living in the mining camps of California, told that her husband had attended a funeral. At the cemetery, "there were six men digging graves. They pointed to a box saying that the man in the coffin was working with them the day before." In and around the mines of Sacramento City, it was reported that a thousand miners died in a single month of 1850.

The remedies against illness were pitifully few. Laudanum (tincture of opium) and camphor were sometimes carried, but the women's diaries give little evidence that the emigrants were well supplied. Catherine Haun's diary tells that her family had with them such medicines as quinine for malaria, hartshorn for snakebites, citric acid for scurvey, and opium and whiskey for everything else. "A little of the acid mixed with sugar and water and a few drops of essence of lemon made a fine substitute for lemonade." Elizabeth Geer's diary confirmed that "no one should travel this road without medicine, for they are sure to have the summer complaint. Each family should have a box of physicking pills, a quart of castor oil, a quart of the best rum, and a large vial of peppermint essence."

Home remedies such as herbs and water baths were common. There were commercial medicines, usually useless, but most of the time the emigrants had nothing at all. One either recovered, or did not. To make matters worse, if cholera did not strike along the way, the diaries provide ample testimony that measles or typhoid or smallpox could be equally deadly. And should one escape these, virtually everyone suffered from some form of dysentery, or, as it was called, the "bloody flux." In the face of such evidence, the bravado of the emigrants seems all the more astonishing.

The settlements of the miners were built in the canyons and gorges of the Sierra Nevada. There, on every tiny "bar" or "flat," the mining camps were struck. Camps were little more than tent sites, near wet ground where rivers had been diverted so that their gravel beds could be washed and sifted. A siding named the "Bar Rich" became an assemblage of men panning for pebbles of gold. It was back-breaking work, but the camps were full of excitement. The rumor of a new strike higher up or farther down along the river was enough to send the men packing off to a better location. The "fat years" were between 1849 and 1852, when a small number of miners, using crude and primitive methods—sometimes no more than a pan and a pick and shovel—could bring out a sizeable amount of gold.

Some of the women who came into the mining camps had powerful ambitions of their own. There were fortunes to be had. Mining camp women worked in primitive conditions, keeping hotels and lodgers, cooking for twenty or fifty men, washing and sewing and demonstrating an intrepid determination to earn their own money.

When Luzena Stanley Wilson and her husband arrived in Nevada City, California, a "row of canvas tents lined each of the two ravines. . . . The gulches [were] . . . alive with moving men." They settled their wagon under some trees, not being "rich enough" for the "luxury" of a tent, and Luzena went to work washing off the dirt of the journey. "I scrubbed till my arms ached, before I got the children back to their natural hue." "I remember filling my wash-basin three times with fresh water before I had made the slightest change apparent in the color of my face." Her husband did not stop to wash but set out to find some wood to make a roof for his family.

While he was gone, Luzena lost no time in setting herself up in business:

> As always occurs to the mind of a woman, I thought of taking boarders. There was a hotel nearby and the men ate there paid $1 a meal. . . . With my own hands I chopped stakes, drove them into the ground, and set up my table. I bought provisions at a neighboring store and when my husband came back at night he found . . . twenty miners eating at my table. Each man as he rose put a dollar in my hand and said I might count on him as a permanent customer. I called my hotel "El Dorado."

Working together with her husband, Luzena served from seventy-five to two hundred boarders at twenty-five dollars a week. "I became luxurious and hired a cook and waiters." More than an innkeeper, Luzena became a banker as well, handling gold dust for the men. "Many a night have I shut my oven door on two milk-pans filled high with bags of gold dust and I have often slept with my mattress lined. . . . I must have had more than two hundred thousand dollars lying unprotected in my bedroom." Money-keeping soon turned to money-lending, and Luzena would have rivaled J. P.

Morgan, had history given her the chance. She lent money out "at such extravagant rate of interest"—no less than 10 percent a month—that even she was surprised at the brisk rate of business.

There were eighteen months of prosperity. Then fire swept through the town, leaving eight thousand miners homeless. Luzena and her husband were wiped out. They picked up their children and what they had in their pockets and started all over again. The mining camps were precarious ground for empire building, and we lose sight of Luzena in the desolate "rag towns" of the mining country in those years.

Mary Jane Megquier was older than most of the other women who went West, but she had an indomitable desire to make a fortune of her own in the gold rush. She had been married in Maine in 1831, and when she and her physician husband decided to go to California, she left her children with relatives and sailed for California via Panama. In her letters to her daughter from Panama, Mary Jane wrote: "Womens help is so very scarce that I am in hopes to get a chance by hook or crook to pay my way. . . . a woman that can work will make more money than a man, and I think now that I shall do that . . . for the quicker the money is made the sooner we shall meet." Her loneliness for her children comes forward in an experience she had in Panama: "Saw a beautiful child, she put out her hand, I asked her mother to give her to me, she said I could have her for one hundred dollars. . . . I should have taken her, it is the only thing I have seen in Panama I wanted."

In San Francisco, the doctor and his wife opened a hotel, and the money poured in:

> Some days we have made fifty dollars but I have to work mighty hard, a family of twelve boarders two small rooms with very few conveniences. We came to this house the third of July I have not been into the street since. . . . I intend to stay only long enough to make a small pile of the dust which will not overrun two years. . . . it is the most God forsaken country in the world, not one redeeming trait excepting gold. . . . I do not sit down until after eight o'clock at night and three nights out of the week I have to iron. I do not go to bed until midnight and often until two o'clock. . . . [There are] twenty in the family.

Six months later, the hotel was still flourishing, but the work that went into making it a success seemed beyond endurance. In June, Mary Jane wrote to her daughter far away in Maine:

San Francisco June 30, 1850

Dear Daughter

I should like to give you an account of my work if I could do it justice. We have a store in the size of the one we had in Winthrop, in the morning the boy gets up and makes a fire by seven o'clock when I get

Mary Jane Megquier (seated at right).

up and make the coffee, then I make the biscuit, then I fry the potatoes, then broil three pounds of steak, and as much liver, while the woman is sweeping and setting the table, at eight the bell rings and they are eating until nine. I do not sit until they are nearly all done. I try to keep the food warm and in shape as we put it on in small quantities, after breakfast I bake six loaves of bread (not very big) then four pies, or a pudding, then we have lamb, for which we have nine dollars a quarter, beef, and pork, baked turnips, beets, potatoes, radishes, salad, and that ever lasting soup, every day, dine at two, for tea we have hash, cold meat bread and butter sauce and some kind of cake and I have cooked every mouthful that has been eaten excepting one day and a half that we were on a steamboat excursion. I make six beds every day and do the washing and ironing you must think I am very busy and when I dance all night I am obliged to trot all day and had I not the constitution of six horses I should [have] been dead long ago but I am going to give up in the fall weather or no as I am sick and tired of work.

The account is not unusual for women in the mining towns. It describes the work of many. Mollie Dorsey Sanford, who accompanied her husband to the silver mines of Colorado, wrote: "My husband is to do the black-smithing for the company, and as was arranged I am to cook for the men. My heart sinks within me when I see 18 or 20, and no conveniences at all."

Narcissa Whitman, describing how her mother as a missionary's wife had to cook and keep house for ten or more "loose" men, wrote:

I often think how disagreeable it used to be to [her] to do her cooking in the presence of men sitting about the room. This I have to bear ever since I have been here. . . . at times it seems as though I cannot endure it any longer. . . . the cooking and eating room [is] always filled with 5 or more [men]. They are so filthy they require a great deal of cleaning wherever they go, and this wears out a woman very fast. . . . I hardly know how to describe our feelings at the prospect of a clean comfortable closet to pray in [alone].

Whitman's note tells us that it was not merely the physical work which the women found difficult; it was that there was no closet for solitude, no corner to preserve modesty or privacy.

For other women, the gold rush was no time for the niceties of person or of conscience. Margaret Frink, like Mary Megquier, was living proof that women as well as men responded to the siren call of gold. She started out in Indiana, lured, she wrote, by the "talk of money in California." She had heard "rumors a woman could get $16 a week for cooking for one man." When she reached Sacramento she opened a hotel, and by 1851 she had made her profit, sold the hotel, and bought a dairy with twenty-five cows. A

Two matrons meet at the muddy crosswalk of Cutler and Water Streets in Helena, Montana. Their dress suggests their determination to civilize that wild mining camp.

spirited entrepreneur, she established her domain by ordering a "cottage" to be sent by ship around Cape Horn and then from San Francisco to Sacramento.

Some of the best accounts of the California mining camps were those published by Louise Clappe under the pseudonym "Dame Shirley." Her letters tell of the courageous women who lived there. In a "canvas house" lived a sixty-eight-pound woman who "earnt her old man (all of 21 years old) nine hundred dollars in nine weeks, clear of all expenses, by washing! . . . To look at the tiny hands of Mrs. B. you would not think it possible."

But not all women fared as well as Mrs. B. . Clappe also told of "the long woman":

When a few weeks on the journey she had buried her husband who died of cholera after 6 hours' illness. . . . when I knew her she was living under a large tree . . . and sleeping at night, with all her family, in her one covered wagon. The oldest was but fifteen years of age and the youngest a nursing babe of six months. She had eight sons and one daughter. . . . She owned nothing in the world but her team, and yet she planned all sorts of succesful ways to get food for her rather large family. She used to wash shirts and iron them on a chair in the open air. . . . But the gentlemen . . . paid her three or four times as much as she asked . . . she accumulated quite a handsome sum in a few days. She made me think of a long-legged, very thin hen, scratching for dear life, to feed her never-to-be satisfied brood.

The migration for the gold fields almost always started out with a whoop of expectation. Rebecca Nutting Woodson remembered that "the California gold fever was getting pretty high by that time. Mr. Hickman and [my] father made their minds to fit out and start as soon as was safe in the spring of 1850. The older ones expect[ed] to amass very large fortunes. . . . us young ones expect[ed] to have a whole lot of fun and pleasure."

Rebecca's family and their longtime friends the Hickmans set out together, and spirits were high. "Us women folks was busy cooking up chickens and nice things for starting on oh we was going to have just a happy time." The sense of expectation was heightened by a prairie wedding and chivaree:*

On May 21st David Parker and Catherine Hickman was married. Father went to Hanesville and got a preacher. Such a Chivarie as they got that night was enough to awaken the Seven Sleepers. The newly married couple occupied a wagon for sleeping apartments. The first notice that they had of any disturbance was when the most of the men and women in the company took hold of the wagon the men at the tongue pulling the women at the back pushing and ran the wagon a half mile out on the prairie. Then the fun began. Such banging of cans shooting of guns, etc. and every noice conceivable was resorted to. The disturbance was kept up until midnight when the crowd dispersed leaving the happy couple out on the prairie to rest undisturbed until morning when they came walking into camp amid cheers and congratulations.

The wedding and the celebration were soon forgotten, however, when cholera touched the wagon train at the Rocky Mountains. The victim was a family man who had come from Iowa where he had left a wife and children. Members of the company took apart his wagon "so as to get boards to put in his grave and over the sides of him."

*The chivaree was an adaptation of the medieval *charivari*. The tradition of raucous noise making seemed particularly popular at wedding celebrations on the frontier.

"Father had a great deal of advice from an old Mountaineer [about] how to use precautions against Cholera I remember that one was to take a large quantity of peper sauce and put some in every bit of water we drank. . . . I do not know how many cases of it father took along He always thought it was a great help to keep from taking Cholera. When we was coming down the mountain there was several of us took sick with mountain fever I took it before we crossed the summit of the Rockies." The saving powers of pepper sauce were not tested by many diarists, but neither do the diaries reveal that other medicines were plentiful.

The family managed to reach Nevada City, California, on September 29, 1850. Rebecca's family built a wooden house and took in boarders from among the miners the first winter. Her mother and sisters who had cooked for their own family and their hired hands all summer, now cooked for paying boarders all winter.

A little over a year later, Rebecca was married. "Father went and got the [preacher] to come and marry us—Father moved away the next morning after I was married leaving me a girl of a little more than 16 years to cook and do the house work for 20 men sometimes more—On the 22nd of April 1853 our first child was born there on Bear River We called him William Henry—He was the pride of our lives—He was so much company to me as I had been sometimes 5 months at a time I did not see the face of a white woman So anyone can guess how much I enjoyed my baby with his big black eyes and dimpled face." Another son was born a year later. Scarcely more than eighteen, Rebecca Woodson was already the mother of two small sons, and lived in a mining camp full of men. When another family with ten children moved nearby, she and the older girls became bosom friends. "We did not think we could start to make a new dress or start piecing a new quilt without consulting each other. Oh those happy days."

Susan Parrish described the gold mines as "a kind of pot of gold . . . that we set out to find. . . . It took the form of a California gold mine or a cattle ranch extending over miles of New Mexico. It was never definite, but it lay always with alluring promise somewhere in the great West." Her father, she remembered, "was a wanderer after rainbows most of his life. . . . We were [a] happy care-free lot of young people. . . . It was a continuous picnic and excitement was plentiful." But the journey would have a curious twist.

Intending to reach Los Angeles, the family decided to turn to the southern route, and at Santa Fe there was a discussion of whether to follow a newly surveyed trail that went through the Soccorro mountains. Parrish, Oatman, and two other families chose the new route. "We set out on a faintly blazed trail over which no emigrant party had gone before. . . . I think I shall never forget the scenery in the Santa Cruz mountains. To me

Mining camps bore such names as "El Dorado" and the "Bar Rich," but the miners called them "Rag towns" or "flats." Women hauled water, cooked for twenty or more hungry men, and sometimes stored gold dust in milk pails.

the most beautiful spot in our journey of thousands of miles was found among the stately pines on the mountain top where a natural fountain poured its crystal waters into a granite basin fully six feet across." Just past Tucson, Royce Oatman decided to press on alone to try to reach Fort Yuma.

> Mrs. Oatman was seized with the pains of childbirth. During the anxiety for her comfort, no one noticed the approach of 17 Apache braves . . . who murdered Mr. and Mrs. Oatman, Lucy, her five-year old brother, two year old sister, new-born baby. Olive and Mary Ann were carried away by the savages. When the murders were discovered by the wagons that followed, there was no way of digging graves in the sunbaked ground, so the bodies were placed beneath a great pile of rocks.

The Parrish family reached Fort Yuma some time later. Susan Parrish recalled, "the day of our arrival was filled with anxiety and fear. My father was very ill and the bloody flux had so wasted my little sister, Lucy, that we hardly hoped for her life. That night, just a few hours after our arrival, another traveler joined us in our pursuit of the pot of gold. She was my little sister, Gila, whom we named in honor of the river near her birthplace."

There were two women, both pregnant when their families started out together from Iowa for California. The husband of one of them, anxious to get his wife to a settlement before her time of delivery, determined to hurry ahead, and was murdered by Apaches. The second family made no special preparation for the impending birth. Indeed, they named the child after the river of her birthplace. The account is as nonchalant as a discussion of potatoes or daisies.

The story has a strange sequel, for many years later, Parrish tells that an Indian captive was discovered. "They found the girl in her bark dress seated on the river bank. At the approach of the white men she buried herself in the sand." Olive Oatman had been tattooed about the chin and arms according to the practice of the Mohave Indians, to whom she had been sold for blankets by the Apaches who had first captured her. "At every opportunity [she sought] to flee back to her Indian husband and children. . . . For four years she lived with us, but she was a grieving, unsatisfied woman who somehow shook ones' belief in civilization. In time we erased the tatoo marks from her face but we could not erase the wild life from her heart. Perhaps we were wise in sending her to Oregon to her relatives. She must have forgotten as the years went by for in time she married a Mr. Fairchild, a banker from Texas."[43]

The Parrish family never actually mined. When they arrived in southern California they discovered that there were "continuous calls for accomda-

Olive Oatman was tattooed on the chin and arms in the fashion of the Mohave women. The marks, which lasted a lifetime, were made by piercing the skin and pressing charcoal into the wounds.

tions," and they opened a hotel on the road between Los Angeles and San Bernadino. There, one year after her arrival in 1851, Susan Parrish married "an emigrant from New York" who stopped at the hotel to find a night's rest. She seemed to regret that life turned her from the boisterous life of the mines; other women would have congratulated her on her good fortune.

By 1852, news of gold was intertwined with reports of disease. Word of the cholera epidemic spread quickly. Yet pioneers held fast to a conviction that their own strength would somehow bear them through the trials to come, and gold was a powerful incentive. The zeal of the emigrants to reach the gold fields was so great that Caroline Richardson wrote "A great many are packing thru on horses and mules or on foot. One boy had come all the way packing thru on a cow!" Richardson found the overland journey glorious. She wrote of "hills and rocks . . . flowers, mountains and valleys. . . . The ground here is covered with artemesis." She noted the wild roses, geraniums, and amaranth. At the South Pass, when the altitude began to lay snow down on the Trail, Richardson wrote that she and the others "gathered snow for a snowballing." Gleefully she observed that the travelers were "as high as we shall probably be in the world." When the emigrants reached Salt Lake City they "pitched a tent in a potato patch . . . Found a fiddler . . . and got together enough people for two sets of cotillions . . . Danced till eleven." On July 19 Caroline wrote that although it had rained, "Some of our boys procured a violin and we danced on the green by moonlight."

Other women noticed the scenery and were moved by the majesty of the western landscape. They saw and named each wild flower, each variety of herb and grass. But few failed to note the graves passed along the way. Even the light-hearted Caroline Richardson records more than eighty grave sites. Sometimes the entry was terse: "passed five graves." Sometimes the distinction was drawn between an old grave and a new grave. Sometimes the account was more detailed: "Saw a new grave covered with prickly pear today—this is the most respect to the dead we have seen on the road and was a lot to the person who had to do it." "A man told me that the graves would average one a mile on the cutoff we have traveled."

Richardson's diary testifies that it was not only cholera that proved deadly; it could as easily be poisonous water (June 13) or the bite of a rattlesnake (June 19) or dysentery (September 18). "We picked and ate large quantities of gooseberries—very large. The Co[mpany] all complaining especially the children who are vomitting." Cholera and gold, that was the strange mix that characterized the lives of the emigrants of the Overland Trail during the years of the gold rush.

Lodisa Frizzell, her husband, and four sons started in Illinois. "I have been reading the various guides of the rout to California," she wrote, "and they have not improved my ideas of the *pleasure* of the trip." She "dreamed of being attacked by wolves and bears," and her strong resolve quite melted by the time she reached the South Pass of the Rockies:

> the heart has a thousand misgivings & the mind is tortured with anxiety & often as I passed the fresh made graves, I have glanced at the side boards of the waggon, not knowing how soon it might serve as a coffin for some one of us.

The qualities of mind and heart that led men and women to choose to make the two-thousand-mile journey are difficult to recapture. An intense hunger for land and for gold and a heady confidence in their own strength combined to catapult the emigrants across a continent. They refused to be discouraged. With a boundless, even foolhardy courage, they suppressed the drama of their personal lives for the larger drama that lay before them. And in that moment of exchange, they were buoyant in the faith that the future was expansive and prosperous.

NOTES

1. Ray Allen Billington, *Westward Expansion: A History of the American Frontier,* 4th ed. (New York, Macmillan, 1974), pp. 431–433.

2. Ibid., p. 436.

3. Sidney Lens, *Radicalism in America* (New York, Crowell, 1969), p. 91.

4. Verne Bright, "The Folklore and History of the Oregon Fever," *Oregon Historical Quarterly,* 1951: 241.

5. Billington, pp. 321–22, 406.

6. Bright, 246.

7. Ibid.

8. Billington, pp. 323–24.

9. Ibid., p. 445.

10. Bright, 243.

11. Ibid., 251–252.

12. Ibid., 252.

13. Kathryn Troxel, "Food of the Overland Emigrant," *Oregon Historical Quarterly* (1955): 13. If a family were large, the quantity of supplies needed was significantly greater. Later guidebook writers, for example, advised taking 400 and 800 pounds of flour and 100 pounds of sugar.

The most widely-read guidebooks among the emigrants were Lansford Warren Hastings, *The Emigrants Guide to Oregon and California* (Cincinnati, 1845); Overton Johnson and William H. Winter, *Route Across the Rocky Mountains, with a Description of Oregon and California* (Lafayette, Indiana, 1846); Hosea B. Horn, *Horn's Overland Guide* (New York, 1852); Andrew Child, *Overland Route to California* (Milwaukee, 1852); Joel Palmer, *Journal of Travels over the Rocky Mountains* (Cincinnati, 1848); Joseph E. Ware, *The Emigrants' Guide to California* (St. Louis, 1849); J. M. Shively, *The Road to Oregon and California Across the Rocky Mountains,* reprinted in Dale Morgan, *Overland in 1846, Diaries and Letters of the California-Oregon Trail,* 734–42.

14. For a good description of the outfitting needed for the overland journey see Faragher, *Women and Men on the Overland Travel*, pp. 20–24 and Mattes, *The Great Platte River Road*, pp. 40–50.

15. Faragher, *Women and Men on the Overland Trail*, p. 17.

16. Mattes, p. 23.

17. James Evans, quoted in Mattes, pp. 162–163.

18. George Gibbs, quoted in Mattes, p. 240.

19. "By both men's and women's accounts, there was a lot of fighting on the Trail; nearly every diary recorded at least one incident somewhere along the road when a male party member got into a fistfight. Indeed, fighting among the men was one of the best noted trail phenomena." Faragher, *Women and Men on the Overland Trail*, p. 101. See also Jeffrey, *Frontier Women*, p. 42.

20. Faragher, *Women and Men on the Overland Trail*, p. 11.

21. Ibid., ch. 1; see also Mattes, ch. 3.

22. Faragher writes of his sample of women's diaries: "Not one wife initiated the idea [of migrating]; it was always the husband. Less than a quarter of the women writers recorded agreeing with their restless husbands; most of them accepted it as a husband-made decision to which they could only acquiesce. But nearly a third wrote of their objections and how they moved only reluctantly" (*Women and Men on the Overland Trail*, p. 163). On the other hand, Julie Roy Jeffrey found not only that women *participated* effectively in the decision-making process, but that "evidence corroborates female power to affect decision making. . . . Whatever ideology had to say about the necessity of female submission, women felt free to disrupt male emigration project and . . . had bargaining powers." (See *Frontier Women*, pp. 30–31.) The debate on the participation of women in the decision to go West is an important one insofar as it presents a major testing of the relationship between husband and wife in America at mid-century.

23. Agnes Stewart's diary corroborates the observations of Carroll Smith Rosenberg, whose seminal article "The Female World of Love and Ritual: Relations between Women in Nineteenth Century America" treats the question of same-sex relationships. All through women's overland diaries one comes upon examples of women spending their days in the company of other women and living a large portion of their emotional life well within a wholly female affectional circle. (*Signs* 131 (1975): 1–29).

24. See Verne Bright, "The Folklore and History of the Oregon Fever," 241–53.

25. See Faragher, *Women and Men on the Overland Trail*, p. 34–35. Also Faragher, "Midwestern Families in Motion: Women and Men on the Overland Trail to Oregon and California, 1843–1870" (Ph.D. diss., Yale University, 1977), p. 59.

26. Mary Kelsey's story is taken from George R. Stewart's *The California Trail*, pp. 19–29.

27. See Ruth Barnes Moynihan, "Children and Young People in The Overland Trail," *Western Historical Quarterly* 6 (1975): 279–94. Also Georgia Willis Read, "Women and Children on the Oregon Trail in the Gold Rush Years," *Missouri Historical Review* 39 (1944): 1–23.

28. Verne Bright, "The Folklore and History of the Oregon Fever," 243.

29. Ibid., 241.

30. For descriptions of buffalo stampeding other emigrant wagon trains, see Mattes, pp. 98–99, 253–59.

31. The story of the Whitman massacre, next to the story of the Donner Party, was probably the most widely-circulated on the frontier. When Marcus Whitman treated children for measles, white children (more resistant to the disease) tended to recover while Indian children often died. Indians were convinced Whitman had poisoned their children. Troubled relations between Catholic and Protestant missionaries, with Indian tribes pulled by each group, exacerbated contacts with the Indians until the massacre itself erupted.

32. See Faragher, *Women and Men on the Overland Trail*, pp. 29–30. Jeffrey points out that the splitting of parties almost always seemed ominous and threatening to women who had formed new and fragile support systems among the women of the wagon train. See *Frontier Women*, pp. 41–42.

33. Stewart, pp. 146, 151, 154.

34. Accidents to children who fell out of wagons and under the wheels or the hooves of oxen are common accounts in the diaries. See Stewart, p. 154, for an account of a young boy whose broken leg became gangrened. The child died after a crudely-performed amputation. Faragher finds that "children were pretty much allowed and encouraged to shift for themselves, to grow as they might, with relatively little parental or maternal involvement in the process" (*Women and Men on the Overland Trail*, p. 59). On the other hand, Faragher writes that "children [are] little mentioned in overland diaries and reminscences" (pp. 59 and 79), while Jeffrey writes: "it is not surprising that journals often mentioned children," and described them as "frightened, weeping or disagreeable" (*Frontier Women*, p. 40). Judging from my own survey, I would say that children older than seven or eight years were left to care for themselves, while younger children were within the circle of their mother's care and concern. Jeffrey's conclusion that "part of women's exhaustion was psychological" is certainly true. Diaries record every illness or accident to a child.

35. See Andrew J. Rotter, "Matilda, for God's Sake Write!: Women and Families on the Argonaut Mind," *California Historical Quarterly* 58 (1979): 136–39.

36. Charles Rosenberg, *The Cholera Years: The United States in 1832, 1849 and 1866* (Chicago: The University of Chicago Press, 1962), p. 115.

37. Ibid., p. 116.

38. Ibid., p. 115.

39. Mattes, p. 84.

40. Ibid.

41. Ibid.

42. Ibid., p. 85.

43. Mohave women were tattooed on their chins and arms. The markings were made by piercing the skin and forcing charcoal or dye into the wounds.

FAMILIES IN
TRANSIT II,
1851–1855

To the observer with a discerning eye, significant changes had come about in the emigrant parties that assembled along the Missouri River towns of 1852 and 1853. In all the activity of those "jumping-off places" where women and children peered out of wagons that rumbled through the streets, where trappers, gold-seekers, and Indians mingled, where the blacksmiths' shops were open from dawn till dark getting the teams ready for the long journey, where hotels were overcrowded—amid all that hubbub, certain changes could be observed. Wagon trains seemed to be made up of larger family units. There were now herds of cattle and sheep, and extra wagons packed with provisions. The companies and their outfits were grander.

Nancy Wilson's family traveled with twenty-five wagons and teams, "nearly all of them ox teams of five yoke each wagon." These families were a proper emblem of American industry and enterprise. "Our wagons were big and strong, and had good, stout bows, covered with thick, white drilling so there was a nice room in each wagon, as everything was clean and fresh and new." There was an aesthetic to wagon-building, an aesthetic of self-sufficiency and pride. "Most of the emigrant wagons had the names of the owners, places where they were from, and where they were bound, marked in large letters on the outside of the cover."

These families were more than farmers. They were ready to run a business, raise and sell a herd of sheep, manage a hotel, open a carpentry shop, trade a horse, sell a farm. Their knowledge and their skills were not only those needed for breaking ground, but for trading and selling and relocating. These families were comfortable in the towns as well as on the farms. They had waited prudently before they sold their farms and set out for Oregon or California. No acting from quick enthusiasm here, just the careful determination that the right time had come.

Caroline Richardson, a sharp observer of the road, wrote of passing 23,000 sheep, and Helen Marnie Stewart was told at Fort Kearney that there had been 13,000 "head of people," and with them "90,000 stock." Rebecca Ketcham wrote: "All around us on each side of the river were sheep, cattle, horses, wagons, men, women and children—more cattle and sheep than I ever saw before in my life: drove after drove, thousands, yes, tens of thousands. . . . It is astonishing to see what a multitude is moving on." The westward movement was now not only a major demographic surge, but also a monumental movement of capital and of goods.

The Trail had become a commercial road. Trappers and Indians ran ferries and bridges and supply stations. From April through October, five dollars per wagon and fifty cents a head for oxen were standard fees at difficult river crossings. The ferrymen and bridge-keepers made the way easier for the emigrant, but they also raised the cost of the passage. Charlotte Pengra wrote that by May 10, 1853, "our expenses here and fitting out for the rest of the journey has cost us nearly 75 dollars—persons starting this journey should have at least 150 dollars."

Within this massive movement of people, the westward migration remained a migration of families. Branches of families were gathered in from different states. The overwhelming importance of the journey was sufficient to reknit families that had seen children marry and settle a hundred, or even a thousand miles distant. The overland crossing could be made with a wife's family or with a husband's family. Kinship was honored in either direction, so long as the destination was California or Oregon. And the families of old friends and neighbors were gathered in. The extra men who were working their passage across the continent were drawn into the family—their "character" was read with much care, and their willingness to work was closely studied. What was of deep significance was the coming together for the start of the historic journey.

Women continued to perceive themselves as existing primarily in the presence of other women. Most readers who have examined these diaries at length have found themselves wondering whether the writer were married at all, whether the odd initial that appears occasionally on a page represents a member of the wagon train or the diarist's husband. Women's daily routine—the baking, the washing, the cooking, the caring for the children, looking for herbs and berries and roots, visiting the sick—all of these were performed with women who traveled in the company. Within a loosely formed, makeshift "women's sphere," even the depressing necessity of having to do men's chores could be absorbed as long as women could make a social fabric of their lives on the Trail.

Cecelia McMillen Adams made the overland crossing with her husband and her parents, her twin sister, her brother-in-law and his wife, and others of her extended family; but she spent virtually the whole of her time with her twin sister. Her husband is mentioned only twice in her diary, once when she fears he may be drowned, and once when she tells that he had gone ahead to get help. In the company of eight wagons, sixteen men and ten ladies and several children, "P[erthenia] and I walked on ahead of the rest of the company," "P[erthenia] and I climbed one of the hills" "P[erthenia] done some washing and I baked bread and pumpkin and apple pies," "P[erthenia] and myself . . . have some jolly times even if we are in a wilderness." The women rode in the wagons or walked together. They tended each other and the children. Sometimes they saddled a horse and rode to a neighboring wagon train in order to help a woman who was in childbirth or ill. It was not domesticity by Victorian standards, for it included some highly unfeminine chores. But the domestic sphere of the Overland Trail was one that involved the close bonding of women and the separation of the women from the men.

As the days settled into a semblance of routine, it became apparent that women's work had a different rhythm from the men's work. The women began their day before dawn, to start the fires, put on the kettles of water, and begin breakfast. The women and the older children milked the cows. By the time the coffee was boiled, the beans warmed and the bread baked, the men were about, gathering in the herds.[1]

Helen M. Carpenter was a bride on her honeymoon. "Although there is not much to cook," she wrote, "the difficulty and inconvenience in doing it, amounts to a great deal—so by the time one has squatted around the fire and cooked bread and bacon, and made several dozen trips to and from the wagon—washed the dishes . . . and gotten things ready for an early breakfast, some of the others already have their night caps on—at any rate it is time to go to bed. In respect to women's work, the days are all very much the same—except when we stop . . . then there is washing to be done and light bread to make and all kinds of odd jobs. Some women have very little help about the camp, being obliged to get the wood and water . . . make camp fires, unpack at night and pack up in the morning —and if they are Missourians they have the milking to do if they are fortunate enough to have cows. I am lucky in having a Yankee for a husband, so am well waited on."

Cecilia McMillen Adams and Dr. William Adams.

Sometimes the line of wagons stretched as far as the eye could see. Oxen were essential to the success of a passage. If they died, or became lame, or too weak to draw the wagons, a family might be stranded a hundred, or a thousand miles from its destination. Cooking over an open fire was difficult at best—more so in a strong wind.

Although cooking was not new to women, cooking in the *open* was. Lodisa Frizzell wrote: "it goes agin the grane." The women soon discovered that cooking over a campfire was far different from cooking on a stove. Two forked sticks were driven into the ground, a pole laid across and a heavy kettle swung upon it. Pots fell into the fire and families soon became accustomed to food that was burned. There were no tables, and all preparation was on the ground. As Frizzell noted: "All our work here requires stooping. Not having tables, chairs or anything it is very hard on the back."

Esther Hanna, eighteen years old and a minister's wife, wrote in her diary of winds that were "very high and piercing. . . . Had to haul our water and wood for night. . . . I have also had to bake tonight. It is very trying on the patience to cook and bake on a little green wood fire with the smoke blowing in your eyes so as to blind you, and shivering with cold so as to make the teeth chatter."

The travelers of 1852 and 1853 had particularly wet summers.[2] Beginning in the early spring, the rains poured down on the wagons. The women kept noting that the bedding had no time to dry out and that children were continually suffering from earaches and fevers. Charlotte Stearns Pengra's diary carries this account:

> Our tent was completely drenched and some of our things that were inside, such as bedding folks and so forth you who have never experienced the pleasure of being awakened sundry times during the night by the falling of pearly drops into their faces, can scarcely imagine the exquisite pleasure, such as awaking affords, especially when it brings the consciousness of a hard thunder storm raging without and the certainty that there is nothing but the thickness of cotton cloth to shelter us from the pelting rain.

Velina Williams wrote, tersely: "Tis a perfect mud-hole, beds and children completely soaked." Lucy Rutledge Cooke noted: "All clothes had to remain wet. Even babies." Women and small children slept under the wagons when the rains were heavy, but there was simply no accommodation that insulated one from the weather.

Cooking in the rain was especially taxing. The weeds and buffalo chips were wet and would not burn. "There is nothing to eat but crackers and raw bacon." In heavy rain, the women might dig a hole in the ground, jam in a hollow ramrod to serve as an air shaft, and then fill the hole with small rocks and bake the bread on these. The food had the pungent smell of ashes or sagebrush or buffalo chips and smoke. James Clyman told of one wife who "having kneaded her dough, she watched and nursed the fire and held an *umbrella* over the fire and her skillet with the greatest composure for near 2 hours and baked enough bread to give us a very plentiful supper!"

By midsummer, fourteen hundred miles behind them and another thousand still ahead, the emigrants found the journey was taking its toll. Women were walking alongside of the wagons to lighten the loads, or walking behind the wagons, in choking clouds of dust, to gather the weeds and buffalo chips needed to start their fires. If the routine work of the Trail were any indication of what life held in store for women on the frontier of the new territories, it is small wonder many had grown suspicious of the promises of a bright tomorrow.

The usual fare for breakfast on the Trail was bread or pancakes, fried meat, beans, and tea or coffee. Pancakes were made with flour, water, and baking soda, and cooked in a large frying pan or baking kettle. If bread were baked, it was placed in a skillet or Dutch oven with an iron lid. The ingenuity of the overland women was enormous, but sometimes even that ingenuity could be defeated, as when one traveler noted that mosquitoes got into the dough and turned it black.

Nevertheless, the emigrant women displayed an astonishing versatility. Lucy Cooke rolled out her pie dough on the wagon seat beside her while they were traveling. Cecelia Adams wrote that on one Sunday in June, she had "cooked beans and meat, stewed apples and baked suckeyes [pancakes] . . . besides making Dutch cheese, and took everything out of the wagon to air." Jane D. Kellogg, who was on her honeymoon, recalled that "our provisions consisted of hard sea biscuit; crackers; bacon, beans, rice, dried fruit, teas, coffee and sugar." Charlotte Stearns Pengra was explicit about her chores, recording meal by meal what she had prepared. April 29, 1853: "I hung out what things were wet in the waggon, made griddle cakes, stewed berries and made tea for supper. After that was over made two loaves of bread stewed a pan of apples prepared potatoes and meat for breakfast, and mended a pair of pants for Wm. pretty tired." May 8: "baked this morning and stewed apples this afternoon commenced washing . . . got my white clothes ready to suds. . . . I feel very tired and lonely." By May 14, Charlotte was thinking she had become derelict in her duties: "gathered up the dishes, and packed them *dirty* for the first time since I started." On May 18, with a burst of determination, Pengra "washed a very large washing, unpacked dried and packed clothing—made a pair of calico cases for pillows and cooked two meals—done brave, I think. Those who come this journey should have their pillows covered with dark calico and sheets colored, white is not suitable."

After the evening meal, the women's work began again, the unpacking of the bedding and the tents, the preparing of the next day's food, sewing torn spots in the canvas, collecting berries if there was still enough light. After dinner, the beds had to be made up, the wagons cleaned out and aired to prevent mildew.

Although a goodly portion of wagon parties started out their journeys with scrupulous adherence to Sabbath observance, the demands of the road soon made such rituals impractical. Stopping for Sunday rest made the travelers feel vulnerable to Indian attacks, and as the season advanced into midsummer and early autumn, the chance of being caught in the mountains by early snows made any delay even more risky. Sundays soon were marked simply by a reading from the Bible during lunchtime stops before the emigrants moved on, honoring the inexorable timetable that brooked no interruption—not even for God.

Surprisingly little is revealed in the diaries about the care of infants and small children. What is preserved shows that the women used all their ingenuity to combat the discomforts of the journey. "For sores about the mouth a concoction of sage, borax, alum and sugar." But the crying of babies must have been a continual sound in the wagons. Were there not always blisters and mosquito bites, teething and coughs, earaches, diarrhea —all of the "ordinary" ills of childhood?

The omission from the women's diaries of prescriptions for the care of infants and small children is puzzling. In so many other respects these overland diaries were intended as instruction manuals for family members or neighbors and friends who might wish to follow, so that one would expect the women to pass along those experiences concerning the care of children—advice for the maddening problems of traveling for five or six months out of doors with small children and infants. Perhaps the children were part of that private world that women committed to oral exchanges, talking with one another as the wagons rolled mile after mile on those long, hot days. The realm of children would then have been consigned to the oral tradition along with information about menstruation, marriage, and pregnancy and childbirth. So much of the woman's world was omitted from written accounts—even from the diaries. So much of the woman's world in the nineteenth century was hidden by elaborate taboos.

In most parties women washed as opportunity presented itself. The banks of a river would be lined with women who carried their kettles, their washtubs, and piles of unwashed linen. If there were fuel to spare, they heated their water, but generally they had to contend with hard soap and cold water. Days of sun, wind, soap, and water could be a painful combination. Rebecca Ketcham wrote: "Camilla and I both burnt our arms very badly while washing. They were red and swollen and painful as though scalded with boiling water. Our hands are blacker than any farmer's and I do not see that there is any way of preventing it, for everything has to be done in the wind and sun."

Jane Kellogg remembered that the women preferred to do their washing in the evening, and that they "put heavy weights on [the clothes] or wore them just as they dried. We were not particular about our looks." Caroline Richardson "washed by full moon in river. Beau[tiful]." But for America E. Rollins, the wash days were nightmares. "Oh! horrors how shall I express it; it is the dreded washing day . . . but washing must be done and procrastination won't do it for me."

Gathering berries was another routine chore. On more than one occasion, women who had gone in search of berries or fuel lost their way. Richardson was once lost in a terrain with no tree to mark the horizon, and two other women in her party wandered for ten miles through deep ravines. They managed somehow to return, by luck or by their pioneer skills or, as Richardson judged in her diary, by virtue of their very stubbornness, for they "stuck with it and came thru."

The work of the road was physically wearing, but worse was the feeling among some women that the journey was a backsliding into conditions that would have been intolerable at home. Each day on the Trail seemed to turn women more into hired hands than Christian housewives.

Miriam Davis, who settled in Kansas with her husband and children in 1855, wrote: "I have cooked so much out in the sun and smoke that I hardly know who I am and when I look into the little looking glass I ask, 'Can this be me?' Put a blanket over my head and I would pass well for an Osage squaw." One of the women traveling with Davis had been stricken with rheumatism by exposure to the weather. She could not even care for her own child. "I picked a lovely bouquet of prairie flowers and carried it to her but she couldn't take it into her hand." Driven by the exquisite punishment of the Trail, women tried to hold together fragments of their accustomed life. They tried to maintain a circle of female care and companionship. But for many, the overland journey seemed an assault on feminine propriety, a hurtful experience to be endured. The open country left many women feeling unprotected and vulnerable. Older women were most pained by the experience. Younger women had different priorities. Unmarried girls found opportunities to share with the young men and boys a brief period of free companionship. Young girls sang together by the campfires and played mouth organs, guitars, and fiddles. It is in the diaries of the *younger* women that one finds the willing—sometimes the eager—acceptance of new roles and a broader definition of what a woman might effectively do.

Lydia Milner Waters wrote: "I . . . learned to drive an ox team on the Platte [River] and my driving was admired by an officer and his wife. . . . I heard them laughing at the thought of a woman driving oxen." When she climbed the hills with the boys and young men, "sometimes my feet would slip off the [tree limbs] and I would be hanging by my arms. You may be sure my skirts were not where they ought to have been then. . . . There were many things to laugh about." And Mary Ellen Todd confided to her diary that she had learned to crack the whip while driving the team of oxen, and that there was "a secret joy in being able to have a power that set things going." Mary Eliza Warner, who was fifteen, wrote: "I drove four horses nearly all day. . . . Aunt Celia and I played Chess which Mrs. Lord thought was the first step toward gambling."

Sometimes there was conflict between mothers and daughters as the overland journey led young girls into "loose" behavior. Mothers tried to impose Victorian proprieties, and overland diaries yield many accounts of stern dialogues. Adrietta Hixon wrote:

> While traveling, mother was particular about Louvina and me wearing sunbonnets and long mitts in order to protect our complexions, hair and hands. Much of the time I should like to have gone without that long bonnet poking out over my face, but mother pointed out to me some girls who did not wear bonnets and as I did not want to look as they did, I stuck to my bonnet finally growing used to it.

Her mother's discipline was burdensome, but Adrietta was obedient: "When riding, I always rode aside with my full skirt pulled well down over my ankles. If we had ridden astride, as they do now, people would have thought we were not lady-like. Mother was always reminding Louvina and me to be ladies."

Mollie Dorsey Sanford recalled that "it had occurred to me how much easier I could get through the tangled underbrush if I were a man, and I slipped out into the back shed, and donned an old suit of Father's clothes. . . . it was very funny to all but Mother, who feared I am losing all the dignity I ever possessed."

The overland journey and the western frontier would bring many women into completely new ways of life. There would be lady "cowboys" and lady ranchers. Dorothea Mitchell became a lumberwoman, and dedicated a book about her life "to every woman . . . pondering her ability to compete in what was once a man's work." Elinor Stewart was a homesteader who wrote: "any woman who can stand her own company . . . and is willing to put in as much time at careful labor as she does over the washtub, will certainly succeed."

Whether the issue was riding astride instead of sidesaddle, or wearing trousers when riding or working, or driving teams of cattle, the frontier continually expanded the work assigned to women. And even women born to farm work resented the awful labor that surrounded breaking new land. There is evidence that farm women sometimes worked grueling hours in order to free their daughters from a similar life. Lucinda Dalton, eldest daughter of a Mormon family that settled in Utah in 1857–58, remembered that her mother worked far into the night in order that she attend school and study. In 1870, Jane Jasper wrote to her daughter, who had been sent to a boarding school: "It is no use for me to be thinking and working my life out for you to have the chance for an Education unless you have the sense to appreciate what is done for your future."[3]

Frontier women resisted any form of dress that would accommodate their daily life and work. No change that might seem to bring women closer to the dress of men or of Indian women was tolerated. The word "squaw" appears occasionally in diaries, always as an epithet of utmost disgust. Whereas men sometimes conveyed their sense of social dislocation by complaining they were working like "niggers," women who were resentful of the labor forced upon them by the frontier, expressed their bitterness in the judgment that they saw themselves reduced to the status of "squaws."

In their steadfast clinging to ribbons and bows, to starched white aprons and petticoats, the women suggest that the frontier, in a profound manner, threatened their sense of social role and sexual identity. The dress of the Indian woman was, after all, both chaste and practical. The fervor with which it was rejected suggests something of the anxiety of emigrant women lest the frontier upset the careful balances that had been worked out between husbands and wives in rural communities.

Precisely because work roles were blurred on the frontier, and because women were often called upon to do chores recognized as men's work, dress became a primary mode of asserting the delineation of the sexes. Dress was emblematic of the intention of women to restore the domestic sphere as soon as possible thereby limiting women's work to the house. Starching white aprons on the frontier must have required extraordinary discipline, but those starched aprons betokened delimited work roles that frontier women would not lightly forego.[4]

When families came together for the start of the cross-country journey, it was commonplace for the men to draw up constitutions in which were set down the obligations of each member of the wagon train: how much

Pupils in an Oregon schoolhouse in the 1860s have their picture taken. Schoolhouses were second only to churches in order of community priority. Emigrant children remembered passing around the single piece of slate that a class might have, so that each one might do sums and practice handwriting.

Lady Oscharwasha, also known as "Jennie," was a Rogue River Indian. This artfully posed portrait shows a delicate beaded costume pioneer women might have envied. Jennie did domestic work for women in Jacksonville, Oregon, and died in 1893.

These women wear sturdy men's boots to ward off the melting snows of the Colorado spring. But the young girl's white apron suggests the will power that went into keeping the domestic sphere a palpable reality of frontier life.

provisioning each was to have; how they were to share the work of the journey. Considering these written agreements, historian David Potter has written about the proclivity of Americans to organize themselves into formal associations as need presented.[5]

But historians of overland diaries know that these constitutions, drawn up at the outset of the migration, came apart as frequently as they were constructed. No written constitution ever survived very long against the kinds of uncertainties that beset the travelers. Disputes continually arose over which route to take; which cutoff would be most propitious. Should one detour in favor of advice left nailed to a tree? And even if there were agreement on which route to follow—and there rarely was—quarrels broke out on other issues.[6] The women's diaries repeatedly note that the quarrels always started among the men. Velina Williams, for example, wrote with alarm that "some of the teams started before all were ready, which led to hard feelings and harsh, angry words, which made us all very unpleasant. Oh, that the spirit of forebearance and love were more prevalent in our company." Quarrels appear regularly noted in the diaries of the women who worried because the decision of a husband or father to separate from the wagon train could mean loneliness for a wife who found comfort in the company of other women.[7]

Sometimes, the very largeness of the wagon train brought the necessity of separation, for the cattle of too large a group could not find forage as the summer wore on. Sometimes sheer accident caused families to fall behind. A wheel that needed repair, an axle that had broken, a family member who was sick—any of these mishaps could separate a family from the company. The diaries tell that the emigrants were a people of joiners, but also a people of separatists, and the truer picture of their behavior was that they were continually moving in and out of formal groups. Even when they had signed a constitutional agreement, the accidents of the road, the quarrels or friendships that were struck made for a fluid grouping and regrouping of people.

Most significantly, fluid patterns of grouping and regrouping held true even *within* families. If one considers the intensity of the effort made by families to draw together for the journey, the ease with which they also tended to separate is surprising. The overland histories of two large families —the Stewarts and the Williamses—provide an illustration of this fluidity.

John Stewart started for Oregon from Pennsylvania in 1853. With him were his second wife, Jannet, and his three unmarried daughters, Agnes, Helen Marnie, and Elizabeth. The Stewarts' eldest daughter, Annie, married to John Stewart (no relation to her father), came along with her husband and eleven children, aged one to nineteen. Daughter Mary Stewart Warner, her husband John and three children were also with the family moving West. Elizabeth Stewart would marry Fred Warner in St. Joseph, Missouri, on May 23, at the start of the trip.

Another daughter, Allison, remained behind in Pennsylvania, awaiting the birth of her third child in June of the year the rest of the family left for Oregon. The parting was a sad one; Annie hoped her brood of eleven and Mary's three children would make up to their mother for leaving Allison and her children behind. So close-knit was this clan that five of Annie's eleven children were named for her parents and for her sisters.

With the Stewarts was Mrs. Love (who had known the family for ten years) and her three grown sons, David, James, and John. Helen Marnie

Stewart would marry David Love in Oregon the following year. And Agnes would marry the third of the Warner brothers, Tom. The Stewarts, Warners, and Loves were three tightly-knit families who intended to make the relocation in Oregon as a solid unit. That closeness however, was shattered by chance once the journey had begun.

John and Annie Stewart and their eleven children fell behind almost at the journey's start. They had traveled with the family all the way from Pennsylvania to Missouri, but just after the wedding of Elizabeth and Fred Warner, they lagged behind because their wagons were too heavily loaded. On May 4, the elder Stewarts, the Warners, and the Loves decided to wait no longer. John and Annie would catch up by day's end. But after they had rearranged their wagons, they kept missing the rest of the family. A thousand miles later, they changed their destination and followed the southern route to California. It was a year before the families heard of one another again. The elder Stewarts also departed from the established route, taking a new road through Idaho Territory. Along with hundreds of other emigrants they were brought close to starvation in the Cascade Mountains, and they did not reach Oregon until December.

The diaries of two of the sisters, Helen Marnie and Agnes, remain, along with an incomplete letter written by Elizabeth. The diaries reveal how the women felt about the separation.

Helen wrote: "We come now to the Missouri and cross we travel a peace when Stewart broke his wagon he will have to wait and get it mended we are going and is to wait at the big blue for them." On May 19, "we got to the big blue [river] today," but there is no mention of the Stewarts rejoining the party. On June 16, Helen wrote: "We heard of Stewart today that he sold his little wagon and ware all well and getting along very well I do wish they could ketch up with us." Agnes felt the separation from her sister and her sister's family more sharply. On May 17, two weeks after they lost touch, she wrote: "I wish Stewarts folks were come up to us I don't like to be parted from any of our people when we all get together again I hope we will

Among the overlanders of 1852 was the photographer Peter Britt, who traveled from Illinois to Oregon. He rode horseback and led a wagon in which rested three hundred pounds of fragile and valuable camera equipment. Among his effects was this photograph of the daughters of Joseph Suppiger of Illinois, taken in 1847. It must have pleased him, for he carried it across the country. Britt arrived in Jacksonville, Oregon, with his camera and plates in a makeshift two-wheeled cart. He had a yoke of oxen, a mule, and five dollars left, and this beautiful photograph of two girls from the state he had left behind.

not be parted again." On May 20, she wrote: "O I feel lonesome today sometimes I can govern myself but not always." And on May 21, she wrote again: "Left stewarts folks for good I suppose this seems too hard to bear for mother frets so if he was not so stubborn he might throw away one of those big wagons and we would wait on him yet if it was not for anna and the children I would not care so much but it is hard to leave them." On June 4 there was some word of the Stewarts, and Agnes's diary notes: "Stewart about 60 miles back will never catch up to us now we cannot wait so long for fear of endangering our own fate." Here was the travelers' gnawing fear, the terrible anxiety that compelled wagon parties to abandon the sick and the lost in their relentless movement forward.

The most sharply etched account of the parting is preserved in the fragment of a letter written by Elizabeth Stewart Warner, who made the journey as a wedding trip. Her letter, written sometime between 1856 and 1857, is printed here in its entirety:

Dear Friends,

I want to write you a full and true letter, this I promised to do, but I fear I shall fail, not in the truth but in giveing you a full description of the rout and gurny whitch I have neither memory to remember or head to discribe and I did not keep a journal as I intended, but I will try to give you the heads and particulars as well as I can remember. we left Pittsburgh, march the 17th 1853, and after a tedous gorney we arived in Saint Jo. april the 5th. We thair bought up our cattle at the verious prices from 65 dolls to 85 dollars paid 40 cents per day for the meanest house you could think of human beings living in and we had to steal beg and take watter all over the town we had to pay 10 cts per day for putting our cattles in a yard mud to the knes, and had to drive them more than a mile to watter every day we camped out in the woods and was mutch better of than in Saint Jo. we crossed the Missuri on the fourth of May in the rain. we crosed on a ferry boat and was to cross the next but ther was another familie had got into the boat, before them. david Love and fred was just coming to cross on the same boat they had been over to buy another youlk of cattle but were just one minute to late, and well it was for us all for the boat struck a snag and drowned 7 men a woman was standing on the bank, she said to mother, do you see that man with the red warmer on well that is my husband and while she spoke the boat struck and went down and she had to stand within call of him and see him drownd. O my heart was sore for that woman and three miles from the river we saw another woman with 8 children stand beside the grave of her husband and her oldest son so sick that she could not travel annd had to go up the river 12 miles before they could cross we waited for them at the mishen we then all got to-gether and one of stewart's wagons broke down and wes mended next day we had ben telling him that he ought not to presist

The dour expression worn by Agnes Stewart in this posed photograph hid a vivacious young woman who drew the attention of young men in the wagon party. Her sister Helen Marnie wrote in her diary: "Sometimes I think our Agnes is made of lodestone for she draws to her wonder powerful."

Married at thirty-one, Elizabeth Stewart appears to have been older than her bridegroom, Fred Warner.

in taking such big wagons but he would no advice and when we ware
at the mishen the men held a council and determined not to wait for
him for they saw he would never keep up. Our wemen protested
against it but they started and we were obliged to fowlow and I did not
feel so bad when death came and snatched one of us away well we got
through and they only made Salt lake about the half way. it was best
for us to go on but it was hard to part I do not think that Mother will
ever get over it she blames her self for not standing still and she
blames us for not doing the same and she blames the men for leaving
them. mother says that no consequence could never make her do the
like again. But it was shurley best for us to push on we only hea[r]d
where they were by Mrs Grilles letter five days ago we thought mother
would have been satisfied when she herd whare they ware to a cer-
tainy but no we haven't any little Jenett with us and mother clings
to the child with a nervous affection whitch I never saw her show to
any object before. we then proceded 10 wagons in company to the plat
River full for miles in wedth to look at that great flood and think that
when we had followed it almost to its cource we would hardley be half
way, and it is the easiest half of they way by 20 degrees, it was painful
though for faint harts I can tell you. But on we goged each day about
25 or 30 miles and it was a pleasure to travel then we had a very
agreeable company not one jarr amongst us had it not been for the
thought of anna behind it would have been a pleasure trip indeed. we
lost the first ox on sweet watter it was Tom's wheel ox, and what he
called one of his main dependence but poor Sam had done his duty
and then laid him down to rest, some time after that one of David
Loves oxen died and then one of mothers, and when we came to snake
river it was every day and every night sombody had lost an ox, we lost
four in one day and two nights when we got up in the morning we
wemon got the breakfuss and the men went after the cattle, and we
thot at last that we could not dare to see them come back for they
always came back minus someones cattle. then we came to the new
road they talk about the times that tried men souls but if this ware not
the times that tried both men and wemon's souls, well thar was a man
thair meeting his wife and familie, and he was going the new road, it
was a 100 miles nearer, our cattle wer few in number we had enough
provisions to do us but no more Thare were a great many wagons gone
with that man and thare a great many more going and we thought if it
was a nearer and better road we had as much need to go as anybody
well on we went until we came to the first camping place and thair we
found a paper telling how far to the next camping place and then we
came to the blue mountains & these mountains are composed of rocks
of a blue coulur and all broken up as eavenly about the size of a pint
cup, as if they were broken by the hand of man they were hard on the
oxens feet and our feet, for everybody walked here. when we ware
crossing the streams the rocks ware larger some times so large they up
set the wagons into the wattor. when we had crossed the blue

Mountains we came to those hard perplexing lakes. now take the map and look at those lakes which lie between the blue Mountains and the Cascades and you will not see one for every five that theirs on the ground but you will have some little idea. The first one we came to we should have taken the north and instead of that we took the south side and thare we wandered sometimes west. . . . [Elizabeth's letter breaks off here, and we have no diary by Jannet Stewart, her mother.]

The accident of having wagons that were too cumbersome parted mother and daughter and grandchildren, among them a favorite namesake, a child named after her grandmother. Jannet Stewart grieved, knowing that she and the other womenfolk had not been strong enough to oppose the men's decision to push on. She should have remained firm and the women should have stood firm with her.

The Trail wore away at the places where women's emotional lives were most intense. It separated mothers and daughters and grandchildren who were one's heart's delight. And all because the men were stubborn or willful, short-tempered or foolish. The separate spheres of men and women ran parallel so long as life remained set in traditional paths, but the Trail bred dislocation. Elizabeth's letter suggests that it was three years before Jannet Stewart knew for certain that her daughter and her eleven children got through. There were messages from people who had seen them, and there was word that they had stopped at this place or that. But her husband's decision not to wait brought with it an extended time of anguish and uncertainty.

Elizabeth's letter also tells us that the mother would not, or could not, openly dispute her husband's decision. Was it unthinkable that she, a wife of many years, should challenge her husband's judgment? Or was it that she did not believe she could make him understand her need to keep her children with her? Throughout the diaries one finds that dark thread of the women's painful subservience to the authority of husbands and fathers. It lies in these stories and generated a gulf of resentment between husbands and wives.[8]

Elizabeth, on the other hand, was living through a remarkable reality of her own. Married at thirty-one on the eve of the journey, she was pregnant before the journey's end. Her letter with its phrase "it was shurley best for us to push on," carries in it her own predicament. If her mother's need was to keep her daughters by her side, Elizabeth's need was to reach Oregon as early as possible. Luck was not with her, however, for the party was lost in the mountains of Idaho, reduced to starvation and forced to move ahead on foot. Elizabeth would have been in the fifth or sixth month of her pregnancy by December. "It was shurley best for us to push on" is Elizabeth's only intimation of the intensity with which she must have been watching their progress each day, hoping to see herself in some settlement before being delivered of a child in a mountain pass, in the snow.

Much the same story is told in the diaries of two sisters of another extended family. Velina Stearns Williams and Charlotte Stearns Pengra went west with fifteen related adults and eighteen children. Charlotte and Bynon Pengra had only one child, while in the wagons of their kin were families of four and five children. On one particular morning, Bynon Pengra started up early to make good headway; he assumed the others would overtake him before long. As luck would have it, one of the wagons in the larger party stuck fast in the sand that morning, and the men could not pry it loose. Charlotte's diary shows her looking back for the family she left behind. "Our company has not got together and we are persuaded they have taken another road." And on May 13: "Dear Sister, shall we meet again in this world, or is our separation for time? Oh, may Got protect you through all the way. . . ."

The curious fact is that Pengra did not wait, and the wagons of the extended family never caught up. Even more curious is the fact that brothers and sisters of the Stearns family had come from their homes in Ohio and Illinois in order to make the journey together.

Having accomplished this initial coming together, the Stearns family clan, like the Stewart family clan, allowed an accident to separate them. En route, each household again became a nuclear unit, self-determined and self-directed. One must wonder, for example, why the eleven children and the possessions of Annie Stewart should not have been shared among her sisters and brothers who were traveling with fewer encumbrances. Or why Charlotte and Bynon Pengra did not lend the same kind of assistance to the others with whom they were traveling. But the journey once begun, each unit was free to go or stay, move quickly or slowly, keep the threads of the family ties or loose them. The two patterns were strongly felt by frontierspeople: the one, the desire to keep the family together, to keep with kin; the other, to respond to the impulses of the road, to take the chance of the moment and move with freedom.

Charlotte Pengra's diary shows one of the more companionable marriages among the emigrant women. When Charlotte fell ill with dysentery, she notes that her husband cared for her. He "gave me a dose of opium and [we] traveled 22 miles." Bynon kept her in wet bandages, prepared a "Sits bath" for her, "packed" her with cold compresses, and finally "made a good bed in

Charlotte Emily Stearns Pengra.

the wagon" when they had to move on.* Similarly, when dysentery laid her husband low, Charlotte became the teamster for the family. On August 26, when both Bynon and her three-year-old daughter Stella were sick and weak, Charlotte drove the team of oxen. "Though Bynon and Sis is very unwell, they are anxious to go on I drove just before we reached the river I was taken in great pain which resulted in the Dysentery. . . . I have suffered much pain and feel a good deal reduced but all are sick and I must keep up to the last." Bynon tried to drive, but collapsed, and Charlotte again "took my turn and drove until I was quite outdone. . . . I am all used up. dark times for we folks." They had run out of meat and sugar. "I am Somewhat discouraged," wrote Charlotte, "and shall be glad when this journey is ended."

Although Charlotte's Yankee husband was more solicitous of her than were most men born in the West, Charlotte was increasingly despondent in being left alone with three men, after they had separated from the larger family group. "I feel lonely and almost disheartened," she wrote. "I feel very tired and lonely—our folks not having come." It is unusual in the language of the diaries to find so clear a sense of despondency, no matter how dire the circumstances of the road. Charlotte was troubled because she suddenly found herself without the company of another woman. It made her illness and her isolation the more painful.

In some measure, women were distressed at losing the daily exchanges, the comfortable conversation, and the sharing of chores with female kin and friends. But the need of women for other women on the Overland Trail was also more critical. So simple a matter as bodily functions on a terrain that provided no shelter could make daily life an agony of embarrassment when there was no other woman to make of her extended skirt a curtain. Excretion and evacuation could become unspeakable problems without another woman or women to make a curtain of modesty. Resistance to the appearance of bloomers on the frontier becomes more understandable when one considers that the reduced skirts had implications beyond fashion. Long and full skirts on the Trail were soon begrimed and muddy, but they were worn because of their properties as curtains. Two women together, long skirts extended, lent privacy to a third; and even one woman could provide a measure of propriety to a sister on the Trail. But a woman alone, where could she hide from the eyes of the men? There was periodic menstruation—and the lack of water. There was periodic

---

*Hydropathy was based on the belief that water was the natural healer of the body. Proponents advocated bathing, wet compresses, steam, massage, the drinking of cold water and a spare diet. Water-cure establishments became popular in eastern cities. Many diarists refer to taking large quantities of water as a curative for the fevers and dysentery that plagued travelers.

dysentery—and the lack of water. There was occasional childbirth—and the lack of water. And all of these functions were complicated by the absence of shelter and by a lack of privacy. Only in contemplating the utter emptiness of some of the terrain the emigrants crossed can one comprehend the panic felt by women at the prospect of being alone among men. There were days when the horizon was not broken by a tree or hill. There were just miles of flat land. Somehow it seemed as if every vicissitude of the road might be borne as long as a woman could preserve the pale of modesty and privacy. When these were stripped away, those aspects of life that came under the heaviest taboos of society—the bodily functions of excretion and childbirth—were exposed to the eyes of men. The need women felt to travel beside at least one other woman was hardly neurotic; it was a reflection of the very real and essential services, the daily services women performed for each other.

By June, Charlotte's anxieties led her husband to join another family in which there were women, and they traveled with this family until the end of their trip. Charlotte even had a visit from a lady in another wagon: "[Mrs. Smith] wishes the pattern of my sunbonnet, which I gave her with pleasure." The language of the women's diaries carries many covert meanings. In Charlotte's case, the entry meant that the circle of women had been repaired.

Of the ninety-six diarists in the collection we are considering here, only two are by single women traveling alone. Elizabeth Wood, who journeyed to Oregon in 1851, wrote: "I have a great desire to see Oregon . . . the beautiful scenery of plain and mountains, and . . . the wild animals and the Indians, and natural curiosities in abundance." Something of her equanimity can be gleaned from those entries in which she cautioned that "people who do come must not be worried or frightened at trifles; they must put up with storm and cloud as well as calm and sunshine. . . ." But most of all, her special spirit comes through in her description of the Fourth of July on the Trail: "I [wore] a red calico frock, made for the purpose in the wagons; a pair of mackasins, made of black buffalo hide, ornamented with silk . . . and a hat braided of bullrushes and trimmed with white, red and pink ribbon and white paper." Her diary, however, tells us little of her situation or of her life.

The other unmarried female was Rebecca Ketcham, traveling alone from Ithaca, New York, to Oregon. Rebecca had received $240 from friends and relatives to help her reach Oregon, where she intended to become a school teacher. The travelers in her party included two significant members of New York society, Philip C. Schuyler, Jr. and James Van Rennsalaer. In fact, Schuyler's father was one of the benefactors who financed Rebecca's trip. Others in the company were Lucy Dix Schuyler and her husband, and her unmarried sister Camilla. In all, fifteen adults started out.

Rebecca joined the overland group at Independence, Missouri, having traveled herself by stage coach from Oswego to Elmira, Dunkirk, Erie, Cleveland, Columbus, Cincinnati and St. Louis. Her transportation cost her $34.58. "I almost wonder how I could have undertaken such an expedition," she wrote. She was of good spirits, and little daunted by the vastness of her enterprise. She spent time with eighteen-year old Philip Schuyler, and shared the washing with Camilla Dix.

Although there were four women traveling in the group, Rebecca's place among them seems strangely insecure. Her diary shows that instead of being in the wagons with the women, she was excluded by them and often found herself riding horseback with the men. At one point, riding an old and tired horse, she wrote: "The wagons soon passed me, and then I was with that slow horse behind all the rest. I felt angry and hurt both, and very much afraid. I had been told females were in great danger of being taken by the Indians because they think a high ransom will be paid for them. For myself I have no particular desire to go among the Indians in that way. . . . Well I thought it would be a very easy matter for them to knock me off and take my horse, if they did not care to take me."

Rebecca discovered fairly soon that she had been bilked out of part of her travel money, as she had been charged more than the others for joining the party, and was required to work besides. Indignantly, she wrote: "I had the curiosity to ask James how much [Mr. Gray]* charged him for taking him over. . . . He said from $50 to $100. Thinks I to myself, if that is the case, I don't work any more. . . . Charge me $150 and then expect me to work my way. I think I shall find more time to write hereafter."

Rebecca shared the work of the wagon party and apparently shared their food as well. There was considerable uncertainty, however, about what provisions were supposed to be covered by her $150: "I supposed we were to be furnished with mattresses—but instead of that we were furnished with nothing, only the men and boys two blankets apiece."

Rebecca tried to reassure herself that "if one is prepared with a good stock of patience and cheerfulness," any difficulty could be overcome. Her toughness shows in her account of one of her smaller troubles: "In jumping off the horse alone today, I caught my dress in the horn of the saddle and

*William H. Gray was the captain of the wagon train. More experienced than most, he had crossed the country several times. See Clifford M. Drury, ed., "Notes and Documents: Gay's Journal of 1838," *Pacific Northwest Quarterly* 29 (1938): 277–82.

tore almost half of the skirt off. That I must mend tonight. I have had no dress on since the day we came to Westport but my *palm leaf muslin delaine* [a lightweight dress of wool or wool and cotton]. I mean to stick to it as long as I can. It is very dirty and has been torn nearly if not quite twenty times. . . . As long as I look as well as the rest, I don't care."

Her journey through a rainstorm, however, brought her to the verge of tears, not so much because of the hardship, but because of the carelessness for her well-being evidenced by both the men and women of her company:

Rainstorms coming on: I was riding a horse: But when the shower came on, instead of taking me in the carriage, Mr. Gray . . . let me have his rubber overcoat. He . . . fixed it for me himself. It covered my shoulders and arms and a very little of one side of my skirt. Mrs. Godley took my sunbonnet into the carriage and let me have an old one of hers without pasteboard. . . . My feet and almost the whole of my lap were uncovered. When Mr. Gray fixed me he said I would get all wet and muddy, and when I came into camp he would laugh at me. I told him I could laugh as hard as he could, and so it proved. I think I felt as much of a disposition to laugh as he did. I *dont* think he felt quite as much like crying as I did though. . . . We drove through mud holes, when we stopped everything was wet. . . . my feet and limbs cold as ice, and my face and head like fire.

We cannot discern from the diary why Rebecca Ketcham should have been excluded by the women. Had the women known her in the small social circles of Ithaca and determined that she was not of their class? Yet she was well-educated and the Schuylers were among those who had advanced her the money for her trip. Why had she traveled alone, by stage, from Elmira to Independence, Missouri? Was her journey the close of some ill-fated romance? Certainly the ladies would have been more sympathetic. By any standards we can reconstruct, her experience seems extraordinary.

It is clear that she expected better care, and on many a day she wrote of being close to despair. "Was very faint and sick at my stomach. . . . Oh how I thought of Cynthia and her dear Mother! If they had been with me I don't believe I would have sat there all that time without a word of care or sympathy. . . . [Oh] the loneliness I felt. . . ."

Although Rebecca Ketcham's diary is lively with vivid accounts of her surroundings and details of the journey, the antagonism of the other women depressed her deeply, and time and time again she confided to her diary her feelings of being outcast by them. "So many times I feel so wronged, so illy treated that I hardly know how to restrain my feelings, and the effort I make to say nothing depresses my spirits very much." She went on stoutly, determined to make good on her decision to go to Oregon despite her bad luck. Perhaps she took some comfort in observing that on this particular wagon train there seemed to have been little chivalry for *any* woman: "Last night for supper we had stewed peaches. They were all eaten up before we ladies had any. This morning we had rice and apples boiled together. They were also eaten up before we got any. . . . After starting we were not at all sociable." Poor Rebecca Ketcham. She seems to have found her way into an unhappy group of travelers. By August, some of her staunch resolve had ebbed away, and she wrote: "I begin to have some misgivings and fears. I shall be a strange land without one friend."

Nevertheless, Rebecca managed to reach Oregon and become a school-teacher, just as she had intended. Within two years of her arrival, she was married to a gentleman with the remarkable name of Finis E. Mills, a member of the board of trustees for the First Presbyterian Society of Clatsop County. She bore two sons, and in 1855 she and her family returned to her husband's home in Kentucky. The notation of his departure from the Presbyterian Society reads, "Left for Kentucky. Since deceased." And so Rebecca is lost from sight.* Her diary is the flag of independence of a plainspoken lady who went West alone.

If Rebecca Ketcham's experiences were unique, so were her highly personal accounts of them, for most diaries are the careful records of tedious details: washing, baking, unpacking and packing, the number of miles traveled, the presence or absence of grass for the cattle. In resisting emotional display, the diaries reflect a determined insistance upon rationality.

In their diaries, women described themselves as given over to the routine of work. The repetitious accounts of chores provided for some sense of regularity and predictability, and seemed to ward off the unexpected dislocations of the road. Fright, exhaustion, excitement, anxiety rarely find expression. Only on occasion does an account of accident or birth slash through the language of controlled routine, and even death is quickly absorbed by religious prescription and linguistic restriction.

In 1853 a large family started their travels, like Rebecca Ketcham, in Oswego County, New York. Their wagon train was well-equipped and there seem to have been no serious troubles. Celinda Hines appreciated the beauty of the scenery and noted that Chimney Rock, by moonlight, was "awfully sublime," and she wrote with delight that "a great many Indians

---

*Rebecca Ketcham and her party may have joined the wagon party of Celenda Hines in September. The two emigrant groups were close to each other, and the men of the Hines family knew William Gray well. See Leo M. Kaiser and Priscella Knuth, eds., "From Ithaca to Clatsop Plains: Miss Ketcham's Journal of Travel," Part I, *Oregon Historical Quarterly* (1961): 244.

came to camp with fish which they wished to exchange for clothing. We bought a number. . . . They understand and use words swap and no swap. . . . They seem most anxious to get shirts and socks."

August 26 was a day that started pleasantly. The family reached a ferry stop on the Sweetwater River, but because their cash was low, they decided to cross their cattle and wagons themselves, without the help of the ferry. The men began to swim the cattle through the water but they were suddenly caught in a swift current and in plain sight of the helpless party, Celinda's father drowned. Most of the men were near, but none of them dared to go in, the danger was so great. "An Indian Chief being with us with whom Uncle G[ustavus] could talk in the Chinook dialect, took several of his men who were expert swimmers and divers and made every possible exertion to get the body, but were unsuccessful. . . . Uncle G[ustavus] swam in an got Pa's hat." Celinda wrote that "With hearts overflowing with sorrow we were under the necessity of pursuing our journey immediately,

Every emigrant family faced the dangers of crossing swollen rivers, which could hide beds of quicksand. Sometimes a rope was stretched across the river, and sometimes the wagons would be lifted off their wheels and floated on improvised rafts, with horses and cattle swimming alongside. Many a man was drowned at a river crossing in plain sight of his friends and family.

as there was no grass where we were." The emblem of her grief must be read in her notation that "wolves howled."

Celinda consoled herself that her father was "yet living" and that he would "watch over me and continue to guide me." A week later she allowed herself to remark upon the beauty of the scenery, but her diary carries not a single word more of her father's death. Grief was, in Agnes Stewart's phrase, "schooled in."

The same restraint characterizes any number of diaries. Maggie Hall told of a "sad event" when another man of their party drowned at a river crossing, leaving fatherless sons. "Sister Rachel took Frank and Mrs. Bolan took Buck." The diary does not express grief so much as it accounts for the disposition of the children. Esther Hanna understood the terrors of the road when she wrote: "O tis a hard thing to die far from friends & home, to be hurried into a hastily dug grave without shroud or coffin, the clods filled in and then deserted, perhaps to be food for wolves." But what the women needed most was to suppress thoughts that threatened self-control. In Esther's simple phrase, "We must endure [trials] like good soldiers."

As the decade advanced, the women on the Trail began to come from families of some social status. These families carried in their entourage extra "hands" to do the cooking and the driving of ox teams and sheep herds. Harriet T. Clarke and her husband had "seven or eight wagons and two or three hundred head of cattle, and about 100 head of horses." Their company included about thirty work hands, and the ladies traveled on horses outfitted with sidesaddles. They brought with them those aristrocrats of the barnyard, their own white "poland" chickens "to furnish us with eggs all the way." Harriet described that "We rode in a carriage not a spring wagon. . . . They were the first carriages, that ever crossed the plains." This family brought "cook stoves" and a man hired especially to do the cooking. So equipped, it is no wonder Harriet considered that the journey was a "pleasure trip and a perfect delight. . . . In the evening we used to sit around the camp fire and sing and tell stories or go visiting."

Jane Kellogg's party included four ox teams, with three yoke of oxen to each wagon, and "one light horse carriage for mother and Melissa to ride in." Because they had sufficient cash, the Kelloggs were able to afford to pay for the hospitality of settlers along the route and often slept in houses instead of tents.

Harriet Sherril Ward was another traveler who enjoyed the benefit of education and some wealth. She was a hearty woman of fifty, traveling with her husband, her son Willie, who was eleven or twelve, and her seventeen-year-old daughter Frances (or Frankie, as she was called). A married son remained behind; another had gone ahead to California.

As they started out over the Plains states, Harriet commented that she "at once recognized one of George Catlin's beautiful views upon the Mississippi."* The journey, to her educated tastes, was a procession of scenic views. In describing Independence Rock, she wrote: "Cold chills come over me and tears would flow in spite of all my efforts to repress them."

Harriet's diary is inscribed in notebooks made of blue vellum paper. It reveals that her husband paid court to her on the broad expanse of the plains, as, in mid-July, she noted: "Tonight my husband brought in some beautiful flowers. The form & color resembling the snowball & the perfume the night-blooming Jessamine."

Along the way, Frankie played the guitar and sang, "I have something sweet to tell you." In July the Wards were joined by another party: "Miss Sarah & Amelia White passed the eve with us & with Frankie amused themselves with 'The Mansion of Happiness' and it is indeed pleasant to see her again in the enjoyment of young ladies' society whose tastes and feelings are in unison with her own. Miss Amelia has her guitar and I hope that all enjoy some pleasant concerts." Meanwhile, Harriet herself noted that "Mrs. Fox, Mrs. Quigley & Mrs. Howell called to see me!"

It is in these travelers' diaries that one reads of women wearing "bloomers" as a gesture of participation in the fashion of the day—a considerable contrast to Rebecca Ketcham, who had but one dress to wear for the duration of the journey. Harriet Ward took a long walk with Mrs. Singletary, whom "notwithstanding her bloomer dress we found to be a sensible pleasant woman." Jane Kellogg also noted that "we wore bloomers all the way, the better to enable us to walk through the sagebrush. They were made with short skirts and pants reaching to the shoe tops. Everyone wore them." And Lucy Rutledge Cooke similarly counted herself among the women who wore bloomers. But not every women wore them. Bloomers appeared only among those women who could afford special fashions for special occasions. The majority of the overland women wore what clothing they had and prayed that what they wore would not tear. They were too preoccupied with the necessities of the day to consider fashion at all.

Harriet Ward and Harriet Clarke were sharply aware of emigrants of lower social standing on the road. Very rowdy emigrants were described as being from Missouri, and the epithet "Missourians" covered everything

*George Catlin (1796–1872). Both painter and writer, Catlin crossed the prairies to paint the domestic life of the American Indian, whom he considered a vanishing race of men. His paintings also included landscapes of the Western Territories.

that was mean and common. Next to Missourians were the travelers bound for the gold fields. Harriet Clarke wrote that "there were a good many desperadoes among them but they were generally bound for California." She was more sympathetic in noting that the lifelong plight of other women was often marked by hardship. "As we passed the emigrant trains there were always plenty of babies. We saw many women traveling along with their sun-bonnets on, leading children or carrying a child on their hips. . . . We found people with nothing at all, footing it alone, sleeping anywhere they could. They walked because their cattle died, and they had to leave their wagons and cattle behind them and just take a little in their hands, as much as they could carry." There is, however, no indication in Clarke's diary that any person in her party offered assistance to the women who were walking.

The westward move for many men was the physical expression of a break with the past and a setting out for a new life. The journey occurred when the rhythms of maturity were primed for a change. The determination to go West was either the initial separation from a man's parental family or the second major move, the move "upward" in the search for economic mobility and success. The adventure took on the color of some "dramatic rite of passage to mastery and adulthood" in the life cycle of frontier men.[9]

But the journey could have no natural place in the life cycle of the women. The journey was a violation of life's natural rhythms for women of childbearing years. There was simply no way that the rigorous exertions of the overland journey could be considered "normal" for a pregnant woman. And yet a woman's pregnancy mattered very little to emigrant families; certainly it was not sufficient cause to defer the trip.

Even with the best of care, childbirth was a precarious business in the nineteenth century. It was even more risky on the open road, followed by immediate travel in a wagon with no springs and with very little access to water for drinking or for bathing. Any complications of delivery proved critical. And frailty in the newborn was life-threatening. The prospect of childbirth on the Trail must have meant months of heightened anxiety to women.

Childbirth is seldom mentioned in the diaries of the men, even when the new babies were their own, whereas women's diaries always mention the birth of a child, even when the birth occurred in a neighboring wagon train. Charlotte Pengra and Mrs. Allison "saddled two horses and started to reach a lady in a wagon party two miles back. . . . found the lady quite comfortable in a bed in a wagon with a little daughter—perhaps an hour

Lucy Brown Smith and her child lived in Utah Territory.

old. Gave it a name (Sarah Emily Bondfield) wished her success and rode back."

Birth is described in all of the diaries as a commonplace event. But at the same time it is also shrouded behind a veil of "not telling."[10] One is asked to believe that what is remarkable is not the occasion of the birth, but the historical accident that set that birth beside the Columbia River, or at Independence Rock, or on the Fourth of July.

Helen Marnie Stewart recorded in her diary that they had "traviled half the day and had to stop and Christie Bomgardner had a daughter added to his familie." Ceclia McMillen Adams told, along with a list of her chores, that a birth had occured in one of the neighboring companies. The woman was bearing her first child and the delivery was a difficult one. The diarist recalled that "the child was doubled up in the womb, making it a serious and strenous birth." After the young mother was delivered, her husband could permit her but a day layover, for he remembered that "the Indians there were not friendly."

Adrietta Hixon, who was a young girl when she crossed the continent, was surprised by the arrival of a baby brother on the Trail. "Father did some washing and extra cooking that day," was all Adrietta noticed at first. "Later that evening I heard Father ask Mother what she thought about going on the next day. She answered 'the baby and I can ride as well on this feather bed as not.' The next morning we slowly moved out, often stopping on the way so that Father might attend to mother and the little Elijah." Jane Kellogg, who was not a child but a bride, similarly recalled the arrival of a baby sister born to her mother. "I think it was where, Meacham is [in Oregon] that my baby sister was born, on the 11th of September." The notation of the birth is the only mention in all the diary that her mother was pregnant.

In similar fashion, Annie Belshaw remembered:

> It was on the banks of the great river [Columbia] that a daughter was born to my mother. I cannot give the exact date, as the family Bible which contained the only record of the birth has long since been destroyed . . . but I have a distinct recollection of the event. We were having breakfast by the camp fire on the banks of the river, when some one told us that we had a little sister in the wagon with my mother. It must of been in the early dawn, for I remember the cold grey sky. . . . She was named Gertrude Columbia. However, she was only with us two weeks. Years afterwards my mother told me that they buried the little body by the road side in the Salem hills.

George Belshaw's diary contains no mention at all of his wife's pregnancy, no mention of the birth of the child, and no mention of its death and burial. One must read the diary of his sister-in-law, Maria Parsons Belshaw, for an account of what had happened. Maria wrote that on September 20, 1853, "Mrs. George Belshaw gave birth to a daughter 4 o'clock this morning." Candace Belshaw had been in poor health throughout the pregnancy, but the real concern was for the infant. One week later, Maria wrote: "All well but the baby." She was depressed by the turn of events. "How dreary it seems. Can it be that I have left my quiet little home and taken this dreary land of solitude in exchange." On the October 6, Maria wrote: "[We] came but a short distance on account of George Belshaw losing his infant daughter. She died at 9 a.m. of cancer of the stomach." What a tribute to patriarchy is Maria's note that the loss of the infant should be the father's rather than the mother's!

Still another lady, Mrs. Francis Sawyer, repeated the story told by many diarists: "I saw a lady where we nooned today who had a fine son three days old. . . . The lady was . . . in good spirits. I have heard of several children being born on the plains though it is not a pleasant place for the little fellows to see the light of day."

Whether women resented their lack of control over their own pregnancies cannot be clearly read from the overland diaries. But the matter of family planning was one of increasing importance to middle-class Americans—to those on the frontier as well as to those in the more settled areas of the nation. Census data and demographic studies confirm that birth rates fell as rapidly on the frontier as they did in the cities.[11] "Given the already burdensome tasks of women's work, the additional responsibilities of the children were next to intolerable. Women must have searched for some way of limiting the burden."[12] In 1896, from Palmyra, Wisconsin, Mary Kincaid wrote to Mamie Goodwater: "I got two months before me yet that if I count right I just dread the time coming. . . . O Mamie I wish there was no such thing as having babies."[13]

There is some evidence that toward the closing years of the century, even rural women were beginning to share rudimentary information about birth control. In 1885, Rose Williams and Lettie Mosher exchanged letters between Ohio and North Dakota, with Rose advising: "You want to know of a sure preventative. Well plague take it. The best way is for you to sleep in one bed and your Man in another." But Rose also had information of a more practical sort: "Well now [there is] the thing. . . . I do not know whether you can get them out there. They are called Pessairre or female prevenative if you don't want to ask for a 'pisser' just ask for a female prevenative. They cost one dollar when Sis got hers it was before any of us went to Dak[ota] The directions are with it."[14] The exchange is significant because it suggests that vaginal diaphragms were not only known but were used and

Maria Parsons Belshaw.

commercially available to women of the rural population by 1885.[15]
Overland women, however, lived one and two generations earlier. While
one must assume that sexual abstinence was common enough on the
journey itself, the evidence is that a large portion of the women were
already pregnant at the journey's start.

In trying to understand the attitudes of the women who made the
overland journey and those who lived out their lives on the frontier, one
soon discovers that the women themselves were the major fabricators of
the taboos of their society. In their own diaries they contrived to hide their
fears and anxieties. No diarist opens to another's eyes the doubt, the pain,
or the uncertainties that childbirth must have held.

How these women dealt with the risks of childbirth, how they felt about
the prospect of being delivered by the side of the road, in a tent or in a
wagon, is untold. The women must have watched the horizon anxiously in
the last days of pregnancy, trying to learn if the weather would be calm or
threatening, if the wagons were near or far from water, if another woman
was at hand, if the road was smooth or rocky. Such thoughts, the "powerful
secrets of the culture," as the poet Adrienne Rich has named them, lie in
the interstices of the diaries. No entry tells of the terrors or the uncertain-
ities. Waiting for labor pains to begin on the open road, what woman could
be entirely tranquil?

We know so little about how these overland women handled their
knowledge of the risks to life that came with each successive pregnancy.
One eighteenth-century pioneer daughter grew up with four stepmothers
in succession, each one dying in childbirth.[16] How did she forecast her own
destiny? How did these women absorb the prospects of maternal death in
order to marry and bear, repeatedly, the pregnancies that threatened their
lives? Rural women must have considered death the unseen partner of the
marriage bed. Such women would have a need to believe in God. Each
release from death was a miraculous chance to seize another year in which
to encircle oneself again with the comforting rituals of daily routine.
Perhaps the detailed pattern-making, the recounting of trivial daily tasks
that one finds in the women's diaries was the necessary counterbalance in
a life pitted against catastrophe.

In one particular group of diaries resentment against the decision to go
West seems to surge up and fill the pages. These are the diaries that
contain detailed tabulations of the numbers of graves passed. Traveling
primarily during the years of the cholera epidemic, but also in the later
years as well, these women kept their accounts with a bookkeeper's care for

detail. They noted whether they were passing "old" graves or "new" graves. That distinction was important, for it told them how close death really was. Mrs. Francis Sawyer wrote: "Today we have passed a great many new-made graves & we hear of many cases of cholera. . . . We are becoming fearful for our own safety." Seventeen days later, she noted: "Dr. Barkwell . . . informed us that his youngest child had died on the plains. . . . The trials & troubles of this long wearisome trip are enough to bear without having our hearts torn by the loss of dear ones."

Cholera appears in the diaries of the men, but the men tended to treat the epidemic in aggregate figures. Dr. T. McCollum put the number of burials in 1849 between fifteen hundred and two thousand. Franklin Langworthy estimated cholera victims in 1850 at over one thousand. Ezra Meeker put the number at five thousand for the same year, noting that the "dead lay sometimes in rows of fifteen or more." Abraham Sortore wrote that he was "scarcely out of sight of grave diggers," and Micajah Littleton counted over one hundred thirty graves.[17] The men were moved by the epidemic, but for the women, each single grave was of overpowering importance.

Cecelia McMillen Adams, who kept the diary of her family's journey from Illinois to Oregon in 1852, traced the wagon train's journey as follows:

Child's grave . . . smallpox . . . child's grave. . . . [We] passed 7 new-made graves. One had 4 bodies in it . . . cholera. A man died this morning with the cholera in the company ahead of us. . . . Another man died. . . . Passed 6 new graves. . . . We have passed 21 new-made graves . . . made 18 miles. . . . Passed 13 graves today. Passed 10 graves. . . .

June 25	Passed 7 graves . . . made 14 miles
June 26	Passed 8 graves
June 29	Passed 10 graves
June 30	Passed 10 graves . . . made 22 miles
July 1	Passed 8 graves . . . made 21 miles
July 2	One man of [our] company died. Passed 8 graves made 16 miles
July 4	Passed 2 graves . . . made 16 miles
July 5	Passed 9 graves . . . made 18 miles
July 6	Passed 6 graves . . . made 9 miles
July 11	Passed 15 graves . . . made 13 miles
July 12	Passed 5 graves . . . made 15 miles
July 18	Passed 4 graves . . . made 16 miles

July 19	Passed 2 graves . . . made 14 miles
July 23	Passed 7 graves . . . made 15 miles
July 25	Passed 3 graves . . . made 16 miles
July 27	Passed 3 graves . . . made 14 miles
July 29	Passed 8 graves . . . made 16 miles
July 30	I have kept an account of the dead cattle we passed & the number today is 35
Aug. 7	We passed 8 graves with a week . . . made 16 miles
Sept. 7	We passed 14 graves this week . . . made 17 miles
Sept. 9	We passed 10 graves this week . . . made 16 miles
Oct. 1	Have seen 35 graves since leaving Fort Boise
Oct. 17	Here are 12 graves all together . . . 15.

Virtually the same kind of tally appears in the diary of Maria Parsons Belshaw, in 1853, as she and her husband journeyed from Indiana to Oregon Territory:

Aug. 25	Passed 1 grave . . . we made 12 miles
Aug. 26	Passed 3 graves . . . 1 dead horse. 18 cattle . . . made 13 miles
Aug. 27	Passed 5 graves . . . 1 horse, 23 cattle . . . made 15 miles
Aug. 28	Passed 1 grave . . . 17 cattle . . . made 23 miles
Aug. 29	Passed 5 dead cattle . . . made 15 miles
Aug. 30	Passed 3 graves . . . 6 dead cattle . . . made 6 miles
Aug. 31	Passed 9 dead cattle . . . made 15 miles
Sept. 1	Passed 1 grave . . . 2 dead horses, 21 cattle, made 10 miles
Sept. 2	Passed 8 graves . . . 19 cattle . . . made 12 miles
Sept. 3	Passed 5 graves . . . 8 dead cattle . . . made 20 miles
Sept. 4	Passed 2 graves . . . 8 dead cattle . . . made 17 miles
Sept. 5	Passed 3 graves . . . 3 dead cattle . . . made 17 miles
Sept. 6	Passed 1 grave . . . 3 dead cattle . . . made 17 miles
Sept. 7	Passed 2 graves . . . 3 dead cattle . . . made 17 miles
Sept. 8	Passed 1 grave . . . 3 dead cattle . . . made 18 miles
Sept. 9	Passed 16 graves . . . 1 ox . . . made 16 miles
Sept. 10	Passed 2 graves . . . 2 horses . . . made 16 miles
Sept. 11	Passed 1 grave—4 cattle . . . made 15 miles
Sept. 12–14	Passed 15 dead cattle, 3 dead oxen . . . made 32 miles.

Not even births were recorded with such precise attention.

Lodisa Frizzell, telling of her family's journey to California, writes:

"Passed where they were burying a man; scarce a day but some one is left on these plains." On the seventy-second day she wrote: "The heart has a thousand misgivings, and the mind is tortured with anxiety, and often as I passed the fresh made graves. I have glanced at the side boards of the wagons, not knowing how soon it would serve as a coffin for some one of us."

The epidemic bred a certain hardness. Lucy R. Cooke told that she and another woman had gone to sit with a lady sick with cholera. "June 2, Did what we could. But the next day, the woman's husband had died and there was no one to stay and care for her. Hated to leave her but . . . [we] went on. About an hour after a man rode by and said she was almost dead and the men in whose company she was were digging her grave so as not to lose time. There's humanity on the plains!"[18]

Caroline Richardson, whose diary is full of exuberant life and optimism, did not forego the observation of death.

May 17	. . . saw 2 graves
May 18	There were two old graves close by saw two more at some distance saw one new grave
May 27	started at six, saw three old graves and two new ones. . . .
May 30	Saw several graves today one with inscription. . . . we counted 5 graves close together only one with inscription. . . .
June 1	Graves now are often partly dug up.
June 7	7 new graves today.
June 9	Most graves look as if they were dug and finished in a hurry.
June 16	Men digging a grave for a young girl. It is common to see beds and clothing discarded by the road not to be used again. It indicates a death.
June 20	A young lady buried at [Independence] Rock today who had lost mother and sister about a week ago.

Algeline Ashley wrote of her journey, "I like it better every day," but in the fragment of her diary that remains, recording only twenty-six days between May 29 and June 23 in 1852, she noted passing forty-seven graves.

Esther Hanna was only eighteen, and yet woven into her diary are notations of 102 individual graves, evidence that neither the vitality or the buoyancy of youth were sufficient to allow one to ignore the trials of the overland route.

Nor was cholera the only enemy of the emigrants. Jane Kellogg wrote that "the little children all had measles, and some of the men." And Lydia Rudd told that she met a man who "had buried his wife this morning . . . from the effects of measles." Rudd herself wrote "I am almost dead tonight. I have been sick two or three days with the bowel complaint and am much worse tonight." Cornelia Sharp noted: "Parts of our family sick, ourselves tired and our cattle exhausted." Weakened by exposure, exposed to cholera and measles, susceptible to dysentery, dependent upon unreliable water supplies, the emigrants were vulnerable to all manner of sores, stomach upsets, mountain fevers. Blistered by the sun, chilled by the nights in the mountains and early snows, harrassed by dust and by mosquitoes, the travelers were sorely tried. With exasperation: Lydia Rudd wrote "There was a wasp just stung me on the back of my neck."

The women recorded every accident and every illness that befell them on the trip. They noted the dust storms, the hailstorms, the heat and the mosquitoes: "The sun is melting. . . . The stench occasioned by the dead cattle is [awful]. . . . We are near being eaten alive with mosquitoes, there are thousands of them buzzing about your ears which makes one almost frantic." Esther Hanna "felt today like giving up in despair." Velina Williams got out of her wagon to get a breath of air and walk about a bit when she found herself "standing on a copperhead snake." Helen M. Stewart noted that Hiram McGraw had his ankle crushed by the tongue of the wagon, and Catherine Stansbury Washburn knew of a child who had fallen out of another wagon which had "run over its jaw and shoulder."

There is a kind of murderous precision in the women's recounting of mishap. Surely, the accounts must be viewed as a reflection of the continuing anxieties they felt. But the more one reads these diaries, the more one comes to feel the passionate indictment, the bitter appraisal by the women of the men's determination to make the journey. However bravely the women started, however they mustered their strength to meet the demands of each day, however they rallied to appreciate the splendors of the scenery, the women were intimately affected by the journey's dreadful toll. Their responses depended upon whether their own lives were placed within the processes of childbearing and childrearing, or whether they were still in their girlhood years. Buoyant spirits are almost always in the diaries of unmarried girls and young wives. Accounts shade and darken in the pages of women whose energies were spent nursing and caring for infants and small children.

NOTES

1. See Faragher, *Women and Men on the Overland Trail*, ch. 3, for a description of the different rhythms of men's work and women's work on the Trail.

2. See Donald H. Clark, "Remember the Winter of . . ." *Oregon Historical Quarterly*, 1953: 140–48. See also John Unruh, *The Plains Across*, ch. 12.

3. Lillian Schlissel, "Mothers and Daughters on the Western Frontier," *Frontiers*, III, no. 2 (summer 1978): 29–33.

4. See Carl Degler, *At Odds: Women and the Family in America from the Revolution to the Present* (New York, Oxford University Press, 1980), p. 28; Nancy Cott, *The Bonds of Womanhood: Woman's Sphere in New England, 1780–1835* (New Haven, Yale University Press, 1977), pp. 200–201.

5. David M. Potter, Introduction to *The Trail to California: The Overland Journal of Vincent Geiger and Wakeman Bryarly* (New Haven, Yale University Press, 1962).

6. Stewart, p. 152; Faragher, *Women and Men on the Overland Trail*, p. 28.

7. "Female friendships were broken off as companies separated. When friends parted, women wept. 'We had become so attached to each other having travelled so far together, and being dependent on each other in times of danger and accident,' explained one woman." Jeffrey, *Frontier Women*, pp. 41–42.

8. Jeffrey cites another example of the separation of close female relationships: one woman told that she was separated from her sister because of their husbands' "first class row," and wrote that her sister "did not feel that she would ever be happy again" (*Frontier Women*, p. 42).

9. Howard R. Lamar's essay "Rites of Passage: Young Men and their Families in The Overland Trail Experience, 1843–69," is one of the very few places where evaluation is made of the psychological impact of the overland journey in the life cycle of the emigrants. In *Soul-Butter and Hog Wash and Other Essays on the American West*, Charles Redd Monographs in Western History, No. 8. Thomas G. Alexander, ed. (Provo, Utah, Brigham Young Univ. Press, 1978), 33–68.

10. "Only rarely did frontier women reveal how they felt about pregnancy and birth." Jeffrey, *Frontier Women*, p. 69. "The personal meaning of pregnancy in the lives of 19th century women is not easy to recapture." Carl Degler, *At Odds: Women*

and the Family in America from the Revolution to the Present (New York, Oxford Univ. Press, 1980), p. 59.

11. Carl Degler's discussion of the processes by which population trends changed among nineteenth-century Americans is thorough and intelligent. See ch. 9, "Limiting Fertility," in *At Odds*, pp. 210–226. See also Jeffrey, *Frontier Women*, pp. 57–58.

12. Faragher, *Women and Men on The Overland Trail*, p. 58.

13. Mary Kincaid to Mamie Goodwater, February 28, 1896. Quoted in *To All Inquiring Friends: Letters, Diaries and Essays in North Dakota*, compiled by Elizabeth Hampsten, (Grand Forks, Univ. of North Dakota, 1979), p. 18.

14. Rose Williams to Alliette Mosher, September 22, 1885. Quoted in *To All Inquiring Friends*, p. 122.

15. The diaphragm was invented before the Civil War, but most researchers have doubted that the device was known or used by women of the working-class or farm populations. Thus Degler writes: "Most demographers have believed, on the basis of what we know about the spread of contraceptive knowledge today among social classes, that the upper classes first practiced the more sophisticated—and effective—methods. . . . We still would like to know how far down the social scale the knowledge and practice penetrated." *At Odds*, p. 220. See James C. Mohr, *Abortion in America: The Origins and Evolution of National Policy, 1800–1900* (New York, Oxford Univ. Press, 1978), p. 83. Also James Reed, *From Private Vice to Public Virtue: The Birth Control Movement and American Society since 1830,* (New York, 1978); Robert V. Wells, "Family History and Demographic Transition," *Journal of Social History* 9 (1975): 1–19.

16. Tracey Emslie of New Mexico has been able to trace her family genealogy back to an ancestor born in Wales in 1679. That ancestor, Owen David, came to America in 1708, and his son Enoch was born in 1718. Enoch married four times, each wife dying in childbirth. Emslie is descended from his first wife, Catarina Van Bebler. Ms. Emslie shared this genealogy with the writer. See also *The David Family Scrapbook*, vol. 4, privately printed by Mrs. Jess David, Lakewood, Ohio. This individual case is supported by data for larger communities. Historian Carl Degler writes: "In [1840 and 1850] the death rates for women between the ages of 10 and 35 are greater than those for men, measuring thereby the effects of childbearing on women's chances for life" (*At Odds*, p. 60). It is nevertheless true that most demographic studies are derived from communities in New England areas, with limited research for areas of the Midwest. See Bloomberg, Fox, R. M. Warner and S. B. Warner, "A Census Probe into Nineteenth Century Family History: Southern Michigan, 1850–1880," *Journal of Social History* 5 (1971): 25–28, and Richard A. Easterlin, "Factors in the Decline of Farm Family Fertility in the United States: Some Preliminary Research Results, *Journal of American History* 43 (1976): 600–612. There are few extensive studies of far-western frontier communities. U.S. Census reports, useful to a point, sometimes cloud the very issues one would most like to clarify. In giving information concerning the causes of death, for example, the category "hemorrhaging" is listed, but whether hemorrhaging is related to childbirth or even pertains to female deaths is not indicated.

17. These accounts can be found in Mattes, *The Great Platte River Road*, pp. 84–85.

18. John Unruh tells of Forty-niner Bernard Reid, who "came upon a seventeen year old girl all alone save for her younger brother who lay in their wagon sick with cholera. Both the mother and the father had already died of the dread disease. The oxen were gone and so was the faithless company with which the family had been traveling" (*The Plains Across*, ch. 6).

THE LATER
JOURNEYS,
1856-1867

A dozen or so years after the westward emigration began, the Trail had undergone significant changes. There were trading posts and stagecoach stations, and travel no longer meant empty horizons and utter loneliness. Travel time was shortened by almost a month. By 1856, Salt Lake City was a well-established, efficient community where emigrants could find everything from bathhouses and barber shops to law courts. Telegraph poles were strung the entire length of the route by 1861, and messages could be sped from coast to coast in seconds.

On the other hand, the Indians were a new threat. By the middle of the decade, two hundred thousand emigrants had come across the continent, and in their wake cholera, smallpox, and measles decimated the tribes. Buffalo herds began to move from their habitat, and Indians grew restive about the security of their tribal ways and tribal lands.

The emigrants' fear of the Indians was equaled only by their ignorance of the Indians' ways. They seldom knew, for example, that it was common custom among many tribes to offer strangers a token of hospitality, and Indians often expected such tokens from those who were traveling through their lands. Emigrants almost always wrote of the Indians who came up "begging" to their wagons, and they found the habit "disgusting."

Sometimes the emigrants' ignorance and fear of the Indians was the more dangerous because it was accompanied by a show of arrogance. Helen H. Clark noted of the party she traveled with that when they reached Pawnee-Sioux territory: "There was a white man who boasted that he would kill the first Indian he saw, he soon had opportunity of fulfilling his boast as they saw a squaw & he shot her as he would a wild animal & the

Indians came on and demanded the fellow to be given up and they had to do it and the Indians skinned him alive." Indian attacks, the nightmare of the travelers, began to occur sporadically.

For many of the women, the fear alone could be excruciating. Maggie Hall remembered:

> The boys would go fishing, go hunting. When it was discovered the mothers let up a wail, knew that Indians would kill them, so the Pa's would get out guns and off they would go to find [the] boys. Tried to kick the boys to camp. First chance, those boys would go off again. But those night alarms, when someone would cry "Indians." The guard came running in who had seen the Indians hide behind a bush or heard an arrow, etc. Then in a moment men were loading guns, women crying. A call for volunteers would go out and [they] would circle around. . . . But that scare in the night. . . . It made the women nervous and sick.

Nancy Hunt told of the uncertainty that gripped the emigrants. "We always treated the Indians well and with respect, and they never molested us at any time." But on one particular night, the Indians formed lines on both sides of the emigrants' camp, and in the light of fires "they set up their terrible war-hoop and kept it up until late into the night. . . . Greatly frightened, we made ready for an attack. But . . . they did not molest us at all, except as we suffered in our minds from fright." More experienced travelers would have known the Indians would not attack by the light of the fires, and more experienced travelers might have told the emigrants whether or not the song was really a "war-hoop." Nancy wrote: "At night we placed our weapons of defense by the sides of our beds in our tents. I claimed the ax for mine, and always saw that it was close to me, but I never had occasion to use it on an Indian." Poor Nancy, sleeping every night with an ax-handle by her side to protect herself, her sick husband, and her two small sons. What prolonged terror it must have been. How the howl of a coyote or a wolf must have pierced her sleep.

In other respects, however, overland travel in the 1850s and 1860s presented women with the same problems they had had from the start. Roxana Cheney Foster was born in New Hampshire. A spinster of twenty-six, she had followed an older brother to Illinois where she took a job as a schoolteacher, earning one dollar a week with an arrangement whereby she was to "board around," in the homes of school children in town. A short year after her arrival she was married and her first child was born in 1848. In 1849 talk of gold stirred the hearts of young men of the region, and Roxana's husband with his younger brother went off to find their fortune in California, leaving Roxana and her newborn son alone for two years. Her husband came back to Illinois but in 1852, her father-in-law went to California and sent letters back: "Sell your farm, buy cows, horses, and come to this valley; don't stay in that inhospitable climate. *I would rather eat off a tin plate and live in a tent in California than have the best house and farm in Illinois.*" The letter was not to be resisted. Roxana wrote in her diary: "In April [1853] we had a daughter born. Three months later we sold our farm and . . . then bought our outfit for California. . . . we traveled as far as Council Bluffs with two teams, one with baggage, the other with husband and myself, our boy aged 5 years and Lucy 3 months old." In the Spring of 1854, her family set forth on the Overland Trail. Her diary tells that they had "two wagons, four horses, thirty five head of cattle," but gives not one hint that she was once again pregnant.

Roxana was thirty-six, older than most of the women on the road. She tells only that as they traveled through Utah there was a "nice stream," and one morning in July, with no other wagon near them, "we set up our tent, and before twelve o'clock a boy baby was born to us, probably the first person born in Ogden. We rested three days, then went slowly on."

There was husbandly solicitude in that three-day wait and in their moving "slowly." Such care was not common. When they reached California in September, her baby was eight weeks old and her second child little more than a year. "The Indians," Roxana remembered, "were peaceable all along the route." Did Roxana and her husband talk and decide together to make the overland journey despite her pregnancy? Did Roxana agree that the risks were negligible? Her diary will not tell us.

The summer of '54 found other overland women in the same predicament. Nancy Hunt wrote:

> While the young folks were having their good times, some of the mothers were giving birth to their babes: three babies were born in our company that summer. My cousin Emily Ibe . . . gave birth to a son in Utah, forty miles north of Great Salt Lake, one evening; and the next morning she traveled on until noon, when a stop was made and another child was born—this time Susan Longmire was the mother made happy by the advent of little Ellen. The third birth [was to] the wife of my cousin Jacob Zumwalt who gave birth to a daughter while traveling in the Sierra Nevada. To this baby they gave the name of Alice Nevada.

Roxana Cheney and Emily Ibe, unknown to each other, bore an emigrant son and an emigrant daughter near Ogden, Utah. But where Roxana rested for three days, Emily and the two other new mothers "traveled right along the next day, mothers and babes with the rest of us." Fear of Indian attacks

Roxana Cheney Foster.

led the emigrants to defer even less to the needs of women. Within hours of birth, women were hurried over the Trail.

Sometimes the Trail proved too strenuous for men as well as for women. Nancy Hunt and her husband had decided to settle in California, hoping a milder climate would restore his failing health, but exposure of the road weakened him with every mile. "He was very sick through Nevada. . . . He was a soft kind of man, with little grit or vim in him." By August, the cool winds of the Sierra Nevada and the burning sun of the days had taken their toll. "We laid his body away in the best manner we possible could. . . . But there was no grass for the cattle. We must push on." Like many another woman, Nancy was widowed by the journey. She and her two small sons moved into her parents' wagon, and when they reached the mining camps near Sacramento, she hired herself out to work by the day. "Women were scarce in California." She sold her wagon for "two fifty-dollar California slugs," and was soon earning fifty and then seventy-five dollars a month. A year after her husband's death, Nancy was married again. "I was dressed in white, with embroidered pink flowers." She was twenty-four years old. She would have five more sons. Life surged on for the emigrants. The New Country was a land for survivors.

Along with these women Mary Perry Frost traveled in the summer of '54, but her story was very different. The Indians had begun to burn the grass in an effort to starve the livestock of the travelers, forcing large wagon parties to separate so that better forage could be found. Parties broke into smaller and smaller sections, until Mary's family was in a group of only four wagons.

At what point in the summer of 1854 did the Indians—peaceable in the accounts of Nancy Hunt and Roxana Cheney—determine that the emigrants were a growing threat? Foster, Cheney and Frost traveled the same route during the same summer months. At some point, the Indians made a determination of their own.

We had traveled perhaps an hour. . . . Then Indians . . . came up squarely in front of our train and stopped the teams, but appeared friendly, shaking hands and asking for whiskey; upon being told that we had none they began to talk of trading with the men, and while my father was talking of trading a pistol for a pony, they opened fire on us, shooting my father, my uncle and my father's teamster. . . . Thinking they wanted our horses, they were turned loose and the Indians departed after catching them all. Of those shot, my uncle was killed outright, my father's teamster was shot through the abdomen and lived until the following morning and my father was shot through the lungs and lived until the evening of the fourth day. . . . [He] was buried on the morning [of the fifth day]. The Indians also killed all the men in the forward party, leaving a boy of fourteen with an arrow in his chest. . . . we stopped long enough to dig trenches and rude graves for the burial. . . . The women and children [in the forward party] presented a sickening spectacle, having been burned by the savages.

In the northernmost part of the Oregon Territory, Mary's mother filed a widow's claim and started her new life in a log cabin. Mary and her older brother herded sheep, and to escape the hardships of her mother's home, Mary married when she was only thirteen.

Fear of Indians heightened the tensions of the journey, and tensions could have strange effects on the emigrants. The diary of Mary Rockwood Powers shows that her husband's eccentric behavior was aggravated by the pressures of the journey. Her diary is the more remarkable in that we have along with it a series of letters written to her mother in which Mary's growing panic is made even more clear.

Americus Windsor Powers was a doctor who had been to California before. In 1856 he decided to bring his wife and three children by wagon and also to bring a string of blooded Canadian horses to sell on the coast. His mistake was in thinking he could use the purebred horses to pull the heavy wagons.

Mary and the children started from Wisconsin to Chicago by train. "A few miles from Davenport . . . the locomotive . . . left us. . . . we found the road completely drowned in mud. . . . We had to get out and walk [to Iowa City] and carry our baggage. The lady who was with us had a rifle and another had a carpet bag that weighed nearly 50 pounds. I had the three children." From Iowa City the family traveled by wagon.

By early June, Mary lost track of the days of the week and even the month, and her diary becomes a flow of incident and detail. Americus lent his rifle to a fellow traveler who did not return it, nor did Americus seek its return. He refused to visit a sick child when he was called. Mary tried to keep calm by reading *Pilgrim's Progress* to the children.

By the end of June, it was apparent that the horses were not equal to the task of drawing the wagons across a continent. "Our wagon empty weighs 900 pounds, and even that is too much for the big horses to draw." When Mary urged Americus to buy or borrow an ox team, Americus would promise to do so, and then refuse to deal with the men to make the arrangement. Mary's diary shows her slowly learning the facts of overland travel as her husband became more and more withdrawn. She recounted with exasperation that Americus would not pitch the tent. They all slept in the wagon, but one night a rainstorm beat into the wagon and she "lay for two hours and a half with the ice water running onto me and the hailstones beating upon my head."

The doctor's incompatibility with the other men on the wagon train is noted in the astonishing information that at last "the company went on and left us to get on the best we could." That was an unusual action for a wagon company to take under any circumstances. The diary tells only that "a dissatisfaction among the company has separated us, I forbear giving the details." But to her mother Mary wrote that it was apparent that their horses would not carry them through and their provisions were giving out. Yet "the Doctor told [the other men] that was his business." He would not ask for help, and he would not buy an ox team. Two women on the train bade Mary farewell with tears running down their cheeks when it seemed certain the family was to part from the group. "I felt as though my last friends were leaving me," wrote Mary. To her mother, her anger broke forth: she felt she was in the hands of "a Maniac. . . . Myself and the little ones were at the mercy of a mad man. It did not seem that any man in his right mind would take the course the Doctor was taking." In her diary, Mary wrote only: "I said nothing but thought the more." But she told her mother, "I told the doctor if he didn't do something I should, as for moving from that camp without having some arrangements [for getting a team of oxen] I would not."

Somehow they reached Salt Lake City. There, two men of their old wagon train rode back to find them and talk with Mary. "Mr. Curtis . . . and the other men told me that . . . we should not be left behind. I thanked them from the bottom of my heart, for we were on the most dangerous part of the road." The men were making their commitments to Mary and not to her husband. It was she who had taken hold of the family. Mary wrote to her mother: "For some days the Doctor had been falling into his old sullen mood again, out of humor with everyone. . . . Mr. Curtis and Joseph came to me . . . they offered to take me and the children into their wagon and divide the luggage among the ox teams or they would put in a span for a day or two." Despite all their urging the Doctor would not give up his horses but "put the harness on . . . as a matter of course, and hitched up and drove off as though he was lord of all he surveyed." Mary confided to Mr. Curtis that her husband "had grown so peculiar." The men were "willing to do almost anything to assist us." The next day the men of the wagon train came back and demanded to know if Americus were "a mad man or a confounded fool." The public confrontation seemed to do some good. Americus bought a span of oxen and the family once again joined a wagon train. Mary cooked the last of her dried strawberries, poured them over some fresh-made dumplings, and brought the confection to the two men who befriended her. Whether she had any left for her husband, her diary does not say. It seems possible that at least some part of Americus' manner might have been the result of jealousy. His wife was a pretty young woman and his own behavior had made her the center of attention of the other men.

The family came out of the Sierra Nevada in October of 1856. Not Indians but emotional instability had threatened their lives. Mary wrote to her mother. "My health was most miserable and grew worse very fast. . . . Our journey across the Plains was a long and hard one. We lost everything but our lives."

The June following their arrival in California, Mary gave birth to twins, both of whom died in their first year. "After we returned from the grave, I was sick for a week." Mary remained loyal to her husband, despite his instability, but one year later, she was dead. Americus himself wrote to Mary's mother: "Mary had followed me to a distant land, but the expedition was an unfortunate one; had it succeeded we would have been independent, but since everything went wrong, I did the best I could and so did dear Mary, and we both anticipated better days." Whether or not Mary's mother believed that Americus had done his best, is not known. Whether Mary herself believed him is open to question, for her last instructions were that her children be educated by her mother and her mother's family in Wisconsin. Americus became a recluse and was shot during an ambush in 1886 in the hills of California.

Had Americus stayed home he might have preserved the semblance of a moderate life, but he carried within him that flaw of personality, that eccentric imbalance that made him vulnerable to the dislocations of the road. The frontier adventure tested one's psyche as much as it tested one's strength.

———————————————

One of the most engaging and intelligent of the diarists was Helen Carpenter, a bride of four months who made the crossing in 1857.* With Helen and her husband was a seventeen-year-old black boy who was "sold us by his father the consideration being that Henry receive six months schooling in that [his father] receive $25."

Fashion was a topic of enthusiastic discussion. Helen noted that another bride and groom traveled with the wagon party: "The bride wears hoops —we have read of hoops being worn, but they had not reached Kansas before we left. . . . Would not recommend them for this mode of traveling —the wearer has less personal privacy than the Pawnee in his blanket."

One night in July, Helen wrote that the travelers discovered their fire had

———————————————

*In mature years Helen Carpenter wrote for magazines and published a number of books. Her son became a writer and her daughter a painter.

Helen M. Carpenter.

been built upon a grave site, but they did not trouble to move it, and she wondered whether the callousness bred of the open road would permanently change their natures. Then, in August, her diary records the following story:

> When the sun was just peeping over the top of the mountain, there was suddenly heard a shot and a blood curdling yell, and immediately the Indians we saw yesterday were seen riding at full speed directly toward the horses. . . . father put his gun to his shoulder as though to

shoot. . . . The Indians kept . . . circling . . . and halooing . . . bullets came whizzing through the camp. None can know the horror of it, who have not been similarly situated. . . . [the Indians] did not come directly toward us, but all the time in a circular way, from one side of the road to the other, each time they passed, getting a little nearer, and occasionally firing a shot. . . . Father and Reel could stand it no longer, they must let those Indians see how far their Sharps rifles would carry. Without aiming to hit them, they made the earth fly."

The emigrants moved on fearfully. "Such a mere handful of humanity, four men, four women, three young boys, and three children, one my mothers little six month old baby. In no way could we turn for assistance." They found the marker of a newmade grave and a "bit of board" with the inscription "This man was killed by the Indians, Aug. 7." "It is now 18 days since we have seen a train." On August 23, they found the wagon party. "None . . . can ever know the inexpressible joy and relief . . . on seeing those old dust begrimed wagons." As if to celebrate the occasion, a baby was born in camp that very night. The woman had given birth prematurely and was ill. Helen's mother, nursing her own infant daughter, "at once took the baby and is nursing and caring for it." But not even the proximity of another nursing mother was help enough, and on August 28, "Wilson's little baby was buried beside the road this morning before we started."

There were no further attacks by the Indians, but the travelers' fear persisted. In September, the party ahead of them "found the body of a nude woman on the bank of the slough. . . . A piece of hair rope was around her neck. . . . From appearances it was thought she had been tortured by being drawn back and forth through the slough, by this rope around her neck. The body was given the best burial that was possible, under the circumstances." Whether or not the murdered woman had been tortured as the emigrants imagined, the discovery was gruesome enough. And new stories were presented with each day's travel. On September 7, Helen wrote that traders had told them they had found a woman who had been scalped and left for dead. "The Indians traded the woman's scalp to them, and they sold it to her preservers." After a year or two, noted Helen Carpenter, the scalped woman died of "melancholy."

Helen and her family reached California in October. The baby, now seven months old, "was so afraid of indoors" that she would not sleep in a house. The sound of a clock's ticking terrified her. The Trail left the emigrants—even infants—with some strange legacies.

There was no way of knowing when or where, or whether the Indians might attack. Traveling in the same season, one party might cross peacefully, watchful but untroubled, while just ahead of them, or just behind them, another wagon train was burying its dead. Fear of Indians and concern with childbirth are the strands that run through the diaries of this later period on the Trail.

Catherine and Charles Bell had married in South Norwalk, Connecticut, before they had migrated to Iowa and then joined the overlanders headed for California. Catherine was carrying her first child; the baby was born in August on the banks of the Humboldt River. Considering Catherine's advanced pregnancy, her account of the journey is spirited. "It is very muddy and you had better believe it. . . . I had to get out and spat around in the mud to cook out of doors. But I soon got used to it and then it was only fun for me." They traveled with seventeen wagons, fifty men, eight women, and twenty children. Catherine's party made the crossing with no threat of Indian interference: "I didn't feel afraid of them. I could lay down in the wagon nights and sleep as well as I could in a house." The journey's reward was her newborn son. From California she wrote home: "On the bed lies a little black headed fellow nestling about trying to make me put away my writing and take him up. . . . Charles & myself are both very healthy. I am as fat as a bear."

With the nation poised at the brink of Civil War, emigration continued briskly. Discovery of silver in Nevada drew more adventurers, and the start of the Pony Express between St. Joseph, Missouri, and Placerville, California, began to regularize the route. Among the travelers of 1860, Helen H. Clark was one of the most ebullient. Her diary is an anthem to the self-confidence and optimism of youth. On leaving Illinois in April, she noted in her diary that when she went into a store to "buy some side combs" the clerk had stared at the bloomers she and her cousin were wearing as if men never knew before that women had feet. Helen started the journey with high spirits: "A fiddler comes down fron the other camp to see if a dance on the turf cannot be started. . . . Mr. Upton got down his melodeon and played some—we danced a while and went to bed." Three nights later there was violin music and "Dora and Mary danced the polka." Helen felt her own vitality and stamina as she wrote: "Mother has a headache and is trying to be real [sick] but I hear music in another tent."

Helen's diary, so light and airy in its disposition, follows the irresistible current in women's diaries when it comes to marking gravesites. This preoccupation did not fade with the lessening of the disease. If the gravesites in later years were fewer in number, the accounts of them are often more careful. Thus, even the gay and happy Helen wrote: "Mother and I . . . find 4 graves. One was of T. Rice from Michigan." And on June

2, "We find two names on the one headboard. One was J. R. Morse of Shelby Co., Ill. Oct. 10th, 1859 . . . These graves were dug in the soft prairie & were dug full of holes [by wolves] and one head board was split off." On June 7 and June 13 Helen again noted the graves she passed and the names inscribed on the makeshift headboards. Her mother was greatly affected by the presence of death. "Mother has a foreboding something is going to happen. She asked us how we would feel if when we got there Father should be dead. For my part I cannot imagine any such thing as real."

That same summer, Lavinia Porter, wife of "almost twenty" and married for five years, was traveling with her husband toward Pike's Peak and gold. She had been raised as a southern belle; her husband knew nothing of manual labor. "I had learned how to make a delicate cake or a fancy pudding but never before had I tried to cook a meal." The Trail was a rousing education for both of them. Only indirectly do we discover from her diary that she was pregnant. She tells, with typical reticence, that she had sewn a maternity gown from a blue gingham cover from her feather bed, and another from a flowered dressing gown her husband had considered "too effiminate." The fact of her pregnancy makes two accounts in her diary particularly pointed. Early in their travels, Lavinia wrote:

We passed hundreds of new-made graves in this part of our route. . . . One day we overtook a belated team on its way to one of the distant forts with only a man and his wife. . . . The wife was quite ill in the little tent, having given birth to a child a day or two before, which lived only a day. The father had put it in a rude box and laid it away in its tiny grave by the wayside. The poor mother was grieving her heart out at leaving it behind on the lonely plain with only a rude stone to mark its resting place.

Later in the journey, the party was overtaken by severe bouts of dysentery, the disease that struck almost every traveler. For Lavinia, pregnant as she was, the debilitation must have been extreme. "Becoming so weakened that I could no longer climb in and out of the wagon, I was compelled to keep my bed . . . the jolting motion of the wagon soon became a perfect torture to me, and at last became so unendurable, that I implored my husband to take me out, make my bed on the sand and let me die in peace." They had brought with them no medicine at all. "Not one of us had ever been ill." In their youth and confidence, it had seemed to them nothing could befall them. Lavinia's troubles continued until they met an old prospector with some powerful advice: "What your woman needs is a good, big dose of castor oil. That straightens her out all right." Since there was no castor oil in the wagon, Lavinia remembered some hair tonic, "and I swallowed it down." Amazingly, "it acted like a charm." The dysentery passed and Lavinia went on.

Of the Indians she saw, Lavinia wrote: "I would state here that the Sioux Indians were the finest looking warriors we had seen." And she thoroughly enjoyed the sight of an Indian brave "mostly naked" and wearing a discarded hoop skirt!

The rest of Lavinia's journey was uneventful. Her child was born a Californian.

During the years of the Civil War, able-bodied men were called upon to fight, and the westward emigration dwindled. The garrisons along the overland route were emptied of soldiers, and volunteers took over guard duties. The North released Confederate prisoners to fight the Indians and frontiersmen called them "galvanized Yankees." Yet the emigrants pressed on, six thousand of them. Ignorance of the road had not stopped them in the 1840s; cholera had not stopped them in the 1850s, and neither Civil War nor Indians would stop them now.

The diaries of the women who went overland in the 1860s show how remarkably little had changed in the life of the road. Louisa Rahm wrote that she "washed and baked and had a hail storm." For most emigrants, life and death still hung in a precarious balance. Ada Millington was twelve when her family set out for California. It was a large family; her father, who had five children by his first marriage, was traveling with his second wife and their six children. The youngest was a year and a half old. In addition, there were five young hired hands. And there were Mrs. Millington's sister and brother-in-law, their children, and their hired hands. And there was the brother-in-law's sister, stepfather and mother. The party seemed large and secure. The families were well provided. "We have a nice large tent and a good sheet iron stove. Six cows, three calves and two loose horses." By June, Ada had learned to drive the four-mule team by herself.

Although telegraph and stagecoach had made the route more secure, a common ailment on this particular journey produced disaster. Dysentery, which affected almost everyone at some time or other on the overland journey, wracked the baby's body, and not any of Mrs. Millingtons' knowledge of herbal teas could halt the wasting illness. "The doctor they called says our George had flux and mountain fever and if we had been at home he needn't have died."

The prospect of having to leave their youngest in a grave along the roadside was intolerable. Ada's diary, because it is the diary of a child not yet given to reserve and stoicism, opens the family's pain to our eyes. "We couldn't bear the thought of leaving his little body among the sands of this wilderness surrounded by Indians and wolves. . . . we used spirits of camphor very freely on George's clothes and think we will try to take his body on at least another day. Isaac . . . cut the letters [of his name] on the coffin lid so that it will be easier to identify [when we come back]." The prospect of burial on the road was the most painful burden the emigrants had to bear.

One's natural instinct was to mark a gravesite so as to find the resting place of a loved one again. But no adequate grave could be dug on the road. The sun had baked the ground until digging was like breaking through concrete. Then the rains would come and wash away the shallow graves. No matter what marker one might devise—a pile of rocks, a piece of wood, a shred of cloth—no emblem would survive the weather or the passage of time.

On the other hand, there was also the urgent need to obliterate a grave. The Indians made a common practice of digging up the dead for clothing, spreading cholera among themselves even as they gathered up their trophies. The emigrants came to believe that the greatest service they could do the deceased was to *hide* the gravesite. Some companies dug beneath the road itself so that the ox teams would trample over all evidence of a grave:

> One of the emigrants in our party was named Crowley. He had lost several members of his family by death while crossing the plains, and at one of our camps . . . a daughter, Martha Leland Crowley, died. . . . They buried her beneath a big plane tree on the banks of a small stream which they christened Grave Creek. . . . The oxen were cor-ralled over her grave so that Indians would not dig her up and get her clothing.

But even if a grave escaped the notice of Indians, it was not likely that it would escape the prowling wolves and coyotes. "Col. Nesmith saw the grave in 1848 and said it had been opened [and] that a number of human bones were scattered about." The child's bones had to be reinterred and the grave filled.

There was no time to care for the sick and the dying. Fear of Indians forced families to hurry along. The cattle needed water and grass. The provisions might give out if one lingered. Always, delay for the dying threatened the life of the living.

Popular songs of the 1850s depicted the "happy death" of a good Christian as something that occurred in the bosom of the family. Pioneer family and friends gathered beside the deathbed in order to comfort the dying. (Ada Millington wrote of her baby brother's death, "we all gathered around his little bed in the tent to see him die.") Portraits and photographs of dead family members, particularly infants and young children, became cherished mementos of families, a way of holding on to a life too soon snuffed out. Death along the road was a palpable wound, and it scarred the lives of emigrants who had dared to break so completely with home. Baptism seemed a lesser concern. It might be a required sacrament under stable life conditions, but the emigrants set such practices aside on the journey. Too many other problems seemed more pressing.

On the day of their fourteenth wedding anniversary, the Millingtons discussed where to bury their child. Near the road were three graves on a hill. Ada wrote of how they debated "whether or not to bury George here with other graves where it doesn't seem so lonesome, but if we could get him to Carson City we might be able to send for him from California later. His body is still well preserved so we are taking it on." Finally they reached Carson City:

> Pa, ma and we children went to see George's grave about a mile from town and nearly in the corner of yard next to town. Desolate enough but we are better satisfied than to have left him on Dry Creek. . . . Pa cut 20 notches on each rail near the head of the grave for his age—20 months, and cut some letters and emblems on the board at the head and foot of the grave. Then we went away hoping in a year or so to have him sent to California. . . . Seth who is four cannot take the baby's place.

Years later, faithful to the memory of the dead infant, one member of the family returned to Carson City to bring the coffin for reburial in California, but the cemetery had been obliterated, and no trace was ever found of the grave the father had so lovingly and carefully marked.

Three days after the baby's burial, Ada's mother managed to bake ginger cakes to celebrate the birthday of her six-year-old. Life for the emigrants went on.

By 1863 there were new ways to travel the overland route. Hallie Riley Hodder and her sister rode to Atchison, Kansas, on a "steam car," and from there went on seven hundred miles to Denver, Colorado, by stagecoach. "We changed horses every ten miles at the little stations on the way, and riding nights as well as days we made 100 miles in twenty-four hours and reached Denver on the evening of the seventh day." Hallie spent a year and a half in Colorado and then returned East. "Before leaving Denver, my

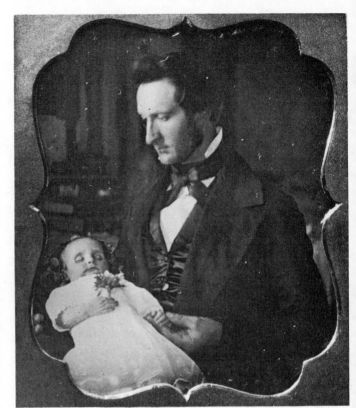

Man with dead child, about 1850. Among a people whose lives were often scarred by the death of children, the photograph quickly became a cherished souvenir. Such pictures might be placed on a mantel or table in a sitting room.

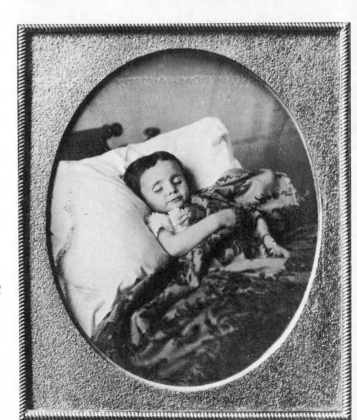

Photograph of dead child, about 1850.

The family of Harvey Andrews visiting the grave of a son who died in childhood. The grave is circled with a picket fence to keep off prowling wolves.

cousin had provided me with a small revolver, and had taught me how to use it. It was loaded and I had taken it from the holster at my belt, so I presume I was ready to use it on myself if we were captured." Hallie apparently saw suicide as the ladylike alternative to killing Indians.

Catherine Wever Collins also traveled West by train. "I left Cincinnati, Ohio, in the Express train last evening . . . and arrived (in St. Louis) about 11 a.m." She left at 4 in the morning and "after due shrieks from the engine [we] launched into the darkness. . . ." Passengers were ferried across the Missouri River and then scrambled as best they could up the banks to the waiting train on the other side. Even travel by train required a certain agility. Catherine reached Atchison, Kansas, at half past one in the morning, and from there for sixty dollars she found a place on the stagecoach. Eleven hectic days after her journey had begun in Ohio, she reached Fort Laramie, Wyoming.

But not all emigrants had changed their mode of travel. Wagons were still the mainstay of travelers. Mary Eliza Warner was fifteen and just the right age to travel. The journey was a lark. Early on a May morning, she wrote in her diary: "I drove four horses nearly all day," and on Sunday, "saw the most magnificent scenery I ever saw." After finishing their work the young people "had a good time singing." When the weather was fine, she and "Aunt Celia," a married lady scarcely out of her teens herself, rode horseback for the sheer fun of it. Surely this was a delicious way to spend the summer months.

Katherine Dunlap was older and she marked the dangers more carefully. "A little girl was jostled out of a wagon run over and killed." Perhaps because she traveled with a small child of her own, she noticed a pine board at the head of a grave with the inscription: "Two children, killed by a stampede." And on July 16, she came upon the grave of an infant. "Oh, what a lonely, dark and desolate place to bury a sweet infant—We read the following inscription on the headboard of the death-sleeping infant: 'Morlena Elizabeth Martess, died Aug. 9th, 1863, born July 7th, 1862. Friends nor physician could save her from the grave." The gravestone carried a plea to all emigrants who might pass to repair the grave, and Katherine noted in her diary: "It *was repaired* and a pen of logs built around it."

Deep in the hills of Idaho and Colorado were two other women whose journeys had brought them to the camps where men were digging for gold and for silver. Each determined to get herself a share of that wealth. Mrs. Theodore Schultz was the "first white woman in [the mining camp]." She started a boarding house and "charged $3.00 per meal and on Sunday [I] often got 200 extra [men]. I worked 18 hours a day lots of times. We had little provisions but bushels of gold dust. I had gold dust everywhere in everything. . . . I threw it in the wood box . . . and under beds." Mrs. Fowler ran a boarding house in Pueblo, Colorado. She charged a dollar a meal, and had all the men she could cook for. Space was so much at a premium that men paid for the privilege of sleeping on the ground *outside* the boarding house. For women who provided a semblance of home—a warm meal and a clean bed—there were fortunes to be made in the mining camps.

Some of the women who worked in the mining camps had come as slaves, like the seventeen-year-old boy sold by his father to Helen Carpenter and her husband. Sometimes whole families had come with their masters, traveling in their own wagons at the end of the long trains, secretly hoping to find a way to freedom in the territories.

Oregon was less hospitable to blacks than many of them had hoped. The territorial legislature passed laws prohibiting admission to black settlers, even though exceptions were made on individual petition. When Oregon was admitted to the union in 1857, a Free Negro Admission Article was proposed for the state's constitution, but it was defeated, and the small number of blacks who had made their way to Oregon lived uneasily until the Emancipation Proclamation of 1863.[1]

California, on the other hand, outlawed slavery within its boundaries in 1850 because miners feared the appearance of slave labor. The mines soon became places where an exotic mixture of races and nationalities shouldered one another in the feverish search for wealth. Mary Ballou wrote home that she lived in a mining camp called "Negro Bar," where "French and Duch and Scoth and Jews and Italions and Sweeds and Chineese and Indians" were all panning for gold.[2] Even before the discovery of gold, California had been settled by men and women of Mexican, Indian, and African descent. Eighteen percent of the population, according to a Spanish census of 1790, were of other than Anglo-American origin. By 1849, San Francisco blacks had formed a "mutual Benefit and Relief Society" of their own. By 1854, that city had three black churches, and within the next decade there were three black newspapers and as many black churches.[3]

Some of the black women who came to western lands we cannot name. Margaret Frink wrote in her journal that somewhere in the Humboldt Sink she saw "a Negro woman . . . tramping along through the heat and dust, carrying a cast iron bake stove on her head, with her provisions and a blanket piled on top . . . bravely pushing on for California."

Some of the black women we do know about. Mary Ellen Pleasants came to San Francisco in 1849. Born a slave in Georgia, she was married to a free black in Boston and came to the West Coast with a sizable fortune. In 1858 she traveled all the way back to eastern Canada, in order to deliver thirty thousand dollars personally into the hands of John Brown, to help him in his crusade to free her people. When she came back to California, she was put off a San Francisco streetcar, and she filed a suit, along with other black women, and eventually compelled the streetcar lines to allow Negroes to ride.[4] "Mammy" Pleasants, as she had come to be called, was a formidable citizen.

Another black emigrant was Clara Brown, who took in washing at the

This black woman, possibly named Emily Butler, was said to be the wife of Charles Blockwell, a white barber, in Jacksonville, Oregon. Her dress indicates she enjoyed considerable status in her community. Photograph by Peter Britt.

Horshoe Bar, in Miner's Ravine, California. Born in Virginia in 1803, she and her mother were sold to a man who was headed West. Several owners later, she purchased her freedom and made her way to St. Louis, Missouri. In 1859, she persuaded a party of gold prospectors to hire her as a cook. At the age of fifty-nine, she rode on the back seat of a covered wagon, slowly making her way across the plains. She arrived in Central City, Colorado, and like the white women who saw in the mining camps a place to make a profitable living, Clara Brown started a laundry. In 1860, she moved the laundry to Mountain City, forty miles away, and paid a prospector to drive her there as his "hired help." After the Civil War, Clara Brown searched for her family, for people she had not seen in almost sixty years. She found thirty-four relatives and brought them, by steamboat and by a wagon she bought and outfitted, across the country to Denver. In later years she sponsored other wagon trains, helping blacks to come West as she had done.[5]

Not all blacks were prosperous, but many were enterprising. Biddy Mason was a slave who trudged from Mississippi to California driving sheep behind the three hundred wagons of her master's wagon train in 1851. She had her own wagon and three daughters. Her master remained in California until 1854, when he decided to take his family and his slaves to Texas. Biddy prevailed upon the sheriff of Los Angeles County to issue a writ preventing her master from taking his slaves out of the state, and she finally secured her freedom through the courts in 1856.

A shrewd businesswoman, Biddy Mason began to purchase property in 1866. Her original investment amounted to only $250, but thirty years later, her heirs refused an offer of $200,000 for only part of the land. In the 1880s, she paid grocery bills for black families who had been left destitute.[6]

Susan Wilson was another slave who came to California by oxteam, traveling across the Plains with three of her children. Addie Stanley came with her parents from Illinois to California in 1852.[7] And Cloye Burnett Logan-Flood came to the Pacific Coast as a slave with a white family in 1853. When she was only eleven she took a horse and rode from Oregon to Shasta, California, alone. As a Californian, she married and raised six children.[8]

Blacks in California opened their own schools and their own churches. Although these women did not leave diaries and journals, there is evidence that they strove to make the western territories a more hospitable environment in which to raise their families.

Despite the uncertainty and danger of travel, despite Indian wars that were now real threats, the emigrants continued to press through the

Clara Brown, about 1860.

Biddy Mason, seated in the doorway, with her family in Los Angeles.

western roads. At the end of the Civil War, twenty-five thousand emigrants made the overland crossing. They were among the last Americans to make the journey by wagon. Cora Wilson Agatz and her family were prosperous Iowa farm people. They had five span of matched mules, a team of horses, a saddle pony and four wagons to carry beds and tables, linen, silver, china, carpets, books, and pictures. They took "canned goods, bacons, hams, bologna sausage, flour, barrels of both white and brown sugar, great cakes of maple sugar. . . ." They had a sheet iron camp stove and an oven and a wagon filled with clothing. Also "a maiden lady devoid of hearing and

Biddy Mason was freed by a California judge in 1856. Four years later, she had a certified copy of the order issued for her keeping.

eyelashes who begged passage for the avowed purpose of finding a lifemate out west, which she did very shortly after her arrival." Cora described the "gymnasium costumes" worn by some of the women. "Short gray wool skirts, full bloomer pants of the same, fastened at the knee, high laced boots, and . . . white stockings which were changed often enough to be kept spotless. Large straw hats finished these picturesque and sensible costumes. When compared with the long, slovenly, soiled calico gowns worn by the other women of the train, these simple costumes elicited many commendatory remarks." What a wonderful picture: these ladies kept their

This old woman put on her best bonnet and claimed the right to lead the team into Baker City, Oregon. The variety of draft animals and their gaunt condition suggests that most of her oxen died on the road.

stockings washed, their high boots laced and their large straw hats in good order through the long journey! Surely they were a far cry from poor Rebecca Ketcham in her one dress, and from Martha Morrison's mother wading through the swamps.

But lest one come to believe the road had become a place of fashion and ease, the diary of Barsina French, the last diary of this collection, reminds us that in 1867, traveling through Apache country along the southern route, the mothers had to take their turns standing guard against the Indians at night. And in the morning, the women cooked what they called "red mud" for coffee at breakfast.

Migration dwindled after 1868. The railroad began to replace the wagon and settlers also began to look to the lands of the middle mountain regions rather than to the coast. It was a time for consolidation and for a different kind of building, not log houses this time, but the fabric of social life—schools and churches and the reweaving of families separated and broken by the migration. It was time for the women to build.

NOTES

1. Alan Clark Miller, *Photographer of a Frontier: The Photographs of Peter Britt* (Eureka, California, Interface California Corporation, 1976), p. 58.

2. Mary Ballou, "I Hear the Hogs in My Kitchen: A Woman's View of the Gold Rush," in *Let Them Speak for Themselves: Women in the American West*, ed. Christiane Fischer (Hamden, Connecticut, The Shoestring Press, 1977), p. 46.

3. Delilah L. Beasley, *The Negro Trail Blazers of California* (New York, Universities Press, 1969), p. 146.

4. Ibid., pp. 95–96. Lawrence B. de Graaf, "Race, Sex, and Region:Black Women in the American West, 1850–1920," *Pacific Historical Review* 49 (1980): 292.

5. Joan Swallow Reiter, *The Women* (Alexandria, Va., Time-Life Books, 1978), p. 131. Also Sheryl and Gene Patterson-Black, *Western Women in History and Literature* (Crawford, Neb., Cottonwood Press, 1978), p. 2. Kathleen Bruyn, *Aunt Clara Brown* (Boulder, Colorado, Pruett Publishing, 1971).

6. Beasley, pp. 109–110; Reiter, p. 213; Miriam Matthews, "TheNegro in California from 1781–1910," unpublished paper.

7. Beasley, p. 122.

8. Ibid., p. 123.

Inez Adams Parker.

EPILOGUE

The settlements that awaited the women in Oregon and California were primitive. "Oregon City" in 1845 was a place where seven or eight families huddled against the winter. Fortunate emigrants found a family willing to share a home until the spring came. Inez Parker remembered that the only shelter her family could find that first winter in Oregon in 1849–50 was with another family with ten children living in two "moderately sized rooms and a loft." Seven girls slept in the loft and the younger children "on the floor in the front room by the fireplace." Her father, in payment for his family's lodging, taught school for all the children and, in the evenings, made chairs, tables, brooms, and bedsteads by the light of a "shallow tin pan of melted tallow, with all but one end of an inch-wide strip of cotton or woolen cloth immersed in it, and the protruding end resting on the edge of the pan ignited for light. . . . later when candle wicking could be had, mother made candles." Such pans were sometimes filled with bear grease; the settlers called them "bitch lights."

Lucy Ann Deady wrote: "We lived on boiled wheat and boiled peas" in the winter of 1846. Martha Morrison remembered her first winter: "We never had a bit of tea or coffee, the coffee made was *pea* coffee."

The first winter was often disheartening. "I had nothing to do but be homesick. . . . There was not a newspaper or book in the country. . . . I ripped up an old dress and sewed it together with ravellings, just to have something to do." Martha Minto recalled that their clothing was weather-worn by the journey, and many of the women felt ashamed.

I think there was only one bolt of calico in Oregon when we came

147

here—That was all the cloth we had for dresses at that time. That was
sold for fifty cents a yard. It was very poor quality of calico. The women
and girls that came here were very destitute. The next summer . . .
my oldest sister and I gathered a barrel of cranberries and I sent them
to Oregon City and got a little piece of blue drilling that made us a
covering. And that was about all; it could hardly be considered dresses,
but it was so we were covered. We did not have any ruffles, I think.
There were no shoes or stockings to buy, and if there were we did not
have the money to pay for them. My sister and I managed to . . . get us
a pair of fine slippers. We used to carry them in our hands and put
them on just before we go to [a] house.

But a hardy enthusiasm for life sustained them. When Martha Morrison
married John Minto, she started housekeeping with "just one stew kettle.
. . . we had that [same] kettle to make coffee, or bread, or to fry meat, for we
had not even a frying pan. We had three butcher knives, that were bought
at Oregon City, nothing else. . . . We had just two sheets and one little bit of
a bed with a few feathers in it. . . . I cut up the sheets to make shirts for my
husband and then we had none. We slept as we could. We had a pile of
straw." Minto went on to recall: "People say they would not have staid they
would go right back. I would like to know *how* we could go back. . . . we
had no horses, not cattle, nor anything to haul us across the plains; we had
no provisions; we could not start out naked and destitute in every way."

The emigrants managed to hang on, and thousands more came each
year. They built flour mills and lumber mills, water mills and blacksmith
founderies. They set up manufacture on unbroken land. Elizabeth Wood,
who came in the summer of '51, wrote, "A lazy person should never think of
going to Oregon."

For many of the emigrant families, reaching Oregon or California was not
the end of their traveling. Roxana Cheney arrived in California in 1854, but
her husband was restless and moved the family to the gold fields in 1856,
and then back again to the Santa Clara valley. Roxana said he wavered
between mining and dairying, and then between dairying and ranching. In
1861 they sold their land and moved to the Bay Area where they built a
farm "fenced with pickets split from redwood driven into the ground by
hard knocks, nearly two miles of this fence and all was the work of my
husband. After seven years of hard work one morning in June, when
everything on the farm was growing and looking splendidly, a [man] from
the city [came] to look at our farm. . . . I set the price so high that we
thought he would not give it, but he bought us out." Roxana and her
husband and four children moved again, and it was not until 1868 that they
finally laid down roots. The restlessness that propelled the emigrants across

The Hager family standing before their log cabin in Oregon Territory. The infant cradled in a halved packing crate sleeps unaware of the austerity of life in the first settlements, but the haunting beauty of the young mother appears in stark contrast to her surroundings.

the continent did not abate when they reached the coast. They moved and moved again, searching for that final geography, that ultimate configuration of land that would make them prosperous. So many roads seemed to lead to success that new beginnings became a way of life.

As soon as they could, the women saw to it that there were schools for their children and churches to solemnize the essential rituals and rhythms of life and death. There was a momentous outpouring of energy and determination that went into making settlements out of wilderness. And the women continued to keep the bonds of family life together. Somehow they found the time to write the letters back home and to keep track of births and birthdays, marriages and deaths. They simply refused to sever the framework of their old lives as they began to build anew.

The diaries, reminiscences, letters and accounts of 103 women have formed the basis of this book (96 overland journeys, 7 exchanges of frontier letters). The accounts are uneven and of different quality, but it is possible to draw some kind of composite picture of the group as a whole.

We know that the overland migration at mid-century was a major transplanting of young families. If any passion drove the women forward, it was the determination to keep their families together. Against the familiar strategy of sending the men on ahead, overland women set themselves to maintain the family's coherence. The decision to go West was not theirs to make, and they were reluctant to embark on a journey that meant a complete break with their old lives, but if the women understood and responded to any principle, it was the need to keep their families together. They picked up their children and traveled that agonizing road so that the family—all the family—might be transplanted in the new country. That purpose, above all, made the hardship bearable.

The overwhelming majority of women who made the overland crossing were married—they went West because they were the wives and daughters of the men who made the journey. In the total group, 73 women (70%) were married; 27 women (26%) were either unmarried or were children; the status of 3 women is unknown. The placement of women within the family determined their lives and the choices available to them. In only 2 cases did women travel the overland trail alone.

In the total census, seventeen diarists (16%) were under the age of fifteen and were traveling with their parents. Nine more were unmarried females between sixteen and thirty, and they also traveled with their families. It is in these accounts of younger female travelers that the most buoyant accounts of the journey are to be found. Youth carried its own resiliency of spirit and of body. Youth adapted to the patterns of work and dress demanded by life on the frontier. The fact that one might not look "the lady" seemed to matter less to those whose years had ingrained those prescriptions only lightly. And the landscape appeared far more magnificent when one was not searching for a lost child or carrying a babe in arms as she walked.

For ten women (10%), the overland journey was a honeymoon, begun within hours or weeks of the wedding ceremony. One diarist told of a honeymoon couple in the wagon train, and another remembered that her own parents had emigrated from Iowa to Illinois on their own honeymoon. The idea of the honeymoon journey was a popular one; it held the prospect of a new life and a new land to those just starting out.

The diaries show that the ages at which overland women married bore a strong correlation to the period during which they traveled. In twenty-five diaries in which we learn the ages of the women at first marriage, the women who traveled in the first years of the emigration married at the earliest ages. Eleven women (40%) who were married between thirteen and eighteen years old traveled between 1844 and 1850. In contrast, nine women (37%) who married between the ages of twenty and thirty-one were among the later emigrants who traveled between 1852 and 1862. The pattern seems to bear out the evidence of the diaries that there were significant differences between the early and the later emigrants. The first travelers were upwardly mobile, but also restless, and their pattern of life was to move from free land to free land. Early marriage was common among these restless people, and it was the pattern that persisted. Among the women whose families traveled in the second decade of the emigration, there was a consistent trend toward later marriage. These families owned and traveled with more property. They were cautious in setting off for new lands; these women were more cautious in setting out upon a new life.

In terms of family size and family formation, the diaries show thirty-two women traveling with 108 children among them. The average overland family in this census was one that held 3.4 children. Only four of these thirty-two families were "mature" families with more than five children. The majority of the wives were young women traveling with small children—young families still in the process of growth.

Among the seventeen diarists who were under the age of fifteen, we find that thirteen traveled in families that held a total of eighty-two children, or an average of 6.3 children per family.[1] When the mature families of the first group are included, we find seventeen mature families with a total of 107 children, or 6.3 children per family.

Thus, family size among thirty-two overland families at the time of migration on was 3.4 children per family. *But seventeen older families provide a model of significantly larger numbers of children, with six or more children completing the family.* (It is important to remember that none of these data include information regarding stillbirths, miscarriages, or infant or early-childhood deaths.)

Strategies of family planning seemed to depend upon each particular family's vision of itself and its future. As long as emigration was a primary intention, large numbers of children provided the model for family formation. But once the family began to understand itself as geographically stable, family size and age of first marriage began to alter toward the formation of smaller family units.[2]

The diaries bear this out, for in fifteen accounts where there is evidence of the size of families after settlement in Oregon and California, one learns that overland women gave birth to between one and nine *more* children during the course of their married lives, or in remarriages. These fifteen women would have 101 more children, again giving an average of 6.7 children per emigrant family.

In contrast, in two instances where we know the family configuration of the *daughters* of overland women, we find that they married later and bore fewer children than their mothers. In one case the overland mother had nine children, while her daughter would have only four. In another, the emigrant mother married at sixteen and had eight children, but her two daughters married at eighteen and twenty respectively and would have seven and four children during their own childbearing years.

The diaries suggest that two different models of family size were operative during the years of the major emigrations in the United States. The first model provided for a family that succeeded in producing six or more surviving children. This family often undertook more than one geographic migration during its period of development and tended to understand its strength as the number of children who could help with the physical labor of clearing the land. Children, however, did not linger in parental families, but broke away by the midadolescent years to start their own families and their own removals to new land. The other model of frontier families seemed to come when families believed themselves geographically stable. At the point where they believed they had come to a satisfactory economic condition, a situation that would allow them to develop their opportunities rather than to search out new ones, family size tended to shrink. The data suggest that the movement toward smaller family formation was one that was agreed upon by both husband and wife and was in considerable measure the mark of the end of emigration.

In considering childbearing through the diaries, we learn that nine of the seventy-three married women were pregnant on the overland journey. In addition, five of the older women, mothers of diarists, were also pregnant, and two others traveled with newborn infants. Thus, 22 percent of the married women who had reached childbearing years in this census were in some stage of pregnancy or had recently delivered. Eighteen other women (21% of the census population of adult married women) wrote that they knew of or personally assisted women in neighboring wagon trains who gave birth on the way.[3]

Accounts of pregnancy appear in the diaries of women from 1844 through 1860. Time is not a factor, nor is class. In this random sample of ninety-seven diarists, fifty women traveled with 191 children, and sixteen were pregnant or had recently given birth on the overland journey. In addition, there are eighteen specific accounts of women in other wagon parties who were also pregnant. Overland women were living through the many stages of the childbearing and childrearing processes, a fact that in no way impeded the decision to make the twenty-four hundred-mile journey.

Two women died on the journey of cholera and two after childbirth, and there are four accounts of women in other wagon trains who also died after they had delivered. Infants seemed to have suffered a somewhat higher mortality rate. The diaries contain detailed accounts of nine infant deaths and one stillbirth following arrival in Oregon, although some of these include infants in other wagon parties.

Children are shown in this census to have been under considerable risk. Nine were seriously injured by slipping off the wagon tongue under the wheels of the wagons or the hooves of the oxen. Three children were caught in buffalo stampedes and two of them died. One child died of an overdose of laudanum. Children are repeatedly reported lost.

The highest risks to life seem to have been borne by the men. 11%— seven husbands, three fathers and one uncle—died during the course of these overland journeys. In addition, nine husbands and fathers in neighboring wagon trains are accounted by the women to have drowned. The husbands of two women died in accidents shortly after their arrival in Oregon and California. The clear sense is that the men—exposed to accident, cholera, typhoid, exposure and exertion, and Indian assault— traveled under the greatest risk on the Trail. *All* of the wives who were widowed at the end of the journey remarried, most of them quickly and two of them twice.

Against the dangers of the road, emigrants sought to travel in company with family, friends, neighbors and co-religionists. Thirty-six of the ninety-six diarists (37%) traveled in assorted patterns of extended families.

Even when it appears on first reading of a diary that a family was traveling alone, closer attention shows that a family member had either preceded the emigrants or had promised to follow them. Families emigrated with their kin or in advance of kin, or moved to meet kin who had gone ahead. Family was trusted above the constitutions and the agreements of the road. But even family would be abandoned if a new course were presented, a new route described, or an unexpected opportunity offered.

Forty women journeyed during the years of the cholera epidemic, and of these, seventeen (43%) recorded the fearful disease by noting in their diaries the individual grave sites they passed. The meticulous care the women gave to recording the death toll of the journey remains one of the major sex-related differences between the diaries of women and men on the overland passage. The fact of death loomed large for the women, and they felt death to be a personal catastrophe. Whereas men in their diaries tended to record the cumulative impact of cholera, the women set themselves to note each and every grave they saw. Men dismissed women's concern as overly sensitive, and tended to erase from their own thoughts evidence of the devastation on the road.

No one who reads the diaries of women on the Overland Trail can escape feeling the intensity with which the women regarded loss of life. Cholera, illness, accident—these were central facts in the minds of the women who were the ritual caretakers of the dying and the dead. In the diaries of such women there is an unmistakable tension and sense of resistance to the journey. These were the women who seemed to judge the overland adventure to be an extravagant expense of human life. They shared the incredulity of Mary A. Jones when her husband showed her by a sweep of his arm at their journey's end "nothing but nature" and a little mud and stick hut. One must suspect that such women subscribed to the journey with obedience and considerable courage, but not by the acquiescence of their spirits. The women observed the rituals of patriarchal deference. Not even Jannet Stewart, married many years, dared to oppose the decision of her husband and the rest of the men when they decided to press on rather than wait for her daughter's wagon and family detained on the road. There are mighty few bravos and huzzahs for the new territory in the accounts of the older overland women.

In only 7 percent of the overland diaries of the women are there records of Indian attacks and these account for the deaths of two men, one woman, and two families. The evidence is that the Indians were universally feared, only sporadically hostile during the most important years of emigration, and more or less continually the guides and purveyors of vital services to the emigrants. The women learned quickly enough to conduct their own barter with the Indians they met, trading shirts for food, pancakes for moccasins.

Some historians have claimed that the traditional image of overland women as "bearing up under suffering rather than enjoying the freedom which western life permitted them is an inaccurate portrayal." And recent research has uncovered evidence of women who independently registered as homesteaders and who homesteaded their lands without the help of men. These were women who "sought economic freedom through land ownership . . . who sought to earn a living by means other than those of schoolteacher, maid, or factory worker." Sheryll and Gene Patterson-Black have found that in Colorado and Wyoming between 1887 and 1908, "an average of 11.9% of the sample of homestead entrants were women." Gusta Anderson Chapin, who came to Dakota Territory in the 1870s, "hauled hay . . . and earned the fabulous sum of a dollar a day breaking land for other settlers, working with oxen and using a walking plow." They point to Clara Brown, who "made enough money in the Colorado gold camps to invest in real estate and to grubstake several prospectors."[4] And women like Margaret Frink, Luzena Wilson and Mary Jane Megquier certainly made the most of the opportunities offered by the gold rush. Historian Dawn Lander has discovered other women who similiarly greeted the adventure of the western frontier with zeal and independent spirit.[5]

But however powerful the attempt to revise history, the period of the Overland Trail migration (1840–60) produces overwhelming evidence that women did not greet the idea of going West with enthusiasm, but rather that they worked out a painful negotiation with historical imperatives and personal necessity.

Within cycles of childbearing and childrearing, women managed a kind of equity in which they placed their lives. Women were neither brave adventurers nor sunbonneted weepers. They were vigorous and given to realism and to stoicism. The West to them meant the challenge of rearing a family and maintaining domestic order against the disordered life on the frontier. Once embarked on the journey, they were determined and energetic in their efforts to make the move a success.

If any idea joined the women to their men, if any expectation made the strenuous journey bearable, it was the idea that the move would bring them and their children a better life. Certainly the women as well as the men had seen the hard winters and the limitations of the land in their old homes. Hope for a new life was the common thread between husband and wife on the journey. Once past the rigors of the Trail itself, once through the first winter crowded in a cabin with other families or still living in a tent, the emigrants found that the "New Country" began to yield its rewards. The land was bountiful, the weather mild, epidemics rare. For those who had resourcefulness, stamina, and good spirits, prosperity emerged out of hard work. It did not take many seasons before emigrant women started to count their fruit trees, their egg money, their land under cultivation, and the prospects of good crops. Many became "boosters," writing home of the wonders of their golden country out West.

Mary M. Colby wrote to her brother and sister in Massachusetts from Lebenon, in Oregon Territory, in 1849:

Dear Brother & Sister:

It is a long time since we have seen each other but I have not forgotten you altho many miles of land and water separate us yet I often wish I could see you and your family and many dear friends in Nashville [New Hampshire]. I suppose you would like to hear how we

By the close of the century about 12 or 15% of western homesteaders were women alone, either unmarried or widowed. This woman in southern California marked the occasion of receiving the patent to her land from the land agent by having her photograph taken.

like this country and how we prosper in the first of our living here. I did not like [it] very well but after we had taken our claim and became settled once more I began to like [it] much better and the longer I live here the better I like [it]. the summer is beautiful and not hot a very little rain tho it is not so warm in the summer here as it is in the States the nights cool and comfotable and I can sleep like a rock. the winters is rather rainy but it is not cold and so bad getting about as it is in the States here the grass is fresh and green the year round and our cattle are all fat enough now for beef their is not a month in the year but I can pick wildflowers or some strawberry blossoms.

As to our prosperity we are getting along as well as one could expect we have a section of land one mile square in the best part of Oregon it is prairie all except a strip of timber on two sides of it with a stream of water running through each pice of timber our stock consists of seven cows one yoke of oxen six calves fifteen hogs and 24 hens; hens here are one dollar a piece eggs are only one dollar per dozen I sold a lot yesterday, for that price butter is from fifty cents to one dollar [a] pound. I think with good health and good economy we shall get along verry well. I cannot say that I wish to go back to the states to live at present if ever. I know when one gets comfortably fixed here they can live as well as they can anywhere else with half of the labor that you do in the states. . . .

I do not wish to brag but I think we shall ere long be as well off for property as some of the family think they are. . . . Our health is good and has been for the most of the time since we have been here the children are healthier than when in Ohio well Ruth I have got two of the pretiest children in the whole family Frances Ann looks like her father and he you know must be pretty for Sabrina said he was Allen James looks as Brother John used to. . . .

I bought home a mirror the other day that I can see my whole body in for the egg [money] we are in the best neighborhood I ever lived in all it wants to make it right is to have some of my friends here. . . . I have got a first rate husband all the fault I find with him he is not lively enough he is verry still that you no is verry different from me but you no a close mouth maketh a wise heart and I believe it we have about 140 acres of our own land under fence 40 of it is improved I suppose he would not sell it for four thousand that is a small price to what some value their claims when our fruit trees begin to bear it seems more like home we have apples pear peaches and plum trees. . . . we live in a dry cabbin it has two rooms and is verry comfortable is as good as the rest of our neighbors have so I am content with it till we can have a better one now. . . . give my love to all your children and please to except a good share your self. . . .

Yours
Mary M. Colby

Please send us a paper now and then.[6]

The diaries of the women are evidence that "power passes down the matriarchal line as surely as it does down the patriarchal line."[7] They show us women who were not merely swept along in the flow of migration, but women who were strong and resilient. They stood their ground as personalities, as actors in the family drama and in the drama that history set before them. In the face of all of the forms of dislocation that commonly accompanied emigration, these women determined to maintain the family as an integral unit. And when disaster struck, when a husband or father died, the women picked up their children and continued on. There was no turning back. The widows filed their claims and held on to the land.

Overland women married, bore their children, and did the work required of them. Their aim was to be sufficient to the needs of the day. They left their homes to make the journey with their men and with their children and in keeping the strands of their families together, they bore new life even on the crest of upheaval, on the road to the New Land. Their legacy to history was the survival of the family on the westward journey.

NOTES

1. According to Faragher, the mean size of emigrating families was 7.6. See *Women and Men on the Overland Trail*, p. 57. Also Faragher, "Women and Men on the Farming Frontier of Illinois: The Political Economy of Sex," unpublished essay.

2. The question of family size is one that currently divides a number of scholars. Although "families with ten or twelve children are pictured as the norm," Jeffrey argues that the picture is a misleading stereotype. Relying upon census data, Jeffrey finds that "Western women's fertility patterns were not very different from those of other women in the country," and points out that other families in the nation were showing a marked reduction in family size, with the average American family falling from 7.04 children in 1800 to 6.14 in 1840 and to 4.24 in 1880 (*Frontier Women*, p. 57). Jeffrey's conclusion is that frontier families had no more than three or four children, and that children on the frontier "were not an asset but a burden."

Faragher, on the other hand, working with diaries and personal narratives, reaches a very different conclusion: "Midwestern farm mothers had relatively large families. The mean family size in the Midwest in 1850 was 5.7. Mean family size of the overland emigrants in this study was a little less, 5.0, mainly because there were so many newlyweds. . . . The mean size of emigrating families in their full childbearing phase was 7.6. In her lifetime, then, a farm woman could expect to raise five or six children of her own. These children helped significantly with the burden of farm work (*Women and Men on the Overland Trail*, pp. 57–58). It is important to remember that no data include information about miscarriages, stillbirths, birth accidents, and infant mortality. One must assume, therefore, that frontier women were pregnant many times in excess of those live births that stand recorded.

James E. Davis's *Frontier America 1800–1840* (Glendale, Calif., Arthur H. Clark Co., 1977) deals with the frontier when it constituted lands east of the Mississippi. He writes that "large households . . . gravitate[d] toward the fresh lands of the West," but he also notes that not all children of frontier households were counted by census takers because "older offspring left to begin their own households before the census taker had a chance to count them as teen-age members of their parent's household" (pp. 103–104).

Demographers who have held that farm households approximated the national average in number of children too often forget that frontier regions contained fewer females. Thus, the national census of 1880 reported the nation's population to be

159

50.4% males and 49.6% females. But the population of Lincoln County, Nebraska, in 1869, was composed of 80.4% males and only 19.6% females, a ratio of 7.5 to 1. Yet the birth rate of Lincoln County matched the national average: 25.9% of the total population were children. Fewer women in Lincoln County produced more children, even though the statistics show equivalency. I am grateful to Frederick Luebke, of the University of Nebraska at Lincoln, for this insight and for his demographic data on women on the Nebraska frontier.

The question of the family size of frontier families is discussed in a growing literature: William Bowen, "The Oregon Frontiersman: A Demographic View," in Thomas Vaughan, ed., *The Western Shore: Oregon Country Essays Honoring The American Revolution* (Portland, Durham & Downey, 1975), pp. 181–197; John Modell, "Family Fertility on the Indiana Frontier, 1820," *American Quarterly* 23 (1971): 615–634; Blaine T. Williams, "The Frontier Family: Demographic Fact and Historical Myth," in Harold M. Hollingsworth and Sandra L. Myres, eds., *Essays on the American West* (Arlington, University of Texas Press, 1969), pp. 40–65; Maris A. Vinovskis' "Socio-Economic Determinants of Interstate Fertility Differentials in the United States in 1850 and 1860," *Journal of Interdisciplinary History* 6 (1976): 375–396, Richard A. Easterlin, "Factors in the Decline of the Farm Fertility in the United States: Some Preliminary Research Results," *Journal of American History* 63 (1964): 600–614. See also W. H. Grabill, C. V. Kiser, and P. K. Whelpton, *The Fertility of American Women* (New York, John Wiley, 1958); and Yasukirchi Yosuba, *Birth Rates of the White Population in the United States, 1800–1860* (Baltimore, Johns Hopkins Press, 1962).

3. Faragher finds much the same situation: "Of the 122 families reconstructed for this study, 16 wives bore children on the trail; this is slightly higher than the general birthrate for the mid-nineteenth century and suggests that neither pregnancy nor expected delivery somewhere out on the road was perceived as a barrier to women's travel" (*Women and Men on the Overland Trail*, p. 139). Faragher's census of overland families yielded 16 births for 74 married women. My own census shows 14 births for 73 married women—the ratios remarkably similar. Faragher's data, therefore, is highly relevant. 16 births for 74 married women converts to a gross birth rate of 215/1,000 (215 live births per 1,000 women). Comparable rates for the U.S. as a whole were: 1840, 222; 1850, 194; 1860, 184. U.S. Bureau of the Census, *Historical Statistics of the United States . . . to 1970* (Washington, D.C., Government Printing Office, 1975), p. 49, see Faragher, p. 238, n. 116.

4. Sheryll and Gene Patterson-Black, *Western Women in History and Literature* (Crawford, Nebr., Cottonwood Press, 1978), pp. 1–2.

5. Dawn Lander, "Women and The Wilderness: Tabus in American Literature," University of Michigan Papers in Women's Studies, vol. *II*, no. 3 (1977): 62–83. Also Dawn Lander Gherman, "From Parlor to Tepee: the White Squaw on the American Frontier," Ph.D. diss., University of Massachusetts, 1975.

6. Mary M. Colby to her Brother and Sister, February, 1849. Bennett Family Papers, Haverhill Public Library, Cambridge, Massachusetts. I thank Alice Kessler-Harris for making the correspondence known to me.

7. Ann Douglas, "Soft-Porn Culture," *New Republic* (August 30, 1980), 28.

THE
DIARIES

This and the following diaries are presented just as they were written. Spelling and punctuation—or lack of punctuation—reflect the common orthography of the period, the women's education, and perhaps the circumstance of writing in a moving wagon.

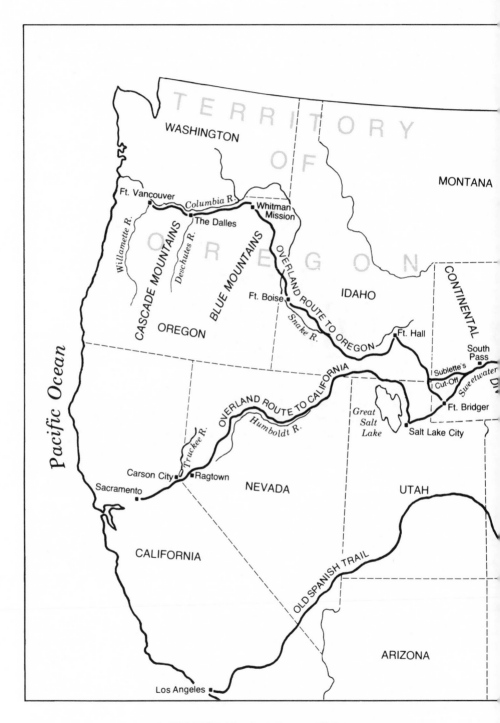

OVERLAND TRAIL

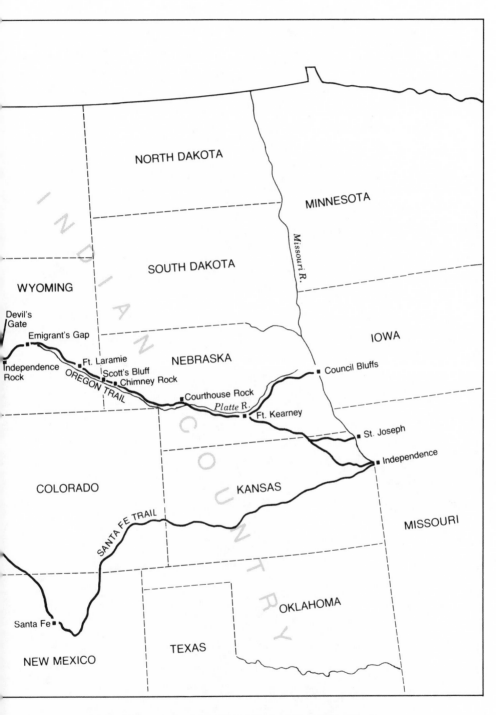

Adapted from a map of the Oregon Trail, 1846, published by the
United States Department of Agriculture, Bureau of Public Roads

A WOMAN'S TRIP ACROSS THE PLAINS IN 1849

Catherine Haun was a young bride when she and her husband, a lawyer, decided to follow the path of the gold rush. Old debts and hopes for a better life in a better climate prompted their move from Iowa. Their buoyant spirits are typical of the emigrants of the flush years of gold rush travel. Her account, moreover, is a reminiscence, dictated to her daughter in later years. Like many emigrants, she remembered details of the road vividly and softened the hardships of the journey in the retelling. Even her story of the woman who escaped from the Indians has the color of romance about it.

Catherine Haun and her husband were educated and from middle-class families. Her wagon train was large, well equipped, and experienced.

CATHERINE HAUN

E arly in January of 1849 we first thought of emigrating to California. It was a period of National hard times and we being financially involved in our business interests near Clinton, Iowa, longed to go to the new El Dorado and "pick up" gold enough with which to return and pay off our debts.*

Our discontent and restlessness were enhanced by the fact that my health was not good. Fear of my sister's having died while young of consumption, I had reason to be apprehensive on that score. The physician advised an entire change of climate thus to avoid the intense cold of Iowa, and recommended a sea voyage, but finally approved of our contemplated trip across the plains in a "prairie schooner," for even in those days an out-of-door life was advocated as a cure for this disease. In any case, as in that of many others, my health was restored long before the end of our journey.

Full of the energy and enthusiasm of youth, the prospects of so hazardous an undertaking had no terror for us, indeed, as we had been married but a few months, it appealed to us as a romantic wedding tour.

The territory bordering upon the Mississippi River was, in those days, called "the west" and its people were accustomed to the privations and hardships of frontier life. It was mostly from their ranks that were formed the many companies of emigrants who traveled across the plains, while those who came to California from the Eastern states usually chose the less strenuous ocean voyage by way of the Isthmas of Panama or around the Horn.

At that time the "gold fever" was contagious and few, old or young, escaped the malady. On the streets, in the fields, in the workshops and by the fireside, golden California was the chief topic of conversation. Who were going? How was best to "fix up" the "outfit"? What to take as food and clothing? Who would stay at home to care for the farm and womenfolks? Who would take wives and children along? Advice was handed out quite free of charge and often quite free of common sense. However, as two heads are better than one, all proffered ideas helped as a means to the end. The intended adventurers dilligently collected their belongings and after exchanging such articles as were not needed for others more suitable for the trip, begging, buying or borrowing what they could, with buoyant spirits started off.

Some half dozen families of our neighborhood joined us and probably about twenty-five persons constituted our little band.

*The Panic of 1837 was followed by prolonged economic depression. The region of the Mississippi valley suffered depressed farm prices well into the next decade.

Our own party consisted of six men and two women. Mr. Haun, my brother Derrick, Mr. Bowen, three young men to act as drivers, a woman cook and myself. Mr. Haun was chosen Major of the company, and as was the custom in those days, his fellow travelers ever afterwards knew him by this title. Derrick was to look after the packing and unpacking coincident to camping at night, keep tab on the commissary department and, when occasion demanded, lend a "helping hand." The latter service was expected of us all—men and women alike, was very indefinite and might mean anything from building campfires and washing dishes to fighting Indians, holding back a loaded wagon on a down grade or lifting it over bowlders when climbing a mountain.

Mr. Bowen furnished his own saddle horse, and for his services was brought free of expense to himself. His business was to provide the wood or fuel for the campfire, hunt wild game and ride ahead with other horsemen to select a camping ground or in search of water. He proved himself invaluable and much of the time we had either buffalo antelope or deer meat, wild turkey, rabbits, prairie chickens, grouse, fish or small birds.

Eight strong oxen and four of the best horses on the farm were selected to draw our four wagons—two of the horses were for the saddle.

Two wagons were filled with merchandise which we hoped to sell at fabulous prices when we should arrive in the "land of gold." The theory of this was good but the practice—well, we never got the goods across the first mountain. Flour ground at our own grist mill and bacon of home-curing filled the large, four-ox wagon while another was loaded with barrels of alcohol. The third wagon contained our household effects and provisions. The former consisted of cooking utensils, two boards nailed together, which was to serve as our dining table, some bedding and a small tent. We had a very generous supply of provisions. All meats were either dried or salted, and vegetables and fruit were dried, as canned goods were not common sixty years or more ago. For luxuries we carried a gallon each of wild plum and crabapple preserves and blackberry jam. Our groceries were wrapped in India rubber covers and we did not lose any of them—in fact still had some when we reached Sacramento.

The two-horse spring wagon was our bed-room and was driven by the Major—on good stretches of road by myself. A hair mattress, topped off with one of feathers and layed on the floor of the wagon with plenty of bedding made a very comfortable bed after a hard day's travel.

In this wagon we had our trunk of wearing apparel, which consisted of underclothing, a couple of blue checked gingham dresses, several large stout aprons for general wear, one light colored for Sundays, a pink calico sunbonnet and a white one intended for "dress up" days. My feminine vanity had also prompted me to include, in this quasi wedding trouseau, a white cotton dress, a black silk manteaux trimmed very fetchingly with velvet bands and fringe, also a lace scuttle-shaped bonnet having a face wreath of tiny pink rosebuds, and on the side of the crown nestled a cluster of the same flowers. With this marvelous costume I had hoped to "astonish the natives" when I should make my first appearance upon the golden streets of the mining town in which we might locate. Should our dreams of great wealth, acquired over night come true it might be embarrassing not to be prepared with a suitable wardrobe for the wife of a very rich man!

When we started from Iowa I wore a dark woolen dress which served me almost constantly during the whole trip. Never without an apron and a three-cornered kerchief, similar to those worn in those days I presented a comfortable, neat appearance. The wool protected me from the sun's rays and penetrating prairie winds. Besides it economized in laundrying which was a matter of no small importance when one considers how limited, and often utterly wanting were our "wash day" conveniences. The chief requisite, water, being sometimes brought from miles away.

In the trunk were also a few treasures; a bible, medicines, such as quinine, bluemass,* opium, whiskey and hartshorn for snake bites and citric acid—an antidote for scurvey. A little of the acid mixed with sugar and water and a few drops of essence of lemon made a fine substitute for lemonade. Our matches, in a large-mouthed bottle were carefully guarded in this trunk.

The pockets of the canvas walls of the wagon held every day needs and toilet articles, as well as small fire arms. The ready shotgun was suspended from the hickory bows of the wagon camp. A ball of twine an awl and buckskin strings for mending harness, shoes etc. were invaluable. It was more than three months before we were thoroughly equipped and on April 24th, 1849 we left our comparatively comfortable homes—and the uncomfortable creditors—for the uncertain and dangerous trip, beyond which loomed up, in our mind's eye, castles of shining gold.

There was still snow upon the ground and the roads were bad, but in our eagerness to be off we ventured forth. This was a mistake as had we delayed for a couple of weeks the weather would have been more settled,

*Bluemass was a quinine derivative.

the roads better and much of the discouragement and hardship of the first days of travel might have been avoided.

Owing partly to the new order of things and partly to the saturated soil, travel was slow for our heavy laden wagons and untried animals. We covered only ten miles the first day and both man and beast were greatly fatigued. As I look back now it seems the most tiresome day of the entire trip.

That night we stopped at a farm and I slept in the farm house. When I woke the next morning a strange feeling of fear at the thought of our venturesome undertaking crept over me. I was almost dazed with dread. I hurried out into the yard to be cheered by the bright sunshine, but old Sol's very brightness lent such a glamor to the peaceful, happy, restful home that my faint heartedness was only intensified. . . . It was a restful scene—a contrast to our previous day of toil and discomfort and caused me to brake completely down with genuine homesickness and I burst out into a flood of tears. . . . I remember particularly a flock of domesticated wild geese. They craned their necks at me and seemed to encourage me to "take to the woods." Thus construing their senseless clatter I paused in my grief to recall the intense cold of the previous winter and the reputed perpetual sunshine and wealth of the promised land. Then wiping away my tears, lest they betray me to my husband, I prepared to continue my trip. I have often thought that had I confided in him he would certainly have turned back, for he, as well as the other men of the party, was disheartened and was struggling not to betray it. . . .

In the morning our first domestic annoyance occurred. The woman cook refused point blank to go any further. Evidently she had not been encouraged by any wild geese for she allowed her tears to be seen and furthermore her Romeo had followed her and it did not require much pursuading on his part to induce her to return. Here was a dilemma! Had this episode happened on the previous morning when my stock of courage was so low and the men were all so busy with their own thoughts—our trip would have ended there.

Our first impulse was that we should have to return, but after a day's delay during [which] our disappointment knew no bounds, I surprised all by proposing to do the cooking, if everybody else would help. My self-reliance and the encouragement of our fellow travelers won the day and our party kept on. Having been reared in a slave state my culinary education had been neglected and I had yet to make my first cup of coffee. My offer was, however, accepted, and as quantity rather than quality was the chief requisite to satisfy our good appetites I got along very well, even though I never became an expert at turning pancakes (slap-jacks) by tossing them into the air; a peculiarly scientific feat universally acquired by the pioneer miners of '49.

At the end of a month we reached Council Bluffs, having only travelled across the state of Iowa, a distance of about 350 miles every mile of which was beautifully green and well watered. We also had the advantage of camping near farm-houses and the generous supply of bread, butter, eggs and poultry greatly facilitated the cooking. Eggs were 2 1/2 cents a dozen—at our journey's end we paid $1 a piece, that is when we had the dollar. Chickens were worth eight and ten cents a piece. When we reached Sacramento $10 was the ruling price and few to be had at that.

As Council Bluffs was the last settlement on the route we made ready for the final plunge into the wilderness by looking over our wagons and disposing of whatever we could spare. . . .

For the common good each party was "sized up" as it were. People insufficiently provisioned or not supplied with guns and ammunition were not desirable but, on the other hand, wagons too heavily loaded might be a hindrance. Such luxuries as rocking chairs mirrors, washstands and corner what-nots were generally frowned down upon and when their owners insisted upon carrying them they had to be abandoned before long on the roadside and were appropriated by the Indians who were always eager to get anything that might be discarded.

The canvas covered schooners were supposed to be, as nearly as possible, constructed upon the principle of the "wonderful one-horse shay." It was very essential that the animals be sturdy, whether oxen, mules or horses. Oxen were preferred as they were less liable to stampede or be stolen by Indians and for long hauls held out better and though slower they were steady and in the long run performed the journey in an equally brief time. Besides, in an emergency they could be used as beef. When possible the provisions and ammunition were protected from water and dust by heavy canvas or rubber sheets.

Good health, and above all, not too large a proportion of women and children was also taken into consideration. The morning starts had to be made early—always before six o'clock—and it would be hard to get children ready by that hour. Later on experience taught the mothers that in order not to delay the trains it was best to allow the smaller children to sleep in the wagons until after several hours of travel when they were taken up for the day.

Our caravan had a good many women and children and although we were probably longer on the journey owing to their presence—they exerted a good influence, as the men did not take such risks with Indians and thereby avoided conflict; were more alert about the care of the teams and seldom had accidents; more attention was paid to cleanliness and sanitation and, lastly but not of less importance, the meals were more regular and better cooked thus preventing much sickness and there was less waste of food.

Among those who formed the personnel of our train were the following families—a wonderful collection of many people with as many different dispositions and characteristics, all recognizing their mutual dependence upon each other and bound together by the single aim of "getting to California."

A regulation "prairie schooner" drawn by four oxen and well filled with suitable supplies, with two pack mules following on behind was the equipment of the Kenna family. There were two men, two women, a lad of fifteen years, a daughter thirteen and their half brother six weeks of age. This baby was our mascot and the youngest member of the company.

. . .

One family by the name of Lemore, from Canada, consisted of man, wife and two little girls. They had only a large express wagon drawn by four mules and a meager but well chosen, supply of food and feed. A tent was strapped to one side of the wagon, a roll of bedding to the other side, baggage, bundles, pots, pans and bags of horse feed hung on behind; the effect was really grotesque. As they had already traveled half across the continent, seemed in good shape and were experienced emigrants they passed muster and were accepted. Not encumbered with useless luggage and Mr. Lamore [sic] being an expert driver his wagon did not sink into the mud or sand and got over grades and through creeks with comparative ease. He required but little help thus being a desirable member of the train.

Mr. West from Peoria, Ill. had another man, his wife, a son Clay about 20 years of age and his daughter, America, eighteen. Unfortunately Mr. West had gone to the extreme of providing himself with such a heavy wagon and load that they were deemed objectionable as fellow argonauts. After disposing of some of their supplies they were allowed to join us. They had four fine oxen. This wagon often got stalled in bad roads much to the annoyance of all, but as he was a wagon maker and his companion a blacksmith by trade and both were accommodating there were always ready hands to "pry the wheel out of mire."

. . .

A mule team from Washington, D.C. was very insufficiently provisioned . . . [by] a Southern gentlemen "unused to work. . . ." They deserted the train at Salt Lake as they could not proceed with their equipment and it was easier to embrace Mormonism than to brave the "American Desert."

Much in contrast to these men were four batchelors Messers Wilson, Goodall, Fifield and Martin, who had a wagon drawn by four oxen and two milch cows following behind. The latter gave milk all the way to the sink of the Humboldt where they died, having acted as draught animals for several weeks after the oxen had perished. Many a cup of milk was given to the children of the train and the mothers tried in every way possible to express their gratitude. When these men lost all their stock and had to abandon their wagon they found that through their generosity they had made many friends. Having cast their bread, or milk, upon the waters it returned, double fold. I remember the evenings' milking was used for supper, but that milked in the morning was put into a high tin churn and the constant jostling that it got all day formed butter and delicious butter-milk by night. We all were glad to swap some of our food for a portion of these delicacies.

After a sufficient number of wagons and people were collected at this rendezvous we proceeded to draw up and agree upon a code of general regulations for train government and mutual protection—a necessary precaution when so many were to travel together. Each family was to be independent yet a part of the grand unit and every man was expected to do his individual share of general work and picket duty.

John Brophy was selected as Colonel. He was particularly eligible having served in the Black Hawk War and as much of his life had been spent along the frontier his experience with Indians was quite exceptional.

Each week seven Captains were appointed to serve on "Grand Duty." They were to protect the camps and animals at night. One served each night and in case of danger gave the alarm.

When going into camp the "leader wagon" was turned from the road to the right, the next wagon turned to the left, the others following close after and always alternating to right and left. In this way a large circle, or corral, was formed within which the tents were pitched and the oxen herded. The horses were picketed near by until bed time when they were tethered to the tongues of the wagons.

While the stock and wagons were being cared for, the tents erected and camp fires started by the side of the wagons outside the corral, the cooks busied themselves preparing the evening meal for the hungry, tired, impatient travelers.

When the camp ground was desirable enough to warrant it we did not travel on the Sabbath.

Although the men were generally busy mending wagons, harness, yokes, shoeing the animals etc., and the women washed clothes, boiled a big mess of beans, to be warmed over for several meals, or perhaps mended clothes or did other household straightening up, all felt somewhat rested on Monday morning, for the change of occupation had been refreshing.

If we had devotional service the minister—protem—stood in the center of the corral while we all kept on with our work. There was no disrespect intended but there was little time for leisure or that the weary pilgrim could call his own.

When possible we rested the stock an hour at noon each day; allowing them to graze, if there was anything to graze upon, or in any case they could lie down, which the fagged beasts often preferred to do as they were too tired to eat what we could give them. During the noon hour we refreshed ourselves with cold coffee and a crust of bread. Also a halt of ten minutes each hour was appreciated by all and was never a loss of time.

However, these respites could not always be indulged in as often the toil had to be kept up almost all day and much of the night—because of lack of water. Night work told very seriously upon the stock—they were more worn with one night's travel than they would have been by several day's work, indeed, invariably one or more poor beasts fell by the wayside—a victim of thirst and exhaustion.

It took us four days to organize our company of 70 wagons and 120 persons; bring our wagons and animals to the highest possible standard of preparedness; wash our clothes; soak several days' supply of food—and say good bye to civilization at Council Bluffs. Owing to the cheapness of eggs and chickens we reveled in their luxuries, carrying a big supply, ready cooked with us.

On May 26th we started to cross the Missouri River and our first real work affronted us. The wheels of the wagon had to be taken off and the bodies carried onto the flat-boats. They were then piled with goods and covered with heavy canvas or rubber sheets to protect the provisions from water. Sometimes two or three small wagons were taken at the same time.

The flat-boats were attached by a pully to a rope stretched across the river to prevent its being carried down stream, and even so row as best the men could, it landed very far down the opposite shore and had to be towed up stream to the landing before the load could be taken off. Ropes were tied to the horns of the oxen and around the necks of the mules and horses to assist them in stemming the current as they swam the river. The women and children sat tailor fashion on the bottom of the raft. Much time and strength was thus consumed and owing to the great size of our caravan we were a week in getting across—as long a time as it takes now to go from the Pacific Coast to Chicago and return.

This was naturally annoying to those safely over, but we were as patient as possible under the circumstances—being fresh and good natured when we started out—but nevertheless we were convinced that our train was too large to admit of much speed even though it might be a safeguard against Indian attacks—a dread always uppermost in our minds. However, on the road some of the more slothful fell behind to augment the following company, since often only a short distance separated its different trains—a few impatient ones caught up with the caravan ahead of us, and during the first few weeks we met emigrants who had become discouraged almost before they were fairly started and were returning homeward. Indeed very few companies "stuck together" the whole trip. When we reached Sacramento not more than a dozen of our original train of 120 were with us.

Finally we were all safely landed upon the west side of the river, on the site of the City of Omaha, Nebraska, but there wasn't no sign of a town there then—only beautiful trees and grass. Several days' travel brought us to the Elkhorn River. . . . The bed of the river was quicksand. . . . Having once entered the water, wagons had to be rushed across to avoid sinking into the quicksand.

The Indians were the first that we had met and, being a novelty to most of us, we eyed them with a good deal of curiosity. One Indian girl of about fourteen years of age wept loud and incessantly for an hour or more until we women sympathizing with her in her apparent grief, gave her a few trinkets and clothes and were astonished at the efficacy of the cure.

The squaws carried their pappooses in queer little canopied baskets suspended upon their backs by a band around their heads and across their foreheads. The infant was snugly bound, mummy-fashion with only its head free. It was here that I first saw a bit of remarkable maternal discipline, peculiar to most of the Indian tribes. The child cried whereupon the mother took it, basket and all, from her back and nursed it. It still fretted and whimpered apparently uncomfortable or ill. The mother then stood it up against a tree and dashed water in the poor little creature's face. By the time that it recovered its breath it stopped crying. No pampered, restless urchin for the Indian household, no indeed.

The bucks with their bows and arrows, beaded buckskin garments and feather head gears were much in evidence and though these prairie redmen were generally friendly they were insistent beggars, often following us for miles and at mealtime disgustingly stood around and solicited food.* They seldom molested us, however, but it was a case of the Indian, as well as the poor, "Ye have always with ye."

During the entire trip Indians were a source of anxiety, we being never sure of their friendship. Secret dread and alert watchfulness seemed always necessary for after we left the prairies they were more treacherous and numerous being in the language of the pioneer trapper: "They wus the most onsartainest vermints alive."

One night after we had retired, some sleeping in blankets upon the ground, some in tents, a few under the wagons and others in the wagons, Colonel Brophy gave the men a practice drill. It was impromptu and a surprise. He called: "Indians, Indians!" We were thrown into great confusion and excitement but he was gratified at the promptness and courage with which the men responded. Each immediately seized his gun and made ready for the attack. The women had been instructed to seek shelter in the wagons at such times of danger, but some screamed, others fainted, a few crawled under the wagons and those sleeping in wagons generally followed their husbands out and all of us were nearly paralized with fear. Fortunately, we never had occasion to put into actual use this maneuver, but the drill was quite reassuring and certainly we womenfolk would have acted braver had the alarm ever again been sounded. . . .

The following night brother Derrick and Mr. Bowen were sleeping as was their custom, under a wagon next to ours and it being very warm they turned their comforters down to the foot of their couch. Behold, next morning the covering was missing! It could hardly have been taken by an animal else some trace of their foot-prints and that of the dragging bedding would have been seen. The Indians with their soft moccasins and the light rapid steps and springing, long strides they take when in retreat seldom left evidence upon the ground.

*Among Indian tribes the sharing of food was a traditional sign of amity and friendship. Haun's response is typical of most emigrants and illustrates the degree to which the travelers often misread and misunderstood the Indians' customs.

This unwelcome call, so soon after the former theft, was anything but reassuring. It was not pleasant to know how shy, steathy and treacherous even these *friendly* Indians were and that they kept such close watch upon our every movement both day and night.

The next night when we retired I had a nervous attack was really so timid that I saw that the canvas of our wagon was snugly together; all strings and fastenings securely tied and—yes, womanlike I added pins here and there, leaving no peekholes: for I just couldn't go to sleep knowing that some bold, prying savage eye might look in at me during the night. Of course I had shut out all ventilation and during the night my husband opened the wagon cover wide enough for not only the savage eye but the whole savage himself to enter! Probably this was done as soon as I had gone to sleep.

Carl West was inclined to sonambulism and these annoying visits from the Indians so worked upon his mind that that night he dreamed that he was attacked by Indians and ran screaming from his wagon. He was bear footed and half clad but he ran so fast that it was all that two of his companions could do to overtake him.

The emigrants were often sorely tried and inconvenienced by losses more or less serious for in spite of the most alert guard it was almost impossible to see the advancing thief crawling, like a snake, on the ground up to his intended prey. . . .

Finally after a couple of weeks' travel the distant mountains of the west came into view.

This was the land of the buffalo. One day a herd came in our direction like a great black cloud, a threatening moving mountain, advancing towards us very swiftly and with wild snorts, noses almost to the ground and tails flying in midair. I haven't any idea how many there were but they seemed to be innumerable and made a deafening terrible noise As is their habit, when stampeding, they did not turn out of their course for anything. Some of our wagons were within their line of advance and in consequence one was completely demolished and two were overturned. Several persons were hurt, one child's shoulder being dislocated, but fortunately no one was killed.

Two of these buffaloes were shot and the humps and tongues furnished us with fine fresh meat. They happened to be buffalo cows and, in consequence, the meat was particularly good flavor and tender. It is believed that the cow can run faster than the bull. The large bone of the hind leg, after being stripped of the flesh, was buried in coals of buffalo chips and in an hour the baked marrow was served. I have never tasted such a rich, delicious food!

One family "jerked" some of the hump. After being cut into strips about an inch wide it was strung on ropes on the outside of the wagon cover and in two or three days was thoroughly cured. It was then packed in a bag and in the Humboldt Sink, when rations were low it came in very handy. Spite of having hung in the Alkali dust and being rather shrivelled looking, it was relished for when hunger stares one in the face one isn't particular about trifles like that.

. . .

Buffalo chips, when dry, were very useful to us as fuel. On the barren plains when we were without wood we carried empty bags and each pedestrian "picked up chips" as he, or she, walked along. Indeed we could have hardly got along without thus useful animal, were always appropriating either his hump, tongue, marrowbone, tallow, skin or chips! . . .

The Indian is a financier of no mean ability and invariably comes out AI in a bargain. Though you may, for the time, congratulate yourself upon your own sagacity, you'll be apt to realize a little later on that you were not quite equal to the shrewd redman—had got the "short end of the deal." One of their "business tricks" was to sell horses or other necessities which were their booty acquired during an attack upon a preceeding train. When we were well along in our journey—in the Humboldt Sink—we overtook emigrants one of whom had swapped his watch with the Indians for a yoke of oxen. A few hours afterwards he found that they had been stolen when left to rest while the owners had gone in search of water. The rightful owners established their claim and after a compromise the oxen were joint property. The watch being the profit of the middleman.

Trudging along within the sight of the Platte, whose waters were now almost useless to us on account of the Alkali, we one day found a post with a cross board pointing to a branch road which seemed better than the one we were on. . . . We decided to take it but before many miles suddenly found ourselves in a desolate, rough country that proved to be the edge of the "Bad Lands" I shudder yet at the thought of the ugliness and danger of the territory. Entirely destitute of vegetation the unsightly barren sandstonehills, often very high and close together formed of great bowlders piled one on top of the other like glaciers, with ravines and gulches between and mighty full of crowching, treacherous Indians, they fairly swarmed and we feared that we had been purposely misled in order that they might do us harm. This, however, could not have been the case for the road often was between precipitous walls hundreds of feet high and had they cared to attack us from the heights above we could have made no effective defense. After the possible massacre had been accomplished their booty would have been our money, clothing, food and traveling paraphernalia—and worse still those of our women who had been unfortunate enough to have escaped death.*

Unlike the Indians of the prairies and plains these mountain inhabitants did not have horses and were expert in concealing themselves, and during our entire trip we were never so apprehensive and terrified. We pushed almost recklessly forward in our endeavor to get back to the road along the river. The unevenness of the surface seemed almost like a maze, and being without a single landmark you can imagine our almost frenzied fear that we might be traveling in a circle. We made our resting stops as brief as possible and the days' work from early dawn until dark.

We saw nothing living but Indians, lizards and snakes. Trying, indeed, to feminine nerves. Surely Inferno can be no more horrible in formation. The pelting sun's rays reflected from the parched ground seemed a furnace heat by day and our campfires, as well as those of the Indians cast grotesque glares and terrifying shadows by night. The demen needed only horns and cloven feet to complete the soul stirring picture!

To add to the horrors of the surroundings one man was bitten on the ankle by a venemous snake. Although every available remidy was tried upon the wound, his limb had to be amputated with the aid of a common handsaw. Fortunately, for him, he had a good, brave wife along who helped and cheered him into health and usefulness; for it was not long before he found much that he could do and was not considered a burden, although the woman had to do a man's work as they were alone. He was of a mechanical turn, and later on helped mend wagons, yokes and harness; and when the train was "on the move" sat in the wagon, gun by his side, and repaired boots and shoes. He was one of the most cheery members of the company and told good stories and sang at the campfire, putting to shame some of the able bodied who were given to complaining or selfishness. . . .

Finally after several days we got back onto the road and were entering the Black Hills Country. . . .

Here we also found fragments of a women's cotton dress tied to bushes and small pieces were scattered along the road. Whether this had been intended as a decoy to lead some of our men into a trap should

---

*Haun's allusion is to the common fear among emigrant women that they would be raped if captured by Indians.

they essay a possible rescue we did not know and the risk was too great to be taken.*

We had not traveled many miles in the Black Hills—the beginning of the Rocky Mountains—before we realized that our loads would have to be lightened as the animals were not able to draw the heavily laden wagons over the slippery steep roads. We were obliged to sacrifice most of our merchandise that was intended for our stock in trade in California and left it by the wayside; burying the barrels of alcohol least the Indians should drink it and frenzied therby might follow and attack us. . . .

The roads were rocky and often very steep from this on to the Great Salt Lake—the distance across the Rocky Mountains. Sometimes to keep the wagons from pressing upon the animals in going down grade young pine trees were cut down and after stripping them of all but the top branches they were tied to the front and under the rear axle. The branches dragging upon the ground, or often solid rock, formed a reliable brake. Then again a rope or chain would be tied to the rear of the wagon and every one, man, woman and child would be pressed into service to hold the wagon back. At other times a chain or rope would be fastened to the front axle and we climbed up impossible bowlders and pulled with might and main while the men pushed with herculanian strength to get the loaded wagons over some barrier. The animals owing to cramped quarters, were often led around the obstacle. Many times the greater part of the day would be consumed in this strenuous and altogether unladylike labor.

And oh, such pulling, pushing, tugging it was! I used to pity the drivers as well as the oxen and horses—and the rest of us. The drivers of our ox teams were sturdy young men, all about twenty-two years of age who were driving for their passage to California. They were of good family connections and all became prominent citizens. One a law student, Charles Wheeler, studied all his leisure time, and often could be seen with his open book as he walked beside his team. One, the whistler, Chester Fall, had been intended for the Ministry and the third Ralph Cushing had run away from college.

The latter was the life of our party and a general favorite with the entire train. I see him now, in my mind's eye, trudging along; his bright countenence and carefree air, an inspiration. The familiar tunes that he played upon his harmonica seemed to soften the groaning and creaking

---

*This macabre note is unusual in diaries of such early travelers.

of the wagons and to shorten the long miles of the mountain road.

"Home Sweet Home," "Old Kentucky Home," "Maryland, My Maryland," "The Girl I left Behind Me," "One More Ribber to Cross," seemed particularly appropriate and touched many a pensive heart. The strains of his ballads went straight to America West's heart even as her sweet voice as she sang at the campfire Cupid used as an arrow with which to pierce Ralph Cushing's manly breast. When the clumsy, heavy wagon of America's father got mired Ralph was among the first to render assistance and towards the end of the journey when we were all enduring great hardships our young couple lent a ray of romance by their evident regard for each other, for "All the world loves a lover." . . .

During the day we womenfolk visited from wagon to wagon or congenial friends spent an hour walking, ever westward, and talking over our home life back in "the states" telling of the loved ones left behind; voicing our hopes for the future in the far west and even whispering a little friendly gossip of emigrant life.

High teas were not popular but tatting, knitting, crocheting, exchanging recepes for cooking beans or dried apples or swapping food for the sake of variety kept us in practice of feminine occupations and diversions.

We did not keep late hours but when not too engrossed with fear of the red enemy or dread of impending danger we enjoyed the hour around the campfire. The menfolk lolling and smoking their pipes and guessing or maybe betting how many miles we had covered the day. We listened to readings, story telling, music and songs and the day often ended in laughter and merrymaking.

It was the fourth of July when we reached the beautiful Laramie River. Its sparkling, pure waters were full of myriads of fish that could be caught with scarcely an effort. It was necessary to build barges to cross the river and during the enforced delay our animals rested and we had one of our periodical "house cleanings." This general systematic re-adjustment always freshened up our wagon train very much, for after a few weeks of travel things got mixed up and untidy and often wagons had to be abandoned if too worn for repairs, and generally one or more animals had died or been stolen.

After dinner that night it was proposed that we celebrate the day and we all heartily join[ed] in. America West was the Goddess of Liberty, Charles Wheeler was orator and Ralph Cushing acted as master of ceremonies. We sang patriotic songs, repeated what little we could of the Declaration of Independence, fired off a gun or two, and gave three cheers for the United States and California Territory in particular!

The young folks decorated themselves in all manner of fanciful and grotesque costumes—Indian characters being most popular. To the rollicking music of violin and Jew's harp we danced until midnight. There were Indian spectators, all bewildered by the (to them) weird war dance of the Pale Face and possibly they deemed it advisable to sharpen up their arrow heads. During the frolic when the sport was at its height a strange white woman with a little girl in her sheltering embrace rushed into the corral. She was trembling with terror, tottering with hunger. Her clothing was badly torn and her hair disheveled. The child crouched with fear and hid her face within the folds of her mother's tattered skirt. The woman could give no account of her forlorn condition but was only able to sob: "Indians," and "I have nobody nor place to go to." After she had partaken of food and was refreshed by a safe night's rest she recovered and the next day told us that her husband and sister had contracted cholera on account of which her family consisting of husband, brother, sister, herself and two children had stayed behind their train. The sick ones' died and while burying the sister the survivors were attacked by Indians, who, as she supposed, killed her brother and little son. She was obliged to flee for her life dragging with her the little five year old daughter.

She had been three days walking back to meet a train. It had been necessary, in order to avoid Indians, to conceal herself behind trees or bowlders much of the time and although she had seen a train in the distance before ours she feared passing the Indians that were between the emigrants and herself. She had been obliged to go miles up the Laramie to find a place where she could get across by wading from rock to rock and the swift current had lamed her and bruised her body.

Raw fish that she had caught with her hands and a squirrel that she killed with a stone had been their only food. Our noise and campfire had attracted her and in desperation she braved the Indians around us and trusting to the darkness ventured to enter our camp. Martha, for that was her name, had emigrated from Wisconsin and pleaded with us to send her home; but we had now gone too far on the road to meet returning emigrants so there was no alternative for her but to accept our protection and continue on to California. When she became calm and somewhat reconciled to so long and uncertain a journey with strangers she made herself useful and loyally cast her lot with us. She assisted me with the cooking for her board; found lodgings with the woman whose husband was a cripple and in return helped the brave woman drive the ox team. Mr. & Mrs. Lamore kept her little girl with their own. . . .

Upon the second day of our resumed travel, still following up the North Platte, Martha spied a deserted wagon some little distance off the road which she recognized as her own. Mr. Bowen went with her to investigate, hoping to find her brother and son. The grave of her sister was still open and her clothing as well as that of her husband, who was in the wagon where he had died, were missing. The grewsome sight drove her almost mad. Mr. Bowen and she did not bury the bodies lest they might bring contagion back to us. No trace of either brother or son could be found. All supplies and the horses had been stolen by the Indians.

Cholera was prevalent on the plains at this time; the train preceding as well as the one following ours had one or more deaths, but fortunately we had not a single case of the disease. Often several graves together stood as silent proof of smallpox or cholera epidemic. The Indians spread the disease among themselves by digging up the bodies of the victims for the clothing. The majority of the Indians were badly pock-marked. . . .

Turning in a southwesterly direction we came to Fort Bridger, named for the celebrated scout. It was simply a trading post for the white and Indian fur trappers. We saw a renegade white man here who having lived for years among the Indians had forgotten his native language and dressing and eating as they did, his long unkept hair and uncouth appearance was loathsome in the extreme; it being hard to distinguish him from his brother Indians. We regarded him with more fear and abhorance than we did a manly buck, and his squaw and family of half-breeds as unfortunates.

It was with considerable apprehension that we started to traverse the treeless, alkali region of the Great Basin or Sink of the Humboldt. Our wagons were badly worn, the animals much the worse for wear, food and stock feed was getting low with no chance of replenshing the supply. During the month of transit we, like other trains, experienced the greatest privations of the whole trip. It was no unusual sight to see graves, carcasses of animals and abandoned wagons. In fact the latter furnished us with wood for the campfires as the sagebrush was scarce and unsatisfactory and buffalo chips were not as plentiful as on the plains east of the Rocky Mountains.

The alkali dust of this territory was suffocating, irritating our throats and clouds of it often blinded us. The mirages tantalized us; the water was unfit to drink or to use in any way; animals often perished or were so overcome by heat and exhaustion that they had to be abandoned, or in case of human hunger, the poor jaded creatures were killed and eaten. . . .

One of our dogs was so emaciated and exhausted that we were obliged to leave him on this desert and it was said that the train following us used him for food.

Before leaving Bear River, knowing of the utter lack of fresh water, we cooked large quantities of bread to be used on the desert. We gave a half loaf each day to each horse until the flour gave out. This was a substitute for grain.

Across this drear country I used to ride horseback several hours of the day which was a great relief from the continual jolting of even our spring wagon. I also walked a great deal and this lightened the wagon. One day I walked fourteen miles and was not very fatigued.

. . . The men seemed more tired and hungry than were the women.

Our only death on the journey occurred in this desert. The Canadian woman, Mrs. Lamore, suddenly sickened and died, leaving her two little girls and grief stricken husband. We halted a day to bury her and the infant that had lived but an hour, in this weird, lonely spot on God's footstool away apparently from everywhere and everybody.*

The bodies were wrapped together in a bedcomforter and wound, quite mummyfied with a few yards of string that we made by tying together torn strips of a cotton dress skirt. A passage of the Bible (my own) was read; a prayer offerred and "Nearer, My God to Thee" sung. Owing to the unusual surroundings the ceremony was very impressive. Every heart was touched and eyes full of tears as we lowered the body, coffinless, into the grave. There was no tombstone—why should there be— the poor husband and orphans could never hope to revisit the grave and to the world it was just one of the many hundreds that marked the trail of the argonaut.

This burial and one I witnessed at sea some years later made a lasting impression upon me and I always think of them when I attend a funeral; such a grewsome sensation was caused by the desolation. The immense, lonesome plain; the great fathomless ocean—how insignificant seems the human body when consigned to their cold embrace! . . . Martha and the lamented Canadian wife had formed a fast friendship while on the plains and the former was a faithful nurse during the latter's illness.

*Haun's account of the death of Mrs. Lamore and of the newborn infant does not mention that the death occurred after childbirth. Her phrase "suddenly sickened and died" is typical of the taboos that shrouded the facts of pregnancy and birth among emigrant women.

The Major found a piece of bacon rind and making a fire of sage brush sticks and buffalo chips, cooked and ate it. The men seemed more tired and hungry than were we women.

Our only death on the journey occurred in this desert. The Canadian woman, Mrs. Lamore, suddenly sickened and died, leaving her two little girls and grief stricken husband. She halted a day to bury her and the infant that had lived but an hour, in this weird, lonely spot on God's footstool away, apparently, from everywhere and everybody.

The bodies were wrapped together in a bedcomforter and wound, quite mummyfied, with a few yards of string that we made by tying together torn strips of a cotton dress skirt.   A passage of the Bible (my own) was read; a prayer offered and "Nearer, My God to Thee" sung. Owing to the unusual surroundings the ceremony was very impressive. Every heart was touched and eyes full of tears as we lowered the body, coffinless, into the grave. There was no tombstone — why should there be — the poor husband and orphans could never hope to revisit the grave and to the world it was just one of the many hundreds that marked the trail of the argonaut.

This burial and one I witnessed at sea some years later made a lasting impression upon me and I always think of them when I attend a funeral; such a gruesome sensation was caused by the desolation. The immense, lonesome plain; the great fathomless ocean — how insignificant seems the human body when consigned to their cold embrace!

Upon this desert there grew a wild, poisonous parsnip. One day we found a stake with a tin cup tied to it, at the head of a grave. The cup had a piece bitten or cut out. There were what seemed to be four graves, but we were not sure whether bodies of persons who had been poisoned by eating the weed

Page from the diary of Catherine Haun.

What more natural than that the dying mother should ask her friend to continue to care for her orphan girls and to make [them] the sisters of her own daughter?

Years afterward when prosperity crowned Mr. Lamore's efforts the three girls were sent "back to the states" to school and Martha's daughter became the wife of a prominent United States Congressman. [Martha's little son was soon reunited with his mother. He had been traded by the Indians to some passing emigrants for a horse. In fact, the child was traveling but a few days' journey behind her in another emigrant train.]*

. . . we reached Sacramento on November 4, 1849, just six months and ten days after leaving Clinton, Iowa, we were all in pretty good condition. . . .

Although very tired of tent life many of us spent Thanksgiving and Christmas in our canvas houses. I do not remember ever having had happier holiday times. For Christmas dinner we had a grizzly bear steak for which we paid $2.50, one cabbage for $1.00 and—oh horrors—some *more* dried apples! And for a Christmas present the Sacramento river rose very high and flooded the whole town! . . . It was past the middle of January before we . . . reached Marysville—there were only a half dozen houses; all occupied at exorbitant prices. Some one was calling for the services of a lawyer to draw up a will and my husband offered to do it for which he charged $150.00.

This seemed a happy omen for success and he hung out his shingle, abandoning all thought of going to the mines. As we had lived in a tent and had been on the move for nine months, traveling 2400 miles we were glad to settle down and go housekeeping in a shed that was built in a day of lumber purchased with the first fee. The ground was given us by some gamblers who lived next door and upon the other side, for neighbors, we had a real live saloon. I never have received more respectful attention than I did from these neighbors.

Upon the whole I enjoyed the trip, spite of its hardships and dangers and the fear and dread that hung as a pall over every hour. Although not so thrilling as were the experiences of many who suffered in reality what we feared, but escaped, I like every other pioneer, love to live over again, in memory those romantic months, and revisit, in fancy, the scenes of the journey.

*Compare this story with that of Olive Oatman, who had been traded by the Apaches for some blankets (p. 69).

Pioneers gathered at the opening of a toll road over the Siskiyou Mountains, Oregon. A horse and rider paid 25 cents and a loaded wagon $1.25.

"NOTES BY THE WAYSIDE EN ROUTE TO OREGON, 1852"

Lydia and Harry Rudd, and their friends—named in her diary only as Henry and Mary—set out for Oregon in 1852. They traveled with no children, although the poem at the end of Lydia's diary suggests that a daughter had died in infancy or early childhood. The couples intended to file for shares of land in Oregon under the Donation Act, which provided that both husbands and wives could enter claims. Lydia, in particular, seems to have been anxious to have land in her own name.

Her diary shows them traveling through the cholera epidemic that swept through the wagon train in June. They also traveled with other sicknesses as well —measles, mountain fever, and dysentery. The bad weather and the constant exposure effected even the young and the strong.

Lydia describes as almost commonplace a pattern of barter with the Indians they met along the road. It is clear that, whatever exchanges the men may have carried on, Lydia Rudd herself made her own bargains with the Indians and exhibited no reticence in doing so. The final leg of her journey—the crossing of the Columbia River —was made in an Indian canoe.

LYDIA ALLEN RUDD

May 6 1852 Left the Missouri river for our long journey across the wild uncultivated plains and unhabited except by the red man. As we left the river bottom and ascended the bluffs the view from them was handsome! In front of us as far as vision could reach extended the green hills covered with fine grass. . . . Behind us lay the Missouri with its muddy water hurrying past as if in great haste to reach some destined point ahead all unheeding the impatient emigrants on the opposite shore at the ferrying which arrived faster than they could be conveyed over. About half a miles down the river lay a steamboat stuck fast on a sandbar. Still farther down lay the busy village of St. Joseph looking us a good bye and reminding us that we were leaving all signs of civilised life for the present. But with good courage and not one sigh of regret I mounted my pony (whose name by the way is Samy) and rode slowly on. In going some two miles, the scene changed from bright sunshine to drenching showers of rain this was not quite agreeable for in spite of our good blankets and intentions otherwise we got some wet. The rain detained us so that we have not made but ten miles today. . . .

May 7 I found myself this morning with a severe headache from the effects of yesterdays rain. . . .

There is a toll bridge across this stream kept by the Indians The toll for our team in total was six bits. We have had some calls this evening from the Indians. We gave them something to eat and they left. Some of them [had] on no shirt only a blanket, while others were ornamented in Indian style with their faces painted in spots and stripes feathers and fur on their heads beeds on their neck brass rings on their wrists and arms and in their ears armed with rifles and spears.

May 8 . . . We have come about 12 miles and were obliged to camp in the open prairie without any wood Mary and myself collected some dry weeds and grass and made a little fire and cooked some meat and the last of our supply of eggs with these and some hard bread with water we made our supper.

May 9 . . . We passed a new made grave today . . . a man from Ohio We also met a man that was going back he had buried his Wife this morning She died from the effects of measels* we have come ten miles

*It is impossible to estimate accurately the backward flow of people. Many diaries mention meeting travelers who were returning to "the States." Measles, it should be noted, could be as dangerous as cholera. Both diseases had devastating effects upon Indian tribes who came into contact with the emigrants.

today encamped on a small stream called Vermillion creek Wood and water plenty Their are as many as fifty waggons on this stream and some thousand head of stock It looks like a village the tents and waggons extend as much as a mile. . . .

Some are singing some talking and some laughing and the cattle are adding their mite by shaking their bells and grunt[ing] Mosquitoes are intruding their unwelcome presence Harry says that I must not sit here any longer writing but go to bed for I will not want to get up early in the morning to get breakfast.

May 10 I got up this morning and got breakfast and before sunrise we had eat in spite of Harry's prophecies to the contrary. . . .

May 11 We had a very heavy fog this morning which cleared up about noon Our men are not any of them very well this morning We passed another grave to day which was made this morning The board stated that he died of cholera. He was from Indiana. We met several that had taken the back track for the states homesick I presume let them go We have passed through a handsome country and have encamped on the Nimehaw river the most beautiful spot that ever I saw in my life I would like to live here As far as the eye can reach either way lay handsome rolling prairies not a stone a tree nor a bush even nothing but grass and flowers meets the eye until you reach the valley of the river which is as level as the house floor and about half a mile wide, where on the bank of the stream for two or three rods wide is one of the heaviest belts of timber I ever saw covered with thick foliage so thick that you could not get a glimpse of the stream through it. You can see this belt of timber for three or four miles from the hills on both sides winding through the prairie like some huge snake. We have traveled twelve miles. . . .

May 12 . . . Our men not much better.

May 13 . . . Henry has been no better to day. Soon after we stopped to night a man came along with a wheel barrow going to California he is a dutchmann He wheels his provisions and clothing all day and then stops where night overtakes him sleeps on the ground in the open air He eats raw meat and bread for his supper I think that he will get tired wheeling his way through the world by the time he gets to California.

May 14 Just after we started this morning we passed four men diging a grave They were packers The man that had died was taken sick yesterday noon and died last night They called it cholera morbus The corpse lay on the ground a few feet from where they were diging The grave it was a sad sight. . . .

On the bank of the stream waiting to cross, stood a dray with five men harnessed to it bound for California, They must be some of the persevering kind I think Wanting to go to California more than I do. . . . We passed three more graves this afternoon

May 15 . . .

May 16 . . . We have not traveled but six miles to day for Henry and myself are not able I am trying to sit up a few minutes to keep up my memorandum. . . .

May 17 . . .

May 18 . . . Henry and myself feel as though we could be crossed off from the sick list this morning Crossed dry sandy [creek] Passed by another newly made grave. If you could see our men now, you would hardly know if they were negroes or white men. (The wind has blown a perfect cloud of dust, covering us all with dirt.)

May 19–31 . . .

June 1 . . . Had another very warm day The warm weather seems to increase the sickness a good many sick and a number of deaths. . . .

June 2 . . . This has been the warmest day that we have had this year We have had a tedious day our road has been sand hills the sand six inches deep in places and the heat almost intolerable. . . .

June 3 . . . Had a fine cool day for traveling but our road has been some sandy passed four graves this morning that the folks died yesterday all out of one train and others sick We also passed another train that were getting ready to bury one of their company

June 4 . . .

June 5 One of the men belonging to our company is quite sick today not any better to night. . . .

June 6 Traveled fourteen miles today had a sprinkle of rain about enough to lay the dust our deaf and dumb man died this morning a few rods from our camp name and place of residence we could not learn for he was too sick to write We found him lying by the side of the road without a person near that ever saw him before We We doctored him what we could but he was to far gone.

June 7 It has been uncomfortably cold riding today We passed three persons this morning that their company said was dying also passed a new grave Traveled fifteen miles encamped on the platte The sick man in our company not any better.

June 8 Left our sick man and his waggon and company behind this morning. . . .

June 9th–10th . . .

June 11 . . . The team that we left with the sick man behind has overtaken us this evening Mr. Chitwood died the next day after we left them. . . .

June 12 Passed five graves this morning and a camp where one of their men was dying The sickness is quite mortal. . . .

June 14 Passed two graves today death caused from the cholera. . . .

June 15 Traveled about three miles today and encamped on the account of our sick ones Henry is not any better and there are three more of our train that are sick We find plenty of wood with our camping ground.

June 16 We have not moved today our sick ones not able to go I went a few rods to a train this evening to see the sick There was two that were very sick The sickness on the road is alarming—most all proves fatal

June 17 I went out to that train again this morning one young lady died last night and the other cannot live but a few hours longer both sisters Their Father an old feeble gray headed man told me that within two weeks he had buried his wife one brother one sister two sons in law and his daughter died last night Past and another that cannot live the day out and he was so week and feeble that he could scarsely walk Our sick ones have not been able to move today Not much better tonight

June 18 We shall not be able to move our sick today they are no better the heat almost insufferable. . . .

June 19 Our sick men a little better some of them today in hopes by tomorrow they will be well enough to move a few miles in the morning

June 20 Traveled about 5 miles and obliged to stop with our sick The Mr. Girtmans not either of them are well The unmarried man cannot get well

June 21 The young Mr. Girtman died today about four o clock his brother not as well Baker worse of the two I do not know when we shall be able to travel any more It begins to look rather discouraging.

June 22 Two of our wagons have gone on to day they could not wait any longer for our company Our sick no better We have given up Mr. Girtman I dont think he will live

June 23 Mr. Girtman died last night about 11 o clock he has left a wife without any relatives but there are two fine men that was in company with her husband and brother that will take good care [of] her Sickness and death in the states is hard but it is nothing to be compared with it on the plains. . . .

June 24–July 3 . . .

July 4 This is the day of our nations jubilee of liberty Traveled ten miles and struck the sweet water* and encamped for the day to celebrate our independence We has some gooseberry sauce for dinner gathered from the bluff Harry killed an antelope. . . .

July 5 . . . Came to independence rock about ten o clock this morning** I presume there are a milion of names wrote on this rock I saw my husbands name that he put on in 1849 At noón we stoped about a fourth of a mile from devils gate I went out to see this wonder and it surpassed anything that ever I saw in my life The sweet water river passes through a gap or gate as it is called of the rocky mountains it has made a channel about two rods in width through the solid rock a quarter of a mile in length the rocks are perpendicular and in places overhanging to the height of more than two hundred feet Traveled fifteen miles encamped on the sweet water good grass and water grease for fuel wood

July 6–July 14 . . .

July 15 . . . Some of the snake indians came to our camp this morning I swaped some hard bread with them for some good berries. . . .

July 16–17 . . .

July 18 . . . Traveled fifteen miles today up and the highest hills that ever I went over passed pine grove about noon Mary and myself got out to prospect a little found a few strawberries. . . .

---

*The Sweetwater River, a tributary of the North Platte, runs through Wyoming.
**Independence Rock, like other natural wonders along the road—Chimney Rock, Court House Rock, Soda Springs, Devil's Gate—is noted by virtually every traveler.

July 19–22 . . .

July 23 . . . Harry was taken with a chill this morning very sick we were obliged to encamp at noon he could not travel encamped on bear river wood water and grass plenty An Indian camp within three rods of us Harry no better tonight.

July 24 . . . Harry is no better this morning very sick called a physician we shall not be able to move him today no better tonight

July 25 . . . Harry is some better this morning but we shall not try to move him today We have all the speckled trout that we can eat caught out of this river Harry is still better this evening tomorrow I traded an apron today for a pair of moccasins of the indians

July 26 . . . Harry is better this morning Traveled with him ten miles today had a good level road encamped on a fork of bear river. . . .

July 27–Aug. 13 . . .

Aug. 14 . . . bought a salmon fish of an indian today weighing seven or eight pounds gave him an old shirt some bread and a sewing needle We have been in the most desolate looking region for a week past that ever I dream was in this world nothing but the digger indians* could live here.

Aug. 15–Sept. 4 . . .

Sept. 5 Traveled eighteen miles today encamped on a slough of powder river poor camp not much grass water nor wood I am almost dead tonight I have been sick two or three days with the bowel complaint and am much worse tonight.

Sept. 6 We have not been able to leave this mieserable place today I am not as well as yesterday and no physician to be had We got a little medicine from a train tonight that has checked the disease some the first thing that has done me any good

Sept. 7 . . . I am some better today so much so that they ventured to move me this for the sake of a better camp Mrs Girtman is also sick with the same disease Our cattle are most all of them ailing there are two more that we expect will die every day

---

*Almost always described as destitute, Indians of the Great Basin region (between the Sierra Nevada and the Rockies) were generally referred to as "Diggers," a reference to their pursuit of roots and perhaps to the semisubterranean houses some of them used in the winter months.

September 8–September 9 . . .

September 10 . . . today Mrs Girtman and myself better

September 11 . . . Traveled fourteen miles today on the blue mountains*
climb up and down the highest hills that ever I saw a person pass over
very steep and rocky moved on grand ronde river encamped on the top
of the mountain to night no water for our stock. . . .

September 12–14 . . .

September 15 . . . Made another start this morning and sickness detained
us again as usual went about four miles and Henry was not able to go
any farther bought one cucumber paid a dime three tomatoes for
another dime twenty cents for four onions

September 16–17 . . .

September 18 . . . Henry has been very sick today

September 19 . . . Henry is not much better today we shall not be able
to move any today Henry is some better tonight Dr. Henry has
overtaken us tonight and we have got medicine from him and I am in
hopes that we shall get able to travel again some day

September 20 . . . We made a start this afternoon and traveled five miles
encamped on the bluffs no wood nor water except what we brought
with us Henry is some better today

September 21–22 . . .

September 23 . . . Henry and myself are just able to move and that is all

September 24–26 . . .

September 27 Traveled down the Columbia [River] about four miles
reached the Deschutes this is a very rapid stream to dangerous to ford
we ferried over our wagons and forded our stock. . . .

September 28 . . .

September 29 It is getting almost too late to try the mountains.
. . . Henry is not as well tonight. . . .

Sept. 30 Made a move of six miles today and encamped on the same
creek We stoped partly on the account of Henrys being sick and partly
because it is fifteen miles from here to the next wood and water and it is
so cold that we cannot get along without wood good camp

*The Blue Mountains rise in northeast Oregon.

Oct. 1 And still on the east side of the mountains and our folks sick and the weather very cold with some rain and it snows on the mountains when it rains here. . . .

Oct. 2 A Frenchman came to us this morning from the mountains yesterday and says that we cannot cross the mountains for the snow he said that seven head of stock died at his fire the night before chilled to death So there is nothing for us to do but to take the back track Made our yesterdays journey back again encamped on the same spot that we did night before last.

October 3–5 . . .

Oct. 6 We have engaged our passage down the Columbia this morning in a canoe with the Indians Left our wagon to be shiped to order after the rush is over The wind blew so heavy that we were obliged to lay by it not being safe to travel in the canoe We left the boat and walked about two miles before we found a convenient place for the boat to land It is to heavily loaded [with] seventeen persons with a quantity of lugage this was about 10 o clock stoped until 3 o clock the wind not quite as heavy expected to travel all night but were again obliged to lay by on the account of the wind

Oct. 7 Made another start in our frail bark early this morning the weather calm our company is rather interesting making the time pass very agreeable the scenery on the shore of the river is very wild and picturesque. . . . The wind again caused us to go on shore about three o clock very anxious to reach the cascade falls tonight within nine miles stoped about two hours and again started the wind still blowing violently not quite safe It was now getting dark and the wind increasing and ran so high the waves washed over the canoe and as high as my head completely drenching us with water Our dark companions then tried to make for the shore but were unable to manage the canoe but fortunately there was more oars on the boat and our men assisted all they could And after a long time we safely made the shore which was more than we expected glad to lay down on the sand in our wet clothes and on our wet bed One Lady was very much alarmed screaming every breath as loud as she could possibly A sorry time*

---

*Lydia Rudd's account of traveling down the Columbia River in an Indian canoe is typical of what many emigrants found to be the last leg of their journey. The weather in October had turned both wet and cold; the river was turbulent. Only the screaming lady makes this account unique.

Oct. 8 started early this morning without any breakfast for the very good reason that we had nothing to eat still three miles from the falls safely landed about eight o clock tired hungry and with a severe cold from last nights exposure something like civilization here in the shape of three or four houses there is an excuse here for a railroad of a mile and half on which to convey bagage below the falls where they can again take water for the steamboat landing Harry packed our bagage down the railroad and the rest of us walked the car is drawn across the railroad by a mule and they will cary no persons but sick We again hired an Indian with his canoe to take us from the falls to the steamboat landing arived about sundown a great many emigrants waiting for a chance to leave the steamboat and several flat boats lying ready to start out in the morning encamped on the shore for the night

October 9–October 13 . . .

October 14 . . . I am so anxious to get some place to stop and settle that my patience is not worth much

October 15–18 . . .

October 19 . . . We have had a very bad day today for traveling it has rained nearly all the time and it has rained very hard some of the time and we have had a miserable road the rain has made the hills very slippery and had to get up and down we have made but eleven miles of travel encamped on the prairie no water for our stock and not much for ourselves

October 21 . . .

October 22 . . . Traveled three miles this morning and reached the village of Salem it is quite a pretty town a much handsomer place than Oregon City and larger. . . .

I am afraid that we shall be obliged to pack from here the rest of our journey and it will be a wet job another wet rainy day I am afraid that the rain will make us all sick I am already begin to feel the affects of it by a bad cold.

October 23 . . . We cannot get any wagon to take us on our journey and are obliged to pack the rest of the way* Mr Clark and wife have found a house to live in and employment for the winter and they will stop here

*Packing meant loading one's immediate possessions on a mule or an ox and riding or walking the last part of the journey.

in Salem It took us until nearly noon to get our packs fixed for packing went about two miles and it rained so fast that we were obliged to stop got our dinner and supper in one meal cooked in a small cabin ignorant people but kind started again just

October 24–25 . . .

October 26 . . . we reached Burlington about two o'clock There is one store one blacksmith shop and three or four dwelling houses We encamped close by found Mr. Donals in his store an old acquaintance of my husbands I do not know what we shall yet conclude on doing for the winter There is no house in town that we can get to winter in We shall probably stay here tomorrow and by the time know what we are to do for a while at least.

October 27 . . . Our men have been looking around for a house and employment and have been successful for which I feel very thankful Harry has gone into copartnership with Mr. Donals in the mercantile business and we are to live in the back part of the store for this winter Henry and Mary are going into Mr. D—— house on his farm for the winter one mile from here Mr. D—— will also find him employment if he wants I expect that we shall not make a claim after all our trouble in getting here on purpose for one I shall have to be poor and dependent on a man my life time.*

TO FRIEND MARGARET

Dear friends you want a keepsake
Of our little one thats gone
Is there ought you would more praise
Than this curl of golden brown[?]

You have often seen her wear it
Looking then the same as now
Curling round her little fingers
As she brushed it from her brow

*In 1850 Congress passed the Donation Land Act which reduced the size of a land claim from 640 to 320 free acres. But the new law allowed a settler to claim another 320 acres for his wife. The demand for brides skyrocketed in the Oregon Territory. Lydia Rudd, however, seemed intent not so much to augment her husband's share as to avail herself, under the provisions of the new Act, of land in her own name. Her diary suggests that other wives in the Oregon frontier felt the same way.

That curly hair and forehead high
Which God to her had given
We never will see them more
Until we meet her in heaven

Oh teach me Father how to bear
This stroke without repinning
That I may meet my angel child
Where countless hosts are shining

Shall we not all meet there to love
With love that has no trembling fears?
In that dear home far, far above
This dark and dreary land of tears?

L. A. Rudd

DIARY OF
MRS. AMELIA
STEWART KNIGHT

An Oregon Pioneer of 1853

Amelia Stewart Knight started from Monroe County, Iowa, and headed for Oregon Territory with her husband and seven children in 1853. Her diary makes no mention of grave sites. Her preoccupation is with the road and her children—Lucy, Jefferson, Plutarch, Seneca, Almira, Chatfield, and Francis. Chatfield was her youngest; she refers to carrying him at the journey's end when the Blue Mountains are too steep to travel by wagon. He is also the child who absorbs much of her energy on the journey, getting scarlet fever and twice falling out of the wagon. At one point in the journey, her daughter Lucy is lost, and at another both Lucy and Almira have poison ivy on their legs.

The picture of the relationship between husband and wife is unusually clear in this diary. When they come to Hot Springs and the road has been dusty, Amelia's husband took her up the river to a place where the water is cool enough for her to bathe.

Her diary shows that the Indians along the way were both much-needed guides and provisioners for the emigrants.

What is not mentioned at all is the fact that at the start of her journey she is already in the first trimester of

AMELIA STEWART KNIGHT

another pregnancy. The diary must be read with this unstated fact in mind. Thus, when she tells that she is too sick to cook or sensitive to the smell of the dead oxen along the road, or that the rainfall has kept them all in wet clothes, or that the mountain passes have forced them to walking and climbing, these details must be weighed in the light of her advancing pregnancy. Amelia Knight delivers her eighth child by the roadside and comes into Oregon with a newborn infant, in a canoe and then a flatboat, across the Columbia River. Her first home is a log cabin with no windows. Her diary contains no word of complaint, just enormous relief that the overland journey is done.

S tarting from Monroe County, Iowa, Saturday, April 9, 1853, and ending Near Milwaukie, Oregon Territory, September 17, 1853.

Saturday, April 9, 1853 STARTED FROM HOME about 11 o'clock and traveled 8 miles and camped in an old house; night cold and frosty.

Sunday, April 10th Cool and pleasant, road hard and dusty.
Evening—Came 8½ miles and camped close to the Fulkersons house.

Monday, April 11th Morn. Cloudy and sign of rain, about 10 o'clock it began to rain. At noon it rains so hard we turn out and camp in a school house after traveling 11½ miles; rains all the afternoon and all night, very unpleasant. Jefferson and Lucy have the mumps. Poor cattle bawled all night.

Tuesday, April 12th Warm and sultry. Still cloudy, road very muddy, traveled 10 miles and camp on Soap creek bottom. Creek bank full; have to wait till it falls.

Wednesday, April 13th Fair weather, have to overhaul all wagons and dry things. Evening—still in camp.

Thursday, April 14th Quite cold. Little ewes crying with cold feet. Sixteen wagons all getting ready to cross the creek. Hurrah and bustle to get breakfast over. Feed the cattle. Hurrah boys, all ready, we will be the

Amelia Stewart Knight.

first to cross the creek this morning. Gee up Tip and Tyler, and away we
go the sun just rising. Evening—We have traveled 24 miles today and
are about to camp in a large prairie without wood. Cold and chilly; east
wind. The men have pitched the tent and are hunting something to
make a fire to get supper. I have the sick headache and must leave the
boys to get it themselves the best they can.

Friday, April 15th Cold and cloudy, wind still east. Bad luck last night.
Three of our horses got away. Suppose they have gone back. One of the
boys has gone after them, and we are going on slowly. Evening—Henry
has come back with the horses all right again. It is beginning to rain;
the boys have pitched the tent and I must get supper.

Saturday, April 16th Camped last night three miles east of Chariton
Point in the prairie. Made our beds down in the tent in the wet and
mud. Bed clothes nearly spoiled. Cold and cloudy this morning, and
every body out of humour. Seneca is half sick. Plutarch has broke his
saddle girth. Husband is scolding and hurrying all hands (and the cook)
and Almira says she wished she was home, and I say ditto. "Home,
Sweet Home." . . .

Sunday, April 17th [This party did not rest on the Sabbath. It continued
to travel over rolling prairies.]

Monday, April 18th Cold; breaking fast the first thing; very disagreeable
weather; wind east cold and rainy, no fire. We are on a very large
prairie, no timber to be seen as far as the eye can reach. Evening—Have
crossed several bad streams today, and more than once have been stuck
in the mud. . . .
    Came 22 miles today. My head aches, but the fire is kindled and I
must make some tea, that will help it if not cure it.

Tuesday, April 19th . . .

Wednesday, April 20th Cloudy. We are creeping along slowly, one wagon
after another, the *same* old gait; and the same thing over, out of one
mud hole into another all day. Crossed a branch where the water run
into the wagons. No corn to be had within 75 miles. Came 18 miles and
camp.

Thursday, April 21st Rained all night; is still raining. I have just
counted 17 wagons traveling ahead of us in the mud and water. No feed

for our poor stock to be got at any price. Have to feed them flour and meal. Traveled 22 miles today.

Friday, April 22nd Still bad weather. no sun; traveling on, mile after mile in the mud, mud. . . .

Saturday, April 23rd Still in camp, it rained hard all night, and blew a hurricane almost. All the tents were blown down, and some wagons capsized. Evening—It has been raining hard all day; everything is wet and muddy. One of the oxen missing; the boys have been hunting him all day. (Dreary times, wet and muddy, and crowded in the tent, cold and wet and uncomfortable in the wagon. No place for the poor children.) I have been busy cooking roasting coffee, etc. today, and have come into the wagon to write this and make our bed.

Sunday, April 24th . . .

Monday, April 25th . . .

Tuesday, April 26th Cold and clear; found corn last night at 2 dollars a bushel. Paid 12 dollars for about half a feed for our stock. I can count twenty wagons winding up the hill ahead of us. Traveled 20 miles and camp.

Wednesday, April 27th A nice spring morning; warm and pleasant; the road is covered with wagons and cattle. (Paid two dollars 40 cts. for crossing a bridge.) Traveled 25 miles. . . .

Thursday, April 28th . . .

Friday, April 29th Cool and pleasant; saw the first Indians today. Lucy and Almira afraid and run into the wagon to hide. Done some washing and sewing.

Saturday, April 30th Fine weather; spent this day in washing, baking, and overhauling the wagons. Several more wagons have camped around us.

Sunday, May 1st Still fine weather; wash and scrub all the children.

Monday, May 2nd Pleasant evening; have been cooking, and packing things away for an early start in the morning. Threw away several jars, some wooden buckets, and all our pickles. Too unhandy to carry. Indians came to our camp every day, begging money and something to eat. Children are getting used to them.

Tuesday, May 3rd . . . here Plutarch is taken sick.

Wednesday, May 4th . . .

Thursday, May 5th . . .

Friday, May 6th . . . Here we passed a train of wagons on their way back, the head man had been drowned a few days before, in a river called Elkhorn, while getting some cattle across and his wife was lying in the wagon quite sick, and children were mourning for the father gone. With sadness and pity I passed those who perhaps a few days before had been well and happy as ourselves. Came 20 miles today.

Saturday, May 7th Cold morning, thermometer down to 48 in the wagon. No wood, only enough to boil some coffee. Good grass for the stock. We have crossed a small creek, with a narrow Indian bridge across it. Paid the Indians 75 cents toll. My hands are numb with cold. . . .

Sunday, May 8th Still in camp. Waiting to cross [the Elkhorn River]. There are three hundred or more wagons in sight and as far as the eye can reach, the bottom is covered, on each side of the river, with cattle and horses. There is no ferry here and the men will have to make one out of the tightest wagon-bed (every company should have a waterproof wagon-bed for this purpose.) Everything must now be hauled out of the wagons head over heels (and he who knows where to find anything will be a smart fellow.) then the wagons must be all taken to pieces, and then by means of a strong rope stretched across the river with a tight wagon-bed attached to the middle of it, the rope must be long enough to pull from one side to the other, with men on each side of the river to pull it. In this way we have to cross everything a little at a time. Women and children last, and then swim the cattle and horses. There were three horses and some cattle drowned while crossing this place yesterday. It is quite lively and merry here this morning and the weather fine. We are camped on a large bottom, with the broad, deep river on one side of us and a high bluff on the other.

Monday, May 9th Morning cold, within 4 degrees of freezing; we are all on the right side of the river this morning. . . .

Tuesday, May 10th . . .

Wednesday, May 11th Evening. It has been very dusty yesterday and today. (The men all have their false eyes on to keep the dust out.) . . .

as far as eye can reach the road is covered with teams. Plutarch is well and able to drive. Came 23 miles.

Thursday, May 12th Thursday Noon—Beautiful weather, but very dusty. We are camped on the bank of Loup Fork, awaiting our turn to cross. There are two ferry boats running, and a number of wagons ahead of us, all waiting to cross. Have to pay three dollars a wagon for three wagons and swim the stock. Traveled 12 miles today. We hear there are 700 teams on the road ahead of us. Wash and cook this afternoon.

Friday, May 13th It is thundering and bids fair for rain. Crossed the river early this morning before breakfast. (Got breakfast over after a fashion. Sand all around ankle deep; wind blowing; no matter, hurry it over. Them that eat the most breakfast eat the most sand. . . .)

Saturday, May 14th . . . Winds so high that we dare not make a fire, impossible to pitch the tent, the wagons could hardly stand the wind. All that find room crowded into the wagons; those that can't, have to stay out in the storm. Some of the boys have lost their hats.

Sunday, May 15th . . .

Monday, May 16th Evening—We have had all kinds of weather today. This morning was dry, dusty and sandy. This afternoon it rained, hailed, and the wind was very high. Have been traveling all the afternoon in mud and water up to our hubs. Broke chains and stuck in the mud several times. The men and boys are all wet and muddy. Hard times but they say misery loves company. We are not alone on these bare plains, it is covered with cattle and wagons. . . .

Tuesday, May 17th We had a dreadful storm of rain and hail last night and very sharp lighting. It killed two oxen for one man. We have just encamped on a large flat prairie, when the storm commenced in all its fury and in two minutes after the cattle were taken from the wagons every brute was gone out of sight, cows, calves, horses, all gone before the storm like so many wild beasts. I never saw such a storm. The wind was so high I thought it would tear the wagons to pieces. Nothing but the stoutest covers could stand it. The rain beat into the wagons so that everything was wet, in less that 2 hours the water was a foot deep all over our camp grounds. As we could have no tents pitched, all had to crowd into the wagons and sleep in wet beds with their wet clothes on, without supper. The wind blew hard all night and this morning presents a dreary prospect surrounded by water, and our saddles have been soaking in it all night and are almost spoiled! . . .

Wednesday, May 18th—Monday, May 23rd . . .

Tuesday, May 24th . . . I had the sick headache all night, some better this morning; must do a day's work.

Wednesday, May 25th—Monday, May 30th . . .

Tuesday, May 31st Evening—Traveled 25 miles today. When we started this morning there were two large droves of cattle and about 50 wagons ahead of us, and we either had to stay poking behind them in the dust or hurry up and drive past them. It was no fool of a job to be mixed up with several hundred head of cattle, and only one road to travel in, and the drovers threatening to drive their cattle over you if you attempted to pass them. They even took out their pistols. Husband came up just as one man held his pistol at Wilson Carl and saw what the fuss was and said, "Boys, follow me," and he drove our team out of the road entirely, and the cattle seemed to understand it all, for they went into the trot most of the way. The rest of the boys followed with their teams and the rest of the stock. I had rather a rough ride to be sure, but was glad to get away from such lawless set, which we did by noon. The head teamster done his best by whipping and hollowing to his cattle. He found it no use and got up into his wagon to take it easy. We left some swearing men behind us. We drove a good ways ahead and stopped to rest the cattle and eat some dinner. While we were eating we saw them coming. All hands jumped for their teams saying they had earned the road too dearly to let them pass us again, and in a few moments we were all on the go again. Had been very warm today. Thermometer at 98 in the wagon at one o'clock. Towards evening there came up a light thunderstorm which cooled the air down to 60. We are now within 100 miles of Fort Laramie.

Wednesday, June 1st It has been raining all day long and we have been traveling in it so as to be able to keep ahead of the large droves. The men and boys are all soaking wet and look sad and comfortless. (The little ones and myself are shut up in the wagons from the rain. Still it will find its way in and many things are wet; and take us all together we are a poor looking set, and all this for Oregon. I am thinking while I write, "Oh, Oregon, you must be a wonderful country." Came 18 miles today.)

Thursday, June 2nd—Sunday, June 5th . . .

Monday, June 6th Still in camp, husband and myself being sick (caused, we suppose by drinking the river water, as it looks more like dirty suds than anything else), we concluded to stay in camp and each take a vomit, which we did and are much better. The boys and myself have been washing some today. The prickly pear grows in great abundance along this Platte River road.

Tuesday, June 7th Rained some last night; quite warm today. Just passed Fort Laramie, situated on the opposite side of the river. This afternoon we passed a large village of Sioux Indians. Numbers of them came around our wagons. Some of the women had moccasins and beads, which they wanted to trade for bread. I gave the women and children all the cakes I had baked. Husband traded a big Indian a lot of hard crackers for a pair of moccasins and after we had started on he came up with us again making a great fuss, and wanted them back (they had eaten part of the crackers). He did not seem to be satisfied, or else he wished to cause us some trouble, or perhaps get into a fight. However, we handed the moccasins to him in a hurry and drove away from them as soon as possible. . . .

Wednesday, June 8th . . .

Thursday, June 9th . . .

Friday, June 10th It has been very warm today. Thermometer up to 99 at noon. . . . one of our hands, left. . . .

Saturday, June 11th . . . we crossed this afternoon over the roughest and most desolate piece of ground that was ever made (called by some the Devil's Crater) (Not a drop of water, nor a spear of grass to be seen, nothing but barren hills, bare and broken rock, sand and dust). . . .

Sunday, June 12th . . . I have just washed the dust out of my eyes so that I can see to get supper.

Monday, June 13th . . .

Tuesday, June 14th . . . Had a great deal of trouble to keep the stock from drinking the poison or alkali water. It is almost sure to kill man or beast who drink it.

Wednesday, June 15th . . . passed Independence Rock this afternoon, and crossed Sweetwater River on a bridge. Paid 3 dollars a wagon and swam the stock across. The river is very high and swift. . . .

Friday, June 17th . . . Have been washing and cooking today. The mosquitoes are very bad here. . . .

Saturday, June 18th . . .

Sunday, June 19th On our way again, Traveling in the sand and dust. Sand ankle deep—hard traveling. . . .

Monday, June 20th . . .

Tuesday, June 21st We have traveled over a very rough, rocky, road today; over mountains close to banks of snow. Had plenty of snow water to drink. Husband brought me a large bucket of snow and one of our hands brought me a beautiful bunch of flowers which he said was growing close to the snow, which was about 6 feet deep. . . .

Wednesday, June 22nd—Saturday, June 25th . . .

Sunday, June 26th . . . Evening—All hands come into camp tired and out of heart. Husband and myself sick. No feed for the stock. One ox lame. Camp on the bank of Big Sandy again.

Monday, June 27th Cold, cloudy and very windy—more like November than June. I am not well enough to get out of the wagon this morning. The men have just got their breakfast over and drove up the stock. (It is all hurry and bustle to get things in order. It's children milk the cows, all hands help yoke these cattle the d——l's in them. Plutarch answers "I can't. I must hold the tent up, it is blowing away." Hurrah boys. Who tied these horses? "Seneca, don't stand there with your hands in your pocket. Get your saddles and be ready.") . . .

Tuesday, June 28th Still in camp waiting to cross. Nothing for the stock to eat. As far as the eye can reach it is nothing but a sandy desert, and the stench is awful. . . . (all along this road we see white men living with Indians; many of them have trading posts; they are mostly French and have squaw wives.) . . .

Wednesday, June 29th Cold and cloudy. The wagons are all crowded up to the ferry waiting with impatience to cross. There are 30 or more to cross before us. Have to cross one at a time. Have to pay 8 dollars for a wagon; 1 dollar for a horse or a cow. We swim all our stock. . . .

Thursday, June 30th—Sunday, July 3rd . . .

Monday, July 4th It has been very warm today. Thermometer up to 110. . . . I never saw mosquitoes as bad as they are here. Chat has been sick all day with fever, partly caused by mosquitoe bites. . . .

Tuesday, July 5th . . . Chatfield is sick yet; had fever all night. . . .

Wednesday, July 6th—Wednesday, July 13th. . . .

Thursday, July 14th It is dust from morning until night, with now and then a sprinkling of gnats and mosquitoes, and as far as the eye can reach it is nothing but a sandy desert, covered with wild sage brush, dried up with heat; however, it makes good firewood. Evening—I have not felt well today and the road has been very tedious to me. I have ridden in the wagon and taken care of Chatfield till I got tired, then I got out and walked in the sand and through stinking sage brush till I gave out; and I feel thankful that we are about to camp after traveling 22 miles, on the bank of Raft River, about dark; river high.

Friday, July 15th Last night I helped get supper and went to bed too sick to eat any myself. Had fever all night and all day. It is sundown and the fever has left me. I am able to creep around and look at things and brighten up a little; the sun has been very hot today. . . .

Saturday, July 16th . . .

Sunday, July 17th We are traveling through the Digger Indians' country, but have not seen any yet. (We crossed Swamp Creek this morning, and Goose Creek this afternoon. Goose Creek is almost straight down, and then straight up again. Several things pitched out of the wagons into the Creek. Travel over some very rocky ground. Here Chat fell out of the wagon, but did not get hurt much.)

Monday, July 18th Traveled 22 miles. Crossed one small creek and have camped on one called Rock Creek. It is here the Indians are so troublesome. This creek is covered with small timber and thick underbrush, a great hiding pleace; and while in this part of the country the men have to guard the stock all night. One man traveling ahead of us had all his horses stolen and never found them as we know of. (I was very much frightened while at this camp. I lay awake all night. I expected every minute we would be killed. However, we all found our scalps on in the morning.) There are people killed at this place every year.

Tuesday, July 19th—Thursday, July 21st. . . .

Friday, July 22nd Crossed the river before daybreak and found the smell of carrion so bad that we left as soon as possible. The dead cattle were lying in every direction. Still there were a good many getting their breakfast among all the stench. I walked off among the rocks, while the men were getting the cattle ready; then we drove a mile or so, and halted to get breakfast. (Here Chat had a very narrow escape from being run over. Just as we were all getting ready to start, Chatfield the rascal, came around the forward wheel to get into the wagon and at that moment the cattle started and he fell under the wagon. Somehow he kept from under the wheels and escaped with only a good or I should say, a bad scare. I never was so much frightened in my life.) I was in the wagon at the time, putting things in order, and supposed Francis was taking care of him. . . .

Saturday, July 23rd We took a fresh start this morning with everything in order, for a good day's drive. Travel about 5 miles and here we are, up a stump again, with a worse place than we ever had before us to be crossed, called Bridge Creek. I presume it takes its name from a natural bridge which crosses it. This bridge is only wide enough to admit one person at a time. A frightful place, with the water roaring and tumbling ten or fifteen feet below it. This bridge is composed of rocks, and all around us, it is nothing but a solid mass of rocks, with the water ripping and tearing over them. Here we have to unload all the wagons and pack everything by hand, and then we are only on an island. There is a worse place to cross yet, a branch of the same. Have to stay on the island all night, and wait our turn to cross. (There are a good many camped on the island.) and there are camps on each side of it. There is no chance to pitch a tent, and this island is a solid rock, so we must sleep the best way we can, with the water roaring on each side of us. The empty wagons, cattle, and horses have to be taken further up the river and crossed by means of chains and ropes. The way we cross this branch is to climb down about 6 feet on rocks, and then a wagon bed bottom will just reach across, from rocks to rocks. It must then be fastened at each end with ropes or chains so that you can cross on it, and then we climb up the rocks on the other side, and in this way everything has to be taken across. Some take their wagons to pieces and take them over in that way.

Sunday, July 24th . . .

Monday, July 25th Bad luck this morning to start with. A calf took sick and died before breakfast. Soon after starting one of our best cows was taken sick and died in a short time. Presumed they were both poisoned with water or weeds. Left our poor cow for the wolves and started on. . . .

Tuesday, July 26th . . .

Wednesday, July 27th Another fine cow died this afternoon. Came 15 miles today, and have camped at the boiling springs, a great curiosity. They bubble up out of the earth boiling hot. I have only to pour water on to my tea and it is made. There is no cold water in this part. (Husband and myself wandered far down this branch, as far as we dare, to find it cool enough to bathe in. It was still very hot, and I believe I never spent such an uneasy sleepless night in my life. I felt as if I was in the bad place. I still believe it was not very far off.) I was glad when morning came and we left.

Thursday, July 28th . . . Chat is quite sick with scarlet fever.

Friday, July 29th—Sunday, July 31st. . . .

Monday, August 1st. . . This evening another of our best milk cows died. Cattle are dying off very fast all along this road. We are hardly ever out of sight of dead cattle, on this side of Snake River. This cow was well and fat an hour before she died. Cut the second cheese today.

Tuesday, August 2nd . . .

[There is no entry for August 3]

Thursday, August 4th . . . Have also a good many Indians and bought fish of them. They all seem peaceful and friendly.

Friday, August 5th . . . (Snake River Ferry) . . . Our turn to cross will come sometime tomorrow. There is one small ferry boat running here, owned by the Hudson's Bay Company. Have to pay three dollars a wagon. Our worst trouble at these large rivers is swimming the stock over. Often after swimming half way over the poor things will turn and come out again. At this place, however, there are Indians who swim the river from morning till night. There is many a drove of cattle that could not be got over without their help. By paying them a small sum, they will take a horse by the bridle or halter and swim over with him. The rest of the horses all follow and by driving and hurrahing to the cattle they will almost always follow the horses, sometimes they fail and turn back. This Fort Boise is nothing more than three new buildings, its inhabitants, the Hudsons Bay Company officials, a few Frenchmen, some half-naked Indians, half breeds, etc.

Saturday, August 6th . . .

Sunday, August 7th . . . The roads have been very dusty, no water, nothing but dust and dead cattle all day, the air filled with the odor from the dead cattle.

Monday, August 8th We have to make a drive of 22 miles, without water today. Have our cans filled to drink. Here we left unknowingly our Lucy behind, not a soul had missed her until we had gone some miles, when we stopped a while to rest the cattle; just then another train drove up behind us with Lucy. She was terribly frightened and so were some more of us when we found out what a narrow escape she had run. She said she was sitting under the bank of the river, when we started, busy watching some wagons cross, and did not know we were ready. And I supposed she was in Mr. Carl's wagon, as he always took care of Francis and Lucy, and I took care of Myra and Chat, when starting he asked for Lucy, and Francis said "She is in Mother's wagon," as she often went there to have her hair combed. It was a lesson to all of us.* Evening—It is near dark and we are still toiling on till we find a camping place. The little ones have curled down and gone to sleep without supper. Wind high, and it is cold enough for a great coat and mittens.

Tuesday, August 9th Came into camp last night at nine o'clock after traveling 19 1/2 miles with enough water in our cans to make tea for supper; men all tired and hungry. I groped around in the dark and got supper over, after a fashion. . . .

Wednesday, August 10th . . .

Thursday, August 11th . . . Frost this morning. Three of our hands got discontented and left this morning, to pack through. I am pleased, as we shall get along just as well without them and I shall have three less to wait on. . . .

Friday, August 12th . . . Came 12 miles today. Crossed Burnt River twice. Lost some of our oxen. We were traveling along slowly, when he dropped dead in the yoke. We unyoked and turned out the odd ox, and drove around the dead one, and so it is all along the road, we are continually driving around the dead cattle, and shame on the man who has no pity for the poor dumb brutes that have to travel and toil month after month on this desolate road. (I could hardly help shedding tears, when we drove round this poor ox who had helped us along thus far,

---

*The loss of a child in all the confusion and disorder of travel was a fear that haunted many mothers, and indeed similar accounts to this one appear in a number of women's diaries.

and has given us his very last step.) We have camped on a branch of
Burnt River.

Saturday, August 13th—Tuesday, August 16th. . . .

Wednesday, August 17th Crossed the Grand Ronde Valley, which is 8
miles across and have camped close to the foot of the mountains. Good
water and feed plenty. There 50 or more wagons camped around us.
(Lucy and Myra have their feet and legs poisoned, which gives me a
good deal of trouble. Bought some fresh salmon of the Indians this
evening, which is quite a treat to us.) It is the first we have seen.

Thursday, August 18th . . .

Friday, August 19th Quite cold this morning, water frozen over in the
buckets. Traveled 13 miles over very bad roads without water. After
looking in vain for water, we were about to give up as it was near night,
when husband came across a company of friendly Cayuse Indians about
to camp, who showed him where to find water. The men and boys have
driven the cattle down to water and I am waiting for water to get supper.
This forenoon we bought a few potatoes from an Indian, which will be a
treat for our supper.

Saturday, August 20th—Tuesday, August 30th. . . .

Wednesday, August 31st . . . It blew so hard last night as to blow our
buckets and pans from under the wagons, and this morning we found
them (and other things which were not secured) scattered all over the
valley. One or two pans came up missing. Everything is packed up ready
for a start. The men folks are out hunting the cattle. The children and
myself are out shivering around in the wagons, nothing for fires in these
parts, and the weather is very disagreeable.

Thursday, September 1st . . . we have encamped not far from the
Columbia River. Made a nice dinner of fried salmon. Quite a number of
Indians were camped around us, for the purpose of selling salmon to the
emigrants.

Friday, September 2nd Came 5 miles this morning, and are now crossing
Fall (or Deschutes* it is called here) River on a ferry boat pay 3 dollars a
wagon and swim the stock. This river is very swift and full of
rapids. . . .

*The Deschutes River is a tributary of the Columbia River.

Saturday, September 3rd Cool and pleasant. Had a fine shower last night which laid the dust and makes traveling much better. Here husband (being run out of money) sold his sorrel mare (Fan) for a hundred and twenty-five dollars.

Sunday, September 4th . . .

Monday, September 5th Passed a sleepless night last night as a good many of the Indians camped around us were drunk and noisy and kept up a continual racket, which made all hands uneasy and kept our poor dog on the watch all night. I say poor dog, because he is nearly worn out with traveling through the day and should rest at night; but he hates an Indian and will not let one come near the wagons if he can help it; and doubtless they would have done some mischief but for him. Ascended a long steep hill this morning, which was very hard on the cattle, and also on myself, as I thought I never should get to the top, although I rested two or three times. . . .

[Within twelve day's time, Amelia Knight would give birth to her eighth child. As the last entries are read, one must imagine her in the final days of her pregnancy, stumbling over rocks and fallen trees, carrying her youngest child.]

Tuesday, September 6th Still in camp, washing and overhauling the wagons to make as light as possible to cross the mountains. Evening—After throwing away a good many things and burning up most of the deck boards of our wagons so as to lighten them, got my washing and cooking done and started on again. Crossed two branches, traveled 3 miles and have camped near the gate or foot of the Cascade Mountains (here I was sick all night, caused by my washing and working too hard).

Wednesday, September 7th . . .

Thursday, September 8th Traveled 14 miles over the worst road that was ever made, up and down, very steep, rough and rocky hills, through mud holes, twisting and winding round stumps, logs and fallen trees. Now we are on the end of a log, now over a big root of a tree; now bounce down in a mud hole, then bang goes the other side of the wagon, and woe be to whatever is inside. There is very little chance to turn out of this road, on account of timber and fallen trees, for these mountains are a dense forest of pines, fir, white cedar or redwood (the handsomest timber in the world must be here in these Cascade Mountains). Many of the trees are 300 feet high and so dense to almost exclude the light of heaven, and for my own part I dare not look to the top of them for fear of breaking my neck. We have camped on a little stream called Sandy. No feed for the stock except flour and by driving them a mile or so, they can get a little swamp grass or pick brush.

Friday, September 9th Came eight and a half miles. Crossed Sandy 4 times; came over corduroy roads, through swamps, over rocks and hummocks, and the worst road that could be imagined or thought of, and have encamped about one o'clock in a little opening near the road. The men have driven the cattle a mile off from the road to try and find grass and rest them till morning. (We hear the road is still worse ahead.) There is a great deal of laurel growing here, which will poison the stock if they eat it. There is no end to the wagons, buggies, yokes, chains, etc. that are lying all along this road. Some splendid good wagons just left standing, perhaps with the owners names on them. and many the poor horses, mules, oxen, cows, etc. that are lying dead in these mountains. Afternoon—Slight shower.

Saturday, September 10th It would be useless for me with my pencil to describe the awful road we have just passed over. let fancy picture a train of wagons and cattle passing through a crooked chimney and we have Big Laurel Hill. After descending several bad hills, one called Lityle Laurel Hill, which I thought is as bad as could be, but in reality it was nothing to this last one called Big Laurel. It is something more than half mile long very rocky all the way, quite steep, winding, sideling, deep down, slippery and muddy, made so by a spring running the entire length of the road, and this road is cut down so deep that at times the cattle and wagons are almost out of sight, with no room for the drivers except on the bank, a very difficult place to drive, also dangerous, and to make the matter worse, there was a slow poking train ahead of us, which kept stopping every few minutes, and another behind us which kept swearing and hurrying our folks on and there they all were, with the poor cattle all on the strain, holding back the heavy wagons on the slippery road. The men and boys all had their hands full and I was obliged to take care of myself and little ones as best I could, there being no path or road except the one where the teams traveled. We kept as near the road as we could, winding around the fallen timber and brush, climbing over logs creeping under fallen timber, sometimes lifting and carrying Chat. To keep from smelling the carrion, I, as others, holding my nose. . . . I was sick all night and not able to get out of the wagon in the morning.

Sunday, September 11th . . .

Monday, September 12th . . .

Tuesday, September 13th Ascended three steep, muddy hills this morning. Drove over some muddy, miry ground and through mud holes and have just halted at the first farm to noon and rest awhile and buy feed for the stock. Paid 1.50 per hundred for hay. Price of fresh beef 16 and 18 cts. per pound, butter ditto 1 dollar, eggs, 1 dollar a dozen, onion 4 and 5 dollars per bushel, all too dear for poor folks, so we have treated ourselves to some small turnips at the rate of 25 cents per dozen. Got rested and are now ready to travel again. . . . there we are in Oregon making our camp in an ugly bottom, with no home, except our wagons and tent. It is drizzling and the weather looks dark and gloomy. . . .

Wednesday, Sept. 14th Still in camp. Raining and quite disagreeable.

Thursday, Sept. 15th Still in camp and still raining. (I was sick all night.)

Friday, Sept. 17th In camp yet. Still raining. Noon—It has cleared off and we are all ready for a start again, for some place we don't know where. . . .

A few days later my eighth child was born. After this we picked up and ferried across the Columbia River, utilizing skiff, canoes and flatboat to get across, taking three days to complete. Here husband traded two yoke of oxen for a half section of land with one-half acre planted to potatoes and a small log cabin and lean-to with no windows. This is the journey's end.

(finis)

"TOURING FROM MITCHELL, IOWA, TO CALIFORNIA, 1862"

Jane Augusta Holbrook was born in Ohio in 1833. She was a descendant of William Bradford, governor of Plymouth Colony from 1622 to 1656. She and Albert Gould had two small sons when they made the overland crossing to California in 1862. They were traveling with Albert's father, his brother Charlie, and Charlie's wife, Lou. It was Lou with whom Jane spent the greatest part of her days. By 1862 the Indians had become hostile, and though they had assisted emigrants in earlier years, they were now unpredictable and sometimes attacked the wagon trains that came through their territories. Jane Gould's descriptions of one of those attacks and the fears that lingered after are part of the power of her diary. Albert was unwell for periods of time along the journey. The strenuous effort of the river crossings and the constant exposure took their toll of his health, and by the time he brought his family to California, he was seriously ill.

JANE GOULD TOURTILLOTT

Sunday, April 27 Left home this morning, traveled through sloughy prairie, found some hay in an old stack, nooned, and went on to camp four miles from Chickesaw. Camped in a grove near a house where we got grain and hay for our teams. The lady of the house offered us some milk but we had that, came sixteen miles.

Monday, April 28 . . .

Tuesday, April 29 When we got up this morning found a white frost on everything. The weather is rather cool for camping yet. Having no stove it is rather unpleasant cooking. Our road is very good today.

Wednesday, April 30 It was raining this morning when we awoke. Had to get breakfast in the rain, having no tent. . . .

Thursday, May 1 Took nearly an hour to build a fire this morning, the ground was very wet and the wind blew cold from the Northwest. Started late. Bought some hay during the forenoon, carried it in bundles. Nooned in a grove, camped for night near an old house which served as a wind breaker. . . .

Friday, May 2–Thursday, May 15 . . .

Friday, May 16 We are to stay some time to recruit our teams at this place. Most of the women of our company are washing. I am baking. I made some yeast bread for the first time for three weeks, which tasted very good after eating hot biscuits for so long.

Saturday, May 17 Awoke this morning, found it raining hard as it could pour down. The men went out of the wagon, made some coffee and warmed some beans and brought the breakfast to the wagon, which we all crowded into. Used a trunk for a table and made out a very comfortable meal. After eating they put the dishes under the wagon where they remained till four o'clock, when the rain ceased and I left the shelter of the wagon for the first time today. It had grown very cold through the day, most of the men were wet through.

Sunday, May 18 The air was pure this morning but very cold. We were all shivering till about nine, when the sun shone out clear and made the air much warmer. I went out with the children to take a walk and gather flowers. We went in a path through the hazel bushes, saw some hazelnuts laying on the ground. We picked up some and cracked [them] and finding them good, gathered two quarts, which were quite a luxury this time of the year. Some of the women are washing, Sunday though it

Gould family.

be. Two gents and ladies of our company went out horseback riding for their health.

Tuesday, May 20 The weather was fair this morning but towards noon it clouded up. Our company all left us to go on. We were detained waiting for a part of our company. While we were preparing our supper it began to rain so that by the time supper was ready we were slightly dampened and what was worse, we had to eat in the rain.

Wednesday, May 21–Thursday, May 29 . . .

Friday, May 30 . . . Lou and I shot at a mark with a revolver. The boys said we did first rate for new beginners. . . .

Saturday, May 31 . . . Gus was fiddling in the evening and two ladies and one gent came over. Albert played some. They wished us to come up to the house and have a little dance but Albert, feeling rather indisposed, we decline the invitation.

Sunday, June 1. . . .

Monday, June 2 . . . Albert went fishing and caught two fish about as long as one's finger. I cooked one for him. His appetite is rather capricious, he not being well.

Tuesday, June 3 . . . In the afternoon we passed a lonely nameless grave on the prairie. It had a headboard. It called up a sad train of thoughts, to my mind, it seems so sad to think of being buried and left alone in so wild a country with no one to plant a flower or shed a tear o'er one's grave. . . .

Wednesday, June 4 Had an early start this morning. A beautiful morning it was too. Clear, bright and warm. We traveled nearly ten miles. I should think, nooned on the Platte banks. The boys waded across on to an island and brought some chips in a sack which were sufficient to get our supper with. . . .

June 5–June 10. . . .

Wednesday, June 11 . . . Lou and I went calling on a new neighbor who has a sick child. . . .

Thursday, June 12 . . .

Friday, June 13 . . . A lady on our train was thrown from her horse and injured quite severely. They sent on ahead a mile for Doctor, who was in the next train.

Saturday, June 14–Sunday, June 22 . . .

Monday, June 23 'Twas somewhat cloudy this morning when we arose. Had a rough road this forenoon. Stopped for noon near the Platte. It is filled with small islands. The boys have gone bathing. There is a grave of a woman near here. The tire of a wagon is bent up and put for a head and foot stone, her name and age is filed upon it. . . .

Tuesday, June 24 Were up rather late this morning, but had a choice breakfast of antelope meat, which was brought us by Mr. Bullwinkle, some that he bought of the Indians. He brought it for us to cook on shares. It was really delicious. We passed through a small Indian village (a temporary one) this forenoon. We saw that they had over a hundred ponies. There were sixteen wigwams. The road has been better today. Nooned on the Platte banks. While we were eating our lunch there was an Indian Chief rode up on a nice mule, his bridle was covered with silver plates, he had the Masonic emblems on it (he the Indian) was dressed in grand style. He had a looking glass and comb suspended by a string, had a fan and silver ornaments made of half dollars made into fancy shapes. I can't describe half the ornaments that he wore. He was real good looking for an Indian. He wore earrings as much as eight inches long. . . .

Wednesday, June 25 . . . The Indians came around, so many that we hardly had a chance to get our dinners. They were very anxious to "swap" moccasins and lariats for money, powder and whiskey, but we had none to trade. Charley traded a little iron teakettle for a lariat. Two of them shot at a mark with Albert's gun. He beat them. . . .

Thursday, June 26–Friday, June 27 . . .

Saturday, June 28 Did not travel today. Stayed over to let the cattle have a chance to rest. Albert set the tire of his wagon wheels and set some shoes on the horses, which made a pretty hard days work for him. He also shortened the reach for his wagon. The smith here only charges ten dollars for shoeing a yoke of oxen. I did a large washing and Lucy did a large quantity of cooking. Made herself nearly sick working so hard. Gus and I took my clothes to the river to rinse them. Was a little island covered with wild bushes nearby. Gus tried to wade over to it—to hang the clothes but it was too deep so we were obliged to hang them on some low bushes close to the river.

Sunday, June 29—Monday, June 30 . . .

Tuesday, July 1 . . . In the night I heard Mrs. Wilson's baby crying very hard indeed, it had fallen from the wagon. It cried for nearly an hour, he struck his head. . . .

Wednesday, July 2—Thursday, July 3 . . .

Friday, July 4 Today is the Fourth of July and here we are away off in the wilderness and can't even stay over a day to do any extra cooking. The men fired their guns. We wonder what the folks at home are doing and oh, how we wish we were there. Albert is not well today, so I drive. I have been in the habit of sleeping a while every forenoon, so naturally I was very sleepy driving. Went to sleep a multitude of times, to awaken with a start fancying we were running into gullies. After going a short distance we came in sight of a mail station, on the other side of the river there were several buildings. They are of adobe, I suppose. Nearly opposite on this side of the river we passed a little log hut which is used for a store. It was really a welcome sight after going four hundred miles without seeing a house of any kind. . . .

Saturday, July 5—Tuesday, July 8 . . .

Wednesday, July 9 . . . We hear many stories of Indians depredations, but do not feel frightened yet. . . .

July 10 . . .

Friday, July 11 . . . There was a little child run over by a wagon in Walker's train, who are just ahead of us. The child was injured quite seriously. . . . They sent for a German physician that belongs to our train, to see the child that was injured. He said he thought it would get better.

July 12—July 19 . . .

Sunday, July 20 . . . The men had a ball-play towards night. Seemed to enjoy themselves very much, it seemed like old times.

Monday, July 21 . . . Our men went to work this morning to building a raft. Worked hard all day. Half of the men in the water, too. . . .

Tuesday, July 22 . . . Went to work this morning as early as possible to ferrying the wagons over. Had to take them apart and float the box and cover behind. The two boxes were fastened together by the rods, one before to tow in and the other to load. Worked till dark. We were the last but one to cross tonight. Got some of our groceries wet, some coffee, sugar dissolved.

July 24–July 25 . . .

Saturday, July 26 . . . Annie McMillen had lagged behind, walking, when we stopped. The whole train had crossed the creek before they thought of her. The creek was so deep that it ran into the wagon boxes, so she could not wade. A man on horseback went over for her, and another man on a mule went to help her on. The mules refused to go clear across went where the water was very deep, threw the man off and almost trampled him, but he finally got out safe, only well wet and with the loss of a good hat, which is no trifling loss here.*

Sunday, July 27 . . .

Monday, July 28 . . . Came past a camp of thirty six wagons who have been camped for some time here in the mountains. They have had their cattle stampeded four or five times. There was a woman died in this train yesterday. She left six children, one of them only two days old.† Poor little thing, it had better have died with its mother. They made a good picket fence around the grave.

July 29–31, August 1–2 . . .

Sunday, August 3 . . . We passed by the train I have just spoken of. They had just buried the babe of the woman who died days ago, and were just digging a grave for another woman that was run over by the cattle and wagons when they stampeded yesterday. She lived twenty-four hours, she gave birth to a child a short time before she died. The child was buried with her. She leaves a little two year old girl and a husband. They say he is nearly crazy with sorrow. . . .**

August 4 . . .

Tuesday, August 5 . . . Did not start very early. Waited for a train to pass.

*There are two versions of the diary entries between April 27 and July 26. One version, edited by Philip K. Lack, said to have been copied from the original diary by Jane Gould's mother, is published in the *Annals of Iowa*. See vol. 37, 37 (Fall 1964, and Winter, Spring and Summer, 1965), 460–76, 544–59, 623–40, 68–75. A copy of the manuscript is deposited with the Iowa State Historical Library. Another version of the first 89 days of travel is reprinted here with permission of Jane Gould Tourtillott's granddaughter, Mrs. Gertrude T. Bradley, Cupertino, California. A copy of this manuscript is deposited with the Bancroft Library, University of California, Berkeley. The Iowa and California branches of the family have lost touch with each other. It is difficult to establish which text is authentic.

†Here Jane Gould's account, like those of other women diarists, avoids associating the woman's death with the mention of childbirth. See the photograph on p. 134 for a picket fence about a child's grave.

**Compare this account with the fate of Catherine Sager Pringle's mother (p. 39) when the wagon overturned shortly after she had given birth.

It seems today as if I *must* go home to fathers to see them all. I can't wait another minute. If I could only *hear* from them it would do some good, but I suppose I shall have to wait whether I am patient or not. . . .

August 6–9 . . .

Sunday, August 10 Traveled five or six miles when we came to Snake River. We stayed till two o'clock then traveled till about four or five, when *we* from the back end of the train saw those on ahead all get out their guns. In a short time the word came back that a train six miles on had been attacked by the Indians, and some killed and that was cause enough for the arming. In a short time were met by two men. They wanted us to go a short distance from the road and bring two dead men to their camp, five miles ahead.

Albert unloaded his little wagon and sent Gus back with them and about forty armed men from both trains, to get them. We learned that a train of eleven wagons had been plundered of all that was in them and the teams taken and the men killed. One was Mr. Bullwinkle who left us the 25th of last month, at the crossing of Green River. He went on with this Adams train. Was intending to wait for us but we had not overtaken him yet. He was shot eight times. His dog was shot four times before he would let them get to the wagon. They took all that he had in his wagon, except his trunks and books and papers. They broke open his trunks and took all that they contained. (He had six.) It is supposed that they took six thousand dollars from him, tore the cover from his wagon, it was oilcloth. He had four choice horses. They ran away when he was shot, the harnesses were found on the trail where it was cut from them when they went. It was a nice silver one. The Captain had a daughter shot and wounded severely. This happened yesterday. This morning a part of their train and a part of the Kennedy train went in pursuit of the stock. They were surrounded by Indians on ponies, two killed, several wounded and two supposed to be killed. They were never found. One of those killed was Capt. Adams' son, the other was a young man in the Kennedy train. Those that we carried to camp were those killed this morning. Mr. Bullwinkle and the two others were buried before we got to the camp. There were one hundred and fifty wagons there and thirty four of ours. Capt. Kennedy was severely wounded. Capt. Hunter of Iowa City train was killed likewise by an Indian. We camped near Snake River. We could not get George to ride after the news, he *would* walk and carry his loaded pistol to help.

Monday, August 11 . . . The two men we brought up were buried early this morning with the other three, so they laid five men side by side in this vast wilderness, killed by guns and arrows of the red demons. The chief appeared yesterday in a suit of Mr. Bullwinkle's on the battlefield. . . .

Tuesday, August 12 Capt. Adams' daughter died this morning from the effects of her wound. Was buried in a box made of a wagon box. Poor father and mother lost one son and one daughter, all of his teams, clothing and four thousand dollars. Is left dependent on the bounty of strangers. . . . In the evening we took in Mrs. Ellen Ives, one of the ladies of the plundered train. Her husband goes in the wagon just ahead of us. She was married the morning she started for California. Not a very pleasant wedding tour. . . .

Thursday, August 13 . . . After going up the canyon about four miles, we came to a wagon that had been stopped. There was a new harness, or parts of one, some collars and close by we saw the bodies of three dead men, top of the ground. They had been dead two or three weeks. Some one had been along and thrown a little earth over them, but they were mostly uncovered again. One had his head and face out, another his legs, a third, his hands and arms. Oh! it is a horrid thing. I wish all of the Indians in Christendom were exterminated. . . .

Friday, August 15 We were aroused this morning at one o'clock by the firing of guns and yelling of Indians, answered by our men. The Capt. calling, "come on you red devils." It did not take us long to dress, for once. I hurried for the children and had them dress and get into our wagon, put up a mattress and some beds and quilts on the exposed side of the wagon to protect us. The firing was from the willows and from the mouth of the corrall. There were two other trains with us. There are one hundred and eleven wagons of all and two hundred or more men. The firing did not continue long nor do any harm. Our men shot a good many balls into the willows but I presume they were not effectual. We sat and watched and waited till morning. Yoked the cattle and turned them out with a heavy guard and several scouts to clear the bushes. Cooked our breakfast and started. There were ball holes through two or three wagon covers. . . . We nooned in a little valley but kept our eyes open to all that might be hidden in the bushes and behind the rocks. . . . In the night we were all startled by the bark of the kiota [coyote], which sounded very much like the Indians when they attacked us last night. The alarm gun was fired, which awakened us all. After a while we concluded it was the wolves and went to bed. Most of the train slept under the wagons, dug a trench and blockaded on the outside of the wagon. Set up flour sacks and all manner of stuff. We hung up a cotton mattress and some quilts, and slept in the wagon. . . . It is not an enviable situation to be placed in, not to know at night when you go to bed, whether you will all be alive in the morning or not.

August 16–20: [Each night the emigrants dug trenches and kept anxious watch for Indians.]

Thursday, August 21 The road was rough some of the way. Some steep hills to pass over. We saw several Indians today for the first time. They were Snakes. One of them said that he was chief. Three of the men in the Newburn train burned their wigwams in their absence. They came on at noon, were very indignant about it and wanted us to pay for it. Capt. Walker told them who it was that burned them. They got quite a good deal of bread and bacon from different ones from our camp. After being in trouble with them for so long, we are glad to let them be friendly if they will. Albert, Lucy and I went a short way from the road and got our arms full of currant bushes laden with fruit, both red and white. We ate what we wished and had nearly two quarts to eat with sugar for supper. They were real refreshing.*

Saturday, August 23 . . . Oh dear, I do so want to get there. It is now almost four months since we have slept in a house. If I could only be set down at home with all the folks I think there would be some talking as well as resting. Albert is so very miserable too, that I don't enjoy myself as well as I would if he was well. There have been Indians around today begging. We are glad to see them do so now, for all we are disgusted with the wretched creatures.

Sunday, August 24–Tuesday, August 26 . . .

Wednesday, August 27 The first thing I heard this morning was that Mr. McMillen was dead. Died at ten last night. He died quite suddenly. Was buried early this morning. They could not get boards to make a coffin. They dug his grave vault fashion made it just the right size for him, high enough for him to lay in, then wider to lay short boards over him. He was in his clothes with a sheet around him. It seems hard to have to

---

*Gathering berries was a chore usually assigned to the children, but after the Indian attack, only the adults risked moving any distance from the wagons.

bury ones friends in such a way. I do feel so sorry for the poor wife and daughter, strangers in a strange land. All of her relatives are in Ohio. . . . [Gus, the friend and hired man of the Goulds, took over the driving of Mrs. McMillen's team.]

Thursday, August 28 . . .

Friday, August 29 . . . We came to where there have been Indian depredations committed. There were feathers strewn around, a broken wagon, and a large grave with stones over it, a bloody piece of a shirt on it. It had probably two or more persons in it. There was a hat and a nightcap found near, also some small pieces of money. It had been done only a few days. We camped after dark on the Humboldt river for which we were very thankful. . . .

Saturday, August 30–Thursday, September 4 . . .

Friday, September 5 . . . Here we are obliged to separate some of the train go the Honey Lake Route and some the Carson River Route We and 24 others go the latter one. The Capt. goes with the former. We seem like a family of children without a father. We think he is the best Capt. on the road. Some could hardly refrain from shedding tears at parting. Tears came into the Capt's. eyes as he bade them good-bye. . . .

Saturday, September 6 . . .

Sunday, September 7 . . . We hear such discouraging account of our road to Carson River, that the female portion of our little train are almost discouraged. We sat by moonlight and discussed matters till near eleven o'clock. Had quite a number of gentlemen visitors during the evening. They say there is no grass between here and Carson River. If not, I don't know what we can do.

Monday, September 8 . . . Some of the train had a dance, but we did not join them.

Tuesday, September 9 When we arose the men told us that if we were in a hurry with our work we might have time to walk up to see [Humboldt] City. So we hurried. Lucy and I. Mrs. McMillen and Annie went to see. Found it a long walk, I should think all of the way up hill. There are some twenty-five buildings. Some of them rough stone and some adobe, some plastered and some not (on the outside) mostly covered with cotton cloth. We called to see a woman who has a sick husband. They are emigrants. Have only been here a week, are waiting for him to recover.

He has the typhoid fever. They wished to cross the Nevada range this fall. Provisions are very high here. Flour is thirteen dollars per cwt., coffe 45 cts. per pound, sugar three pound for a dollar, bacon 35 cts per pound. Mrs. McMillen and Annie went into a house and stayed for a few minutes. When she came out she said she intended to stay there, and in the face of all the opposition we raised, she stayed. There were none of us that had any more than provisions enough to last through and some I fear, *not* enough, so Gus was obliged to stay too. I was sorry to leave him this side of Cal. as long as he started with us, and is an old acquaintance. I was sorry to leave Mrs. McMillen, it does not seem like a good place for a woman to stay, there are only four families here, the rest are single men. We came on six or eight miles and stopped without much grass for noon (I am just as homesick as I can be). I chanced to make this remark and Albert has written it down. . . .

Wednesday, September 10–Saturday, September 13 . . .

Sunday, September 14 . . . Ellen and Will Jones got a chance to go to Virginia City free of charge for which we were very glad, on account of our heavy load. We are nearly out of provisions too. We have to pay five cts. per lb. for hay. Albert sold his wiffletree* and neck yoke for five and a half dollars. We had ten miles to go to get to the desert. . . . Lou and I walked a great deal. The roads are literally lined with wagon irons and keg hoops and piles of bones every five rods. . . .

Monday, September 15 . . . The road is the worst I ever saw. Lou and I walked the whole ten miles, till we came to within a mile of Ragtown. We saw the trees on Carson River and thought we were almost there but we kept going and going and it seemed as if I never could get there.

September 16–18. [They were now passing through the California mining camps.]

Friday, September 19 . . . Were quite surprised to find Ellen here. She had hired out for a month for twenty dollars. Her husband is at Virginia City working for fifty dollars per month. After coming five miles farther we come to another well and a tent for a station. Found Mrs. McMillen here, just ready to go. Went on together a mile and a half. Lou and I and she and Annie walked so as to visit. [Mrs. McMillen decided not to

---

*The wiffletree (or whiffletree) is the pivoted swinging bar to which the traces of a harness are fastened and by which the wagon is drawn.

remain in Humboldt City, but came with Gus all the way to the coast, where the Goulds met her.]

September 20 . . .

Sunday, September 21 . . . There are houses and public wells all along on the road to Empire City, which is ten miles from Dayton. We stayed at Empire all night. This town is not as large as Dayton, but the streets are full of freight wagons. We see a great many fruit wagons here from Cal. There is a quartz mill here also. Money seems to be plenty. Buildings going up fast. Here is the place to make money, especially for a man without a family can get fifty dollars per month, and board, for most any kind of work and mechanics get more.

September 22–30 . . . [The party came through the Great Redwood Forest, where Jane found the Big Tree Hotel already a prosperous inn. She and Lou danced a "schottische" on the surface of a polished giant redwood.]

Wednesday, October 1 Our roads are rather rough. I walked on before the teams two miles or more, called at a farm for a drink and to rest. Had the pleasure of sitting in a large rocking chair, the first time in five months. They have plenty of fruit trees. Albert called for me and bought some fine grapes, and a pail of tomatoes. The lady of the house gave me some roses and verbenas, they were beautiful and fragrant too. . . .

Thursday, October 2 . . .

Friday, October 3 . . . Arrived at the first house in the settlement in the San Joaquin Valley on this road at ten o'clock. The moon shone brightly, we pitched our tent and got supper. In this part of the country all of the water is pumped by power of windmills. The orchards are not as they are in the States, they are so small and the trees so near together. Every garden and orchard has its windmill to irrigate it. . . .

October 4–5 . . .

Monday, October 6 Lou washed today. The men went to town to see what was to be seen and done. Albert came home sick, went to bed and did not sit up but a few minutes, the rest of the day. . . .

Tuesday, October 7 Are still staying here. Albert seems to be no better. I have almost have the "blues" having to camp out and Albert sick too. . . . This day seems long, I can't set myself to sewing although I have so much to do.

Tourtillott family picture, May 13, 1890; top row: True Trevor, Millie Augusta, Ernest Levi; bottom row: Howard Holbrook, Jane Augusta, Walter Wallace.

Wednesday, October 8 Arose this morning with the intention of going to
town. Lou and I went over a few minutes to call on Mrs. Burkett, she
had a visitor from town, she regaled us with some very fine peaches.
Went to town and pitched our tent. A lady called by the fence and told
us of a house to rent, also gave us some green corn, the first we have
had this year. Charlie went with her to the house, made a bargain,
provided it pleased all around, which it did, we picked up and went right
over. Slept in a house the first time for over five months. The house is
one block east of the Lunatic Asylum. The block which intervenes is
vacant. We are to board the owner of the house, Mr. Bray. The house is
very convenient. We pay ten dollars per month rent. The house is over
half a mile from the business part of town.

Farewell to the old Journal.
(Signed) *Jane A. Gould*

[Albert recovered enough to find work at a lumber mill in Santa Clara
County, but he never fully regained his strength. When he died in
February 1863, Jane went to work as a cook for the same lumber camp.
There she met Levi Lancaster Tourtillott, whose ancestors had sailed
from Bordeaux in 1688, fugitive Huguenots escaping religious
persecution. Tourtillott had come to California in 1860. Jane Gould and
Levi Tourtillott married in 1864 and raised five more children, four sons
and a daughter. Jane's children and great-grandchildren live in
California now.]

A SKETCH
OF HER LIFE

Rebecca Hildreth Nutting Woodson was born in New Hampshire in 1835, and she could trace her family back four generations. Her father was a man full of wanderlust and confidence; he took his growing family from Massachusetts through New York State and then on to Ohio. "I shall never forget how much I enjoyed riding on the canals. . . . I [loved] to sit up on the decks of those boats and see the country." The family kept moving; to Cleveland and then to Rock Island, Illinois. In Des Moines her father caught the "gold fever," and along with his sixteen-year-old daughter and her new husband, the families began "fitting out" for California, "the older ones expecting to amass very large fortunes, and us young ones expecting to have a whole lot of fun." "Us women folks was busy cooking up chickens and nice things for starting on. Oh, we was going to have just a happy time." They crossed the country in 1850.

REBECCA HILDRETH
NUTTING WOODSON

I was born at New Ipswich, N[ew] H[ampshire] Dec. 6th 1835.

My Father was Hiram Nutting, Son of Jonas Nutting and Polly Spaulding.

My Mother was Asenath Tenny, daughter of William Tenny and Polly Butterfield.

My Sister Mary Asenath was born on Sept. 8th, 1833.

My Brother Horace Clarke was born on July 14th, 1837. . . .

Our company on starting consisted of Mr. Hickman, his wife, his son Daniel and his wife, his daughters Catherine, Ella and Mary. Mr. Hickman's men to assist him was Amasa Parker, Robert Bailey and Josiah Sharp. Father's men was David Parks and John Russell. Mr. Hickman had three teams two ox teams and a 4 horse team. Father had two ox teams and our buggy horse which became my riding horse. Daniel Hickman had a two horse team. . . . Mr. Hickman built a boat which he used for a wagon bed when he came to streams to cross. They unloaded the boat, corked and pitched it, and crossed our things in it, swimming the cattle. . . .

Us women folks was busy cooking up chickens and nice things for starting on. . . . Oh we was going to have just a happy time.

On May 8, 1850, the men brought down enough of the oxen to move our wagons and after dinner we made our start. . . .

On May 21st David Parks and Catherine Hickman was married. Father went to Kanesville and got a preacher and such a Chivarie as they got that night was enough to awaken the Seven Sleepers. The newly married couple occupied a wagon for sleeping apartments. The first notice they had of any disturbance was when most of the men and women in the company took hold of the wagon, the men at the tongue pulling, the women at the back pushing, and dragged the wagon a half mile out on the prairie. Then the fun began. Such banging of cans shooting of guns and every noise conceivable was resorted to. The disturbance was kept up until midnight when the crowd dispersed, leaving the happy couple out on the prairie to rest undisturbed until morning when they came walking into camp amid cheers and congratulations. . . .

. . . one week later we came to the grave of a young boy a brother of Mr. Davis. We never knew of what he died   a board at the head of his grave simply said Isaac Davis   giving the town in Wis he had come from

We all felt very sad   He had seemed a very nice boy   was so full of life and fun   He was a lovely singer   His singing could be heard for a long distance on still evenings.   He was only 17 years old   He was a handsome boy. . . .

[The "handsome boy" was only two years older than Rebecca when she saw his grave.]

On the 4th of July we came where we had to cross the Platte again. We found afterwards we should not have crossed at all at Fort Larrimia [Laramie] but should have kept up on the North Side. It was not known then. The men unloaded Mr. Hickman's boat and corked and pitched it and took all our things across in it. The wagons they took apart and put them across on the boat. The cattle they swam across. I think the river was at least a half a mile wide. . . .

Mrs. Baker was very much opposed to crossing in the small boat. She wanted to go to the ferry and cross and not have her things disturbed. She was an extraordinary neat woman. While the rest was content to get things fixed comfortable when we camped at night, her tent had to be fixed just so. It was like stepping into a parlor to go in her tent consequently they were always late getting started mornings   the rest almost always had to help them or go and leave them which they would not do. Their wagon must be arranged just so. It was a picnic for the boys to unload their wagon and put the things in the boat. Some would call her attention one way while the others picked up a load and ran with it to the boat when she looked to see after them another lot would go

when they got her things on   they caught her and her little step daughter and put them in the boat   she went screaming   She knew she should be drown[ed] but she wasnt. . . .

I think it was the 9th of July we had the only death in our company. A Mr. Hinton from Iowa He died with Cholera. He had a wife and children in Iowa. It was very sad. I remember I thought so much of his wife I kept thinking of how little she knew of what he was passing through. Some of the company threw away a wagon there so as to get the boards to put in his grave under and over on the sides of him. There we left him, one of many. . . .

Father had a good deal of advice from an old Mountaineer how to use precaution against cholera. I remember that one was to take a large quantity of pep[p]er sauce and put some in every bit of water we drank when the water seemed the least bit brackish. I do not know how many cases of it father took along. He always thought it was a great help to keep from taking cholera. . . .

We got a good deal of wild game   deer buffalo etc. Sometimes herds of Buffalos would get scared and run almost over our tents. . . . mr. Sharp was the most successful man we had along for catching fish. I can remember how we did relish the fish and venison and Buffalo steaks. . . .

[Past Fort Hall] there was indians met at our camping place   some had been to Fort Loring with hides and traded them off   They was going back well supplied with whiskey   another party was going to Fort Loring with furs and things to sell   They met and camped near us. . . .

We came to what was called the Truckey [Truckee] Route. We crossed the Truckey river 11 times in one day. We passed where the Donner party perished 4 years before. We saw their cabin and many relics. It was a lovely valley. The cabin stood on the mountain side just above the valley. We looked and thought of all that company suffered. . . .

We reached Nevada City on Sept 29th. . . . and the men went to work to build us a house. They cut down a large sugar pine tree on the bank of Woods ravine. They sawed and split out enough shakes to build us a comfortable house. I would not like to tell how much timber father sold besides what he used out of the one tree. It would look as if I was exagerating. I am sure it was one or two hundred dollars worth. It was an enormous tree. The men bought it to board up wells (shafts they called them) that they dug to prospect for gold. . . .

We had just got the house so it was near ready to move into when Daniel Hickman [her sister's husband of less than a year] took sick. We moved into the house. We had Dr. Fagan . . . to attend on Daniel. He called other Drs. They called his disease Tyfus fever. I think now it would be called Typhoid. In spite of all we could do he got worse and on the 16th of Nov he died. We buried him where a church was being built. Ther amid the Cedar and the Pine he is resting yet. . . . [Mary Woodson Hickman was widowed at seventeen and moved back to live with her own family.]

We lived that summer (1851) in tents. We had a long shed made of pine boughs for a dining room. We had not less than 40 boarders all summer (in Nevada City). We had a large room made of boughs for a kitchen. George Woodson hauled logs to the [saw] mill. Our boys Robert Bailey, David Parks and John Russell was still with us. . . . That summer, the last of July I got homesick to see my friends the Hickmans. My sister also was anxious to see them. As we could not both leave at once there was so much work—we decided that John Russell and me should go first to visit them and Mary later on. So we started on Sunday morning on two mules. It was a very warm day. We went [into] Grass Valley 14 miles and had dinner and started on. By the middle of the afternoon I began to get very tired. John said the first place we came to where there was a woman living we would stop for the night. There was little road houses all along the road for the accommodation of travelers. We began enquiring at every one if a woman lived there. It was No all the time but there was one at the next house. The next house she had just gone but there was one at the next so it was until eight o clock. They told us there it was 11 miles to where a woman lived! John said we would have our Supper and feed our mules and go on. He helped me off and told me to go in as he wanted to see to feeding the mules. I steped to the door of the shack, a one roomed cabin with a dirt floor and bunks all up the walls [and] a stationary table. There was four or five men sitting in there. When they saw me step to the door they looked at me so wild I was so scared I ran and called John. I told him I could not go in there alone. He let the man attend to the mules and went in with me. We had our supper. The man brought out our mules and we started on again. Our road was only a trail, it was along the foot hills. There was no moon only starlight. I felt so afraid. There was holes all along that had been dug to prospect for gold. They looked like new-made graves. John would persist in singing. (He could not sing but he could screech and he did it well that night.) It seemed to me his voice could be heard for miles. I begged him not to sing but he sang the louder. I suppose he thought it would Sooth[e] my mind. Indeed it had the opposite effect. In all my life I have never ENJOYED so lonesome and fearful a ride. Everything seemed so weird. . . .

At 11 o'clock we came to a very respectable looking canvass house. John called [and] a man came to the door. John asked . . . if a woman lived there. The man said there was. He said we could stay. He took me into the sitting room and called his wife. She came in. She asked if we wished supper. I told her no that I wanted a bed as soon as convenient. I asked her if I could have a bed near to her. She said she would take her children out of their bed and let me sleep in their bed in her room. That suited me. I think I was asleep in five minutes. I knew no more until I heard John's voice in the morning asking where he could find a place to wash. We had breakfast and resumed our journey.

We got to Mr. Hickman's at 11 o'clock. We took them completely by surprise. How I did enjoy meeting my friends. They seemed more than friends to me. We [were] very much in sympathy and felt a strong tie binding us together. I found that Mr. and Mrs. David Parks had a little daughter born the last day of June, 1851. The next day Ella Hickman took a mule and her and John Russell and me went to Marysville 13 miles. It was a small place then. We had dinner at the United States Hotel. I believe it is there yet. . . .

On October 16th, 1851, Robert Bailey and my sister Mary Hickman was married at our house. A Rev Mr. Martin of Nevada City married them. I think he was a Baptist preacher. They staid a short time at home and moved to Ophier [?] near Auburn in Placer Co[unty] where he engaged in mining. . . .

On April 15th, 1852, George Woodson and me was married. The preacher who married us was J[?] A Warren. He was a Presbyterian preacher and lived in Nevada City. Father went and got him to come and marry us. At that time it was not necessary to have any marriage license. I have never for one moment regreted my marriage to George, and so far as I know or believe neither did he ever regret it. We were very happy so long as he lived. Father moved away the next morning after I was married leaving me a girl of little more than 16 years to cook and do the house work for 20 men, sometimes more. Once during the summer after I was married I had to have some sewing done. We hired a collored man to cook for a month so I could do my sewing. We paid him 75 dollars for the months work. The men did very well with the [saw] mill that summer. . . . That fall Sacramento City burned down. The demand for lumber was so great and there was a great many mills built. . . .

On the 22nd of April, in 1853, our first child was born there on Bear River. We called him William Henry. He was the pride of our lives. He was so much company to me as I had been sometimes 5 months at a time I did not see the face of a white woman. So anyone can guess how much I enjoyed my baby with his big black eyes and dimpled face. . . .

On the first day of March, 1854, we moved into our own house. There was just enough roof to cover our beds table stove etc. but no queen was ever more happy than I was. I sat my baby on a rug (he could not even creep) and went to hunt the Spring.

On October 12, 1854, our second son George Franklin was born. . . .

On July 20, 1856, our son Charles Horace was born. . . .

On June 25th, 1858, our Jasper Alonzo was born. . . .

On April 5th, 1860, our Andrew Jackson was born. . . .

On May 6th, 1862 our oldest daughter was born. We named her Mary Frances. . . .

On March 11th, 1864, our Isabell was born. . . .

On Feb. 8th, 1865, our Warren Grant was born. . . .

On the 6th of December, 1867 (my 32nd birthday) our Walter Sherman was born. . . .

[In March, 1865, Rebecca's husband George died at forty-one. They had been married for seventeen years. A year later, on October 27, 1870, she married Frank Ball. She was thirty-six. It was soon apparent that this new marriage was not a happy one. "We did not get along well on account of our children, both having several. I soon found I could not live with him and keep my chidren." Within five months' time, on March 15th, 1871, she left. It was an extraordinary act because by then Rebecca knew she was again pregnant. "On August 21st, 1871, my youngest child, Ernest Eugene Ball was born. As the children could not bear the thought of having him called anything else but Woodson, their name, And as everybody continued to call me Woodson, both him and me have always gone by that name."

The last entry in Rebecca Woodson's narrative is dated 1909. She was living in Santa Rosa, Sonoma County, California. She was seventy-four years old.]

DIARY, 1867

Barsina Rogers was thirteen years old when her family
took the southern route through Arizona Territory in
1867. She was a careful child who noted the water holes
and the strange configurations of the land, but nothing
daunted her as she continued to practice her penmanship and her grammar through the pages of her diary
along the way.

BARSINA ROGERS FRENCH

Names of places in the Ohio
Cincinnatis is the Capitol of Indiana

Names of persons
Mr. Henning is a carpenter

Names of animals
The Elephant is strong

Names of vehicles
Car run fast a ship sail

Names of something invisible
The Wind blows hard

Names of something used as food
Rice is good meat is fresh

Names of something used as drink
Milk is good to make butter from

Education is needed

+ X 3

Jane recites badly because   She does not study

Boys are apt to quarrel when   they are in ill humor

The dog barks loudly for   he saw danger

We shall always be happy if   we try to do right

I will forgive thy fault if   you will not repeat it

Mary and James have left   their books in their desk

Jane has brought her book   to school

Thomas cries because a boy   struck him

Mary dresses her doll and the   robs she looks very well

ex 4 the dog played with   his mate

Jane gave her doll away

Boys play with their ball

Mary added her a nice dress

The Cow eats her hay

Anna reads her "Bible"

The tree is in its prime

John went with his brother

The Ships how med they so il

The fields look gay with   their flower

The ocean

TABLES

The following tables represent an attempt to provide a useful outline of each diary presented in the course of this book. The component categories reflect questions raised in the text.

	Year of Crossing	Age at Crossing	Marital Status: Unknown	Marital Status: Unmarried	Marital Status: Married	Age at First Marriage	Crossing was Wedding Journey	Number of Children	Ages of Children	Pregnant on Journey	Mother was Pregnant	Reports Births to Other Women
1. Ackley, Mary E.	1852	10		✔								
2. Adams, Cecelia Emily McMillen	1852	adult			to a doctor	20		undetermined				✔
3. Adams, Ellen Tompkins	1863	adult			to a doctor			undetermined				
4. Agatz, Cora Wilson	1866	adult			✔			girl—7 boy—14				
5. Allen, Lucinda Cox Brown Spencer	1847	adult			✔	17		3				
6. Ashley, Algeline Jackson	1852	22			✔		✔	undetermined				
7. Bailey, Mary Stuart	1852	adult			to a doctor			one died before journey				
8. Ballou, Mary	1851	adult			✔			2	10–15			
9. Bell, Catherine	1859	adult			✔				baby born in October	✔		
10. Belshaw, Maria Parsons	1853	adult			✔			undetermined				sister-in-law gives birth
11. Behrins, Harriet F.	1851	adult			✔			1				
12. Bennett, Lucy J. Hall	1845	13	✔			17						
13. Bogart, Nancy Hembree Snow	1845	8	✔			16						✔
14. Brown, Clara	1859	adult slave			✔			3				
15. Buck, Mrs. W. W.	1845	adult			✔			undetermined				✔
16. Butler, America Rollins	1852	adult			✔	24		undetermined				
17. Carpenter, Helen	1857	adult			✔		bride of 4 months	mother had 3 or more			mother travelled with 6-month-old baby	✔

Reports Accidents to Children	Reports Children Dying	Travels with Family	Counts Gravesites Passed	Husband or Father Dies En Route	Mother or Other Woman Dies En Route	Remarries	Number of Children in Remarriage	Reports Indian Threat or Attack	Diary	Reminiscence	Moves After Arrival in Oregon or California
		✓			mother dies of cholera					✓	
		travels with family and twin sister	✓							✓	
			✓						✓		
		✓				✓				✓	
		travels with twin sister who married husband's brother		husband dies on trail in 1847		in 1851 and 1859	second marriage—4; third marriage—1; total of 8			✓	
		✓	✓						✓		
			✓						✓		
										✓	
										✓	
	infant dies		✓							✓	
										✓	
		✓								✓	
				father and uncle killed by Indians		at age 54		✓		✓	
										✓	
										✓	✓
				husband dies in California		in 1864			✓		
	tells of infant dying	✓	✓	tells of 2 men dying in accidents					✓		

	Year of Crossing	Age at Crossing	Marital Status			Age at First Marriage	Crossing was Wedding Journey	Number of Children	Ages of Children	Pregnant on Journey	Mother was Pregnant	Reports Births to Other Women
			Unknown	Unmarried	Married							
18. Cazneau, Jane (Montgomery Cora, pseud.)	1852	adult			✔		✔		9 and 16			
19. Clappe, Louise Knapp Smith	1851–52	adult			✔	21						
20. Clarke, Helen E.	1860	adult		✔								
21. Clarke, Harriet T.	1851	19		✔								
22. Collins, Catherine Wever	1863	adult			✔			2				
23. Colt, Miriam Davis	1862	adult			✔			2				
24. Cooke, Lucy Rutledge	1852	adult			✔			1	under 3			
25. Dalton, Lucinda	1857–58	10		✔								
26. Deady, Lucy Henderson	1846	11		✔		17			mother had 4 and newborn		infant born on trail	
27. Duniway, Abigail Scott	1852	17		✔				mother travels with 9 children				
28. Dunlap, Catherine Cruikshank	1864	adult			✔							
29. Findley, Caroline	1847	adult			✔		✔		born in March '48 after arrival	✔		✔
30. Fish, Mary C.	1860	adult			✔			reports man with 10 children				
31. Foster, Roxana Cheney	1853 and 1854	adult			✔	27		3 and infant born July '54 on trail	daughter—1 son—5 newborn	✔		
32. Fowler, Mrs.	1864	adult			✔							
33. French, Barsina Rogers	1867	13		✔				mother has 5				

Reports Accidents to Children	Reports Children Dying	Travels with Family	Counts Gravesites Passed	Husband or Father Dies En Route	Mother or Other Woman Dies En Route	Remarries	Number of Children in Remarriage	Reports Indian Threat or Attack	Diary	Reminiscence	Moves After Arrival in Oregon or California
									✔		
									✔		
		brother	✔						✔		
										✔	
										✔	
									✔		
		✔							✔		father moved to Australia
										✔	
✔	sister died of Laudanum overdose	mother's parents had gone to Oregon								✔	Oregon to California to Oregon
					mother dies of cholera on trail					✔	
	1 fell out of wagon; 2 in stampede		✔		tells of women who die in childbirth				✔		
		friends and church members; father, mother, cousin come in 1850		husband		✔	4			✔	
			✔							✔	
		father and brother had gone in '49 and '52		husband		?				✔	
										✔	
									✔		

	Year of Crossing	Age at Crossing	Marital Status			Age at First Marriage	Crossing was Wedding Journey	Number of Children	Ages of Children	Pregnant on Journey Crossing	Mother was Pregnant	Reports Births to Other Women
			Unknown	Unmarried	Married							
34. Frink, Margaret	1850	adult			✔			2	10, 12 ?			
35. Frizzell, Lodisa	1852	adult			✔			4				
36. Frost, Mary	1854	8		✔		13		parents travelled with 4 (Mary will have 6)				
37. Fulkerth, Abby E.	1863	adult			✔			2 or 3				
38. Geer, Elizabeth Dixon Smith	1847	adult			✔			7				
39. Goltra, Elizabeth Julia Ellison	1853	22			✔			4				
40. Hall, Maggie	1853	adult	✔									
41. Hanna, Esther	1852	adult			✔	18	set out within hour of wedding					
42. Haun, Catherine	1849	adult			✔		✔	parents travelled with children aged 15 years to 6 weeks			✔	✔
43. Helmick, Sarah	1845	adult			✔	21	✔					
44. Hines, Celinda	1853	adult	✔									
45. Hixon, Adrietta Appelgate	1852	9		✔				parents travelled with 9 children			mother's baby born on trail	
46. Hocken-smith, Mrs. M. S.	un-dated	adult			✔							
47. Hodder, Hallie R.	1863	adult		✔								
48. Hunt, Nancy Zumwatt Cotton	1854	23			✔	17 (husband 19)						reports 3 births en route

Reports Accidents to Children	Reports Children Dying	Travels with Family	Counts Gravesites Passed	Husband or Father Dies En Route	Mother or Other Woman Dies En Route	Remarries	Number of Children in Remarriage	Reports Indian Threat or Attack	Diary	Reminiscence	Moves After Arrival in Oregon or California
son lost									✔		
		✔							✔		
				father				father and uncle killed		✔	
										✔	
		✔		husband dies winter of '48 reports of another man dying		in 1849	2nd husband has 10 children			✔	
				husband dies in later years		✔	3			✔	
				reports man drowning; leaves 2 boys orphaned				✔		✔	
		✔								✔	
children hurt in buffalo stampede	reports infant's death	✔			reports woman dying in childbirth					✔	
		✔								✔	Oregon to California to Oregon
		travelled with large family	✔						✔		
		✔								✔	
									✔		
										✔	returns from Colorado
1 child lost		extended family (aunt/uncle travelled with 11 children in 1849)		husband died in 1854		in 1855	5	threatened attack		✔	

	Year of Crossing	Age at Crossing	Marital Status Unknown	Unmarried	Married	Age at First Marriage	Crossing was Wedding Journey	Number of Children	Ages of Children	Pregnant on Journey Crossing	Mother was Pregnant	Reports Births to Other Women
49. Jones, Mary	1846	adult			✔				child born in January 1847	✔		
50. Kellogg, Jane D.	1852	adult			✔		✔					
51. Kelsey, Nancy	1844	18			✔	15		1	1			
52. Ketcham, Rebecca	1853	18 (?)		✔								
53. Kirkwood, Mrs. John	1845	11 or 12		✔		"nearly 15'						
54. Knight, Amelia Stewart	1853	adult			✔			8th child born on trail	newborn to teens	✔		
55. Logan-Flood, Cloye Burnett	1853	child slave		✔				will marry and have 6 children				
56. Mason, Biddy	1851	adult slave			✔			3				
57. Megquier, Mary Jane	1849	adult			to a doctor							
58. Millington, Ada	1862	13		✔		23		will have 10— 7 survive				✔
59. Minto, Martha Ann Morrison	1844	13		✔		15		will have 2 children within 18 months				
60. Norton, Maria Elliott	1859	adult			on arrival							
61. Ohmertz, Millie	1856	adult			✔							
62. Parker, Inez Eugenia Adams	1848	child— under 5		✔								
63. Parrish, Susan Thompson Lewis	1850	17		✔		20		will have 8— 1 survives			mother gives birth on trail	✔
64. Pengra, Charlotte Emily Stearns	1853	adult			✔	26		1	3 yrs.			✔

Reports Accidents to Children	Reports Children Dying	Travels with Family	Counts Gravesites Passed	Husband or Father Dies En Route	Mother or Other Woman Dies En Route	Remarries	Number of Children in Remarriage	Reports Indian Threat or Attack	Diary	Reminiscence	Moves After Arrival in Oregon or California
										✔	
	✔	parents, 2 sisters, and 2 brothers								✔	
										✔	
									✔		
										✔	
son falls out of wagon; daughter lost			✔	reports man who drowns, leaving wife and children						✔	
										✔	
										✔	
										✔	
14-year-old falls under wagon	family's youngest child dies en route	uncle and aunt and 7 children								✔	
										✔	twice
			✔							✔	
										✔	
		friends, church members, and family								✔	
					reports pregnant woman killed by Indians	in 1886	✔	✔		✔	
			✔	reports of a woman's husband dying					✔		

	Year of Crossing	Age at Crossing	Marital Status			Age at First Marriage	Crossing was Wedding Journey	Number of Children	Ages of Children	Pregnant on Journey Crossing	Mother was Pregnant	Reports Births to Other Women
			Unknown	Unmarried	Married							
65. Pleasants, Mary Smith	1849	adult			✔							
66. Porter, Lavinia Honeyman	1860	20			✔	15		2	infant 5	✔		✔
67. Powers, Mary Rockwood	1856	adult			✔			3				
68. Pringle, Catherine Sager	1847	12–13		✔		16		parents travelled with 7			✔	
69. Rahm, Louisa	1862	adult	✔									✔
70. Richardson, Caroline	1852	adult			✔		✔					
71. Rudd, Lydia Allen	1852	adult			✔							
72. Sanford, Mollie Dorsey	1857	adult			✔		✔	parents travelled with 8				
73. Sawyer, Mrs. Francis	1854	adult			✔							
74. Schultz, Mrs. Theodore	1864	adult			✔							
75. Sharp, Cornelia	1852	adult			✔			undetermined				
76. Smith, Ellen	1846	adult			✔	daughter would marry at 15		9	infant to 15			
77. Stewart, Mrs.	1847	adult			✔			6				
78. Stewart, Agnes	1853	21		✔		will marry at 27						
79. Stewart, Annie	1853	adult			✔			11				
80. Stewart, Helen Marnie	1853	17 or 18		✔								born on trail

Reports Accidents to Children	Reports Children Dying	Travels with Family	Counts Grave-sites Passed	Husband or Father Dies En Route	Mother or Other Woman Dies En Route	Remarries	Number of Children in Remarriage	Reports Indian Threat or Attack	Diary	Reminiscence	Moves After Arrival in Oregon or California
						✔				✔	
	infant dies on trail	✔	✔						✔		
child falls under wagon									✔		
Catherine falls under wagon				father dies	mother dies					✔	
									✔		
		✔	✔						✔		
		✔	✔	gun accident; drowning on trail					✔		
									✔		
										✔	
									✔		
									✔		
one child crippled	eldest daughter dies	✔	✔	husband dies of heart attack; uncle also dies						✔	
		twin sister and husband		husband dies on trail		1851 and 1859	4 in 2nd 1 in 3rd			✔	
		✔	✔						✔		
									✔		
		✔	✔						✔		

	Year of Crossing	Age at Crossing	Marital Status			Age at First Marriage	Crossing was Wedding Journey	Number of Children	Ages of Children	Pregnant on Journey	Mother was Pregnant	Reports Births to Other Women
			Unknown	Unmarried	Married							
81. Stone, Elizabeth Hickock Robbins	1864	adult			✔			more than 5				
82. Tabor, Mrs.	1859 –60	adult			✔			1	infant			
83. Todd, Mary Ellen	1853	10–15		✔								
84. Tourtillott, Jane A. Gould	1862	adult			✔		tells of 1	2	8 and 10			2
85. Tuller, Miriam A. Thompson	1845	18			✔	18						
86. Ward, Harriet Sherril	1853	adult			✔			3	oldest is teen			
87. Warner, Mary Elizabeth	1864	15		✔				parents travelled with 4				
88. Washburn, Catherine Amanda Stansbury	1853	adult			✔			infant born on trail		✔		
89. Waters, Lydia Milner	1855	adult			✔							
90. Welch, Nancy	1844	adult			✔	21		2—she will have 11; 5 survive				
91. Whitman, Narcissa	1836 1838	adult			✔			1				
92. Williams, Velina Stearns	1853	adult			✔			4				
93. Wilson, Luzena Stanley	1849	adult			✔			3 (?)				
94. Wilson, Susan	1853	adult slave			✔			3				
95. Woodson, Rebecca Nutting	1850	14		✔		16		will have 7				
96. Wood, Elizabeth	1851	adult		✔								

Reports Accidents to Children	Reports Children Dying	Travels with Family	Counts Gravesites Passed	Husband or Father Dies En Route	Mother or Other Woman Dies En Route	Remarries	Number of Children in Remarriage	Reports Indian Threat or Attack	Diary	Reminiscence	Moves After Arrival in Oregon or California
										✔	
										✔	
										✔	
2 children fall out of wagons	2 infants		✔	reports man dying in accident; husband dies first winter in Oregon		✔	4	✔	✔		
				husband killed by Indians		✔		✔		✔	
		✔						✔			
				reports drowning of father of 8				✔			
✔								✔			
		travelled with people from same county								✔	
								✔			Oregon to California
								✔			
		✔	✔					✔			
								✔			
										✔	
		✔				✔	✔			✔	
								✔			

OVERLAND DIARIES AND OTHER PRIMARY SOURCES

When the overland journey was done and the work of clearing the land was accomplished, the colonial and frontier periods were remembered by the children and grandchildren of pioneers with costumes and nostalgia.

Ackley, Mary E. *Crossing the Plains—Early Days in California*. San Francisco: privately printed, 1928.

Adams, Cecelia Emily McMillen. "Crossing the Plains in 1852." *Transactions of The Oregon Pioneer Association*, 1904, 288–329.

Adams, Ellen Tompkins. Manuscript Diary, 1863. The Bancroft Library, University of California, Berkeley.

Agatz, Cora Wilson. "A Journey Across the Plains in 1866." *Pacific Northwest Quarterly* 27 (1936): 170–74.

Allen, Lucinda Cox Brown Spencer. "Pioneer of 1847." *Transactions of The Oregon Pioneer Association*, 1887, 74–78.

Ashley, Algeline Jackson. "Crossing the Plains, 1852." Manuscript Diary. The Huntington Library, San Marino. Calif.

Bailey, Mary Stuart. "Journal, Ohio to California 1852." Manuscript Dairy. The Huntington Library, San Marino, Calif.

Ballou, Mary. "I Hear the Hogs in My Kitchen: A Woman's View of the Gold Rush." Quoted in Christiane Fischer, *Let Them Speak for Themselves: Women in the American West, 1849–1900*, pp. 42–47. Hamden, Connecticut: Shoe StringPress, 1977.

Behrins, Harriet Frances. "Reminiscences of California in 1851." Quoted in Christiane Fischer, *Let Them Speak for Themselves: Women in the American West, 1849–1900*, pp. 27–41. Hamden, Connecticut: Shoe String Press, 1977.

Bell, Catherine. Manuscript Diary, 1859. The Bancroft Library, University of California, Berkeley.

Belshaw, Maria Parsons. "Reminiscences, 1853." Edited by Joseph W. Ellison. *Oregon Historical Society Quarterly* 33 (1932): 318–33.

Bennett, Lucy J. Hall. Manuscript Diary, 1845. The Huntington Library, San Marino, Calif.

Bogart, Nancy M. Hembree Snow. "Reminiscences of a Journey Across the Plains in 1843. . . ." Manuscript Diary. The Huntington Library, San Marino, Calif.

Brown, Clara. In *"Aunt" Clara Brown*, by Kathleen Bruyn. Boulder, Col.: Pruett Publishing, 1971.

Buck, Mrs. W. W. "Reminiscences, 1845." *Transactions of The Oregon Pioneer Association*, 1894, 67–69.

Butler, America Rollins. "Diary, 1853." Edited by O. Winthur and R. Goley. *Oregon Historical Quarterly*, December 1940, 337–366.

Carpenter, Helen. "A Trip Across the Plains in an Ox Wagon, 1857." Manuscript Diary. The Huntington Library, San Marino, Calif.

Cazneau, Jane [Cora Montgomery]. *Eagle Pass, or Life on the Border*, 1852. Privately printed, n.d. The New York Public Library.

Clappe, Louise Knapp Smith. *Letters of Dame Shirley*, 2 vols. Edited by Carl I. Wheat. San Francisco: Grabhorn Press, 1933.

Clark, Helen E. *Diary*, 1860. Denver: The Denver Public Library, 1962.

Clarke, Harriet. "Narrative, 1851." Manuscript Diary. The Bancroft Library, University of California, Berkeley.

Collins, Catherine Wever. "An Army Wife Comes West, 1863." *The Colorado Magazine*, 31 (1954): 241–273.

Colt, Miriam Davis, *Went to Kansas*. Watertown, New York, 1862.

Cooke, Lucy Rutledge. *Crossing the Plains in 1852.* Modesto, California, 1923. Bancroft Library, University of California, Berkeley.

Dalton, Lucinda. "Autobiography, 1876." Manuscript Diary. Bancroft Library, University of California, Berkeley.

Deady, Lucy Henderson. "Crossing the Plains to Oregon in 1846." *Transactions of The Oregon Pioneer Association*, 1928, 57–64.

Duniway, Abigail Scott. *Pathbreaking: An Autobiographical History of the Equal Suffrage Movement in Pacific Coast States.* 1914. Reprint. New York: Schocken Books, 1971.

Dunlap, Catherine Cruikshank. *Montana Gold Rush Diary, 1864.* Edited by S. Lyman Tyler. Denver: Old West Publishing Co. and University of Utah Press, 1969.

Findley, Caroline. "A Sketch of Pioneer Days, 1847." *Transactions of The Oregon Pioneer Association*, 1926, 23–29.

Fish, Mary C. "Diary, 1860." Manuscript Diary. The Bancroft Library, University of California, Berkeley.

Foster, Roxana Cheney. "The Third Trip Across the Continent, 1854." In *The Foster Family: California Pioneers*. Edited by Lucy Foster Sexton, pp. 187–98. Santa Barbara, Calif.: Schauer Press, 1925.

Fowler, Mrs. "A Woman's Experience in Colorado, 1864." Manuscript Diary. The Bancroft Library, University of California, Berkeley.

French, Barsina Rogers. "Diary, 1867." Manuscript Diary. The Huntington Library, San Marino, Calif.

Frink, Margaret. *Journal of the Adventures of a Party of California Gold-Seekers, Indiana to Sacramento, March 30, 1850 to September 7, 1850*. Oakland, Calif., 1897.

Frizzell, Lodisa. *Across the Plains to California in 1852.* Edited by Victor H. Paltsits. New York: New York Public Library, 1915.

Frost, Mary Perry. "Experiences of a Pioneer, 1854." *Oregon Historical Quarterly*, April 1916, 123–25.

Fulkerth [also Fulkerath], Abby E. "Diary, April–August, 1863, Iowa to California." Manuscript. The Bancroft Library, University of California, Berkeley.

Geer, Elizabeth Dixon Smith. "Diary, 1847." *Transactions of The Oregon Pioneer Association*, 1907, 153–79.

Goltra, Elizabeth Julia Ellison. "Journal of Travel Across the Plains, 1853." Eugene, Ore.; Lane County Historical Society, 1970.

Hall, Maggie. "Diary, 1853." Manuscript Diary. The Bancroft Library, University of California, Berkeley.

Hanna, Esther. Quoted in Eleanor Allen, *Canvas Caravans: Based on the Journal of Esther Belle McMillan Hanna*, 1852. Portland, Ore.: Binfords & Mort, 1946.

Haun, Catherine. "A Woman's Trip Across the Plains, 1849." Manuscript Diary. The Huntington Library, San Marino, Calif.

Helmick, Sarah. "Recollections of Sarah and Helmick Park, 1845." *Oregon Historical Quarterly*, December 1925, 444–47.

Hines, Celinda. "Diary, 1853." *Transactions of The Oregon Pioneer Association*, 1918, 69–125.

Hixon, Adrietta Appelgate. *On to Oregon! A True Story of a Young Girl's Journey into the West*. Idaho: Signal-American Printers, 1947. New York Public Library.

Hockensmith, Mrs. M. S., undated. Manuscript Diary. The Bancroft Library, University of California, Berkeley.

Hodder, Hallie R. "Crossing the Plains in War Time, 1863." *Colorado Magazine* 10 (1933): 131–36.

Hunt, Nancy Cotton Zumwalt "By Ox-Team to California, 1854." *Overland Monthly* 67 (April 1916), pp. 317- 6.

Jones, Mary A. "Story of My Life, 1846." Manuscript Diary. Bancroft Library, University of California, Berkeley.

Kellogg, Jane D. "Memories, 1852." *Transactions of The Oregon Pioneer Association*, 1913, 86–94.

Kelsey, Nancy. Account of 1844 journey, in George R. Stewart, *The California Trail: An Epic with Many Heroes*. New York: McGraw-Hill, 1962.

Ketcham, Rebecca. "From Ithaca to Clatsop," Parts I and II, edited by Leo M. Kaiser and Priscilla Knuth. *Oregon Historical Quarterly*, September and December 1961, 237–87, 337–402.

Kirkwood, Mrs. John. "Diary, 1845." Manuscript Diary. The Huntington Library, San Marino, California.

Knight, Amelia Stewart. "Diary of an Oregon Pioneer of 1853." *Transactions of The Oregon Pioneer Association*, 1928, 38–56.

Lippincott, Jane. *New Life in New Lands*, 1871.

Logan-Flood, Cloye Burnett. Narrative in Delilah L. Beasley, *The Negro Trail Blazers of California*, p. 123. New York: Negro Universities Press, 1919, reprinted 1969.

Mason, Biddy. Narrative in Delilah L. Beasley, *The Negro Trail Blazers of California*, pp. 109–110. New York: Negro Universities Press, 1919, reprinted 1969.

Megquier, Mary Jane. *Apron Full of Gold: Letters from San Francisco, 1849–1856*. Edited by Robert Glass Clelland. San Marino: The Huntington Library, 1949.

Millington, Ada. "Journal Kept While Crossing the Plains, 1862." *Southern California Quarterly* 59 (1977): 13–48.

Minto, Martha Ann Morrison. "Female Pioneering in Oregon, 1844." Manuscript Diary. Bancroft Library, University of California, Berkeley.

Norton, Maria Elliott. "Diary, 1859." Manuscript Diary. Bancroft Library, University of California, Berkeley.

Ohmertz, Millie. "Female Pioneering, April, 1856." Manuscript Diary. Bancroft Library, University of California, Berkeley.

Parker, Inez Eugenia Adams. "Early Recollections of Oregon Pioneer Life, 1848." *Transactions of The Oregon Pioneer Association*, 1928, 17–35.

Parrish, Susan Thompson Lewis. "Following the Pot of Gold at the Rainbow's End, 1850." Manuscript Diary. The Huntington Library, San Marino, Calif.

Pengra, Charlotte Emily Stearns. "Diary, 1853." Eugene, Ore.: Lane County Historical Society, 1966.

Pleasants, Mary Smith. Narrative in Delilah L. Beasley, *The Negro Trail Blazers of California*, p. 95 et passim. New York: Negro Universities Press, 1919, reprinted 1969.

Porter, Lavinia Honeyman. *By Ox Team to California: Narrative of Crossing the Plains in 1860.* Oakland, Calif.: Oakland Enquirer Publishing Company, 1910.

Powers, Mary Rockwood. "A Woman's Overland Journal to California, 1856." *The Amateur Book Collector* I, nos. 1–5 (September 1950–January 1951).

Pringle, Catherine Sager. Diary, 1847. Manuscript Diary. University of Washington Library; typed copy, The Huntington Library, San Marino, Calif.

Rahm, Louisa. "Diary, 1862." Photocopy. Bancroft Library. University of California, Berkeley.

Richardson, Caroline. "Diary, 1852, From Nebraska to California." Manuscript Diary. Bancroft Library, University of California, Berkeley.

Rudd, Lydia Allen. "Notes by the Wayside En Route to Oregon, 1852." Manuscript Diary. The Huntington Library, San Marino, Calif.

Sanford, Mollie Dorsey. *The Journal of Mollie Dorsey Sanford in Nebraska and Colorado Territories, 1857–66.* Lincoln, Nebr.: University of Nebraska Press, 1976.

Sawyer, Mrs. Francis. "Diary." Manuscript Diary. Bancroft Library, University of California, Berkeley.

Schultz, Mrs. Theodore. "Anecdotes of Early Settlements in Northern Idaho, 1864." Manuscript Diary. Bancroft Library, University of California, Berkeley.

Sharp, Cornelia A. "Crossing the Plains from Missouri to Oregon in 1852." *Transactions of The Oregon Pioneer Association,* 1903, 171–88.

Smith, Ellen. "A Brief Sketch and History of an Oregon Pioneer, 1846," told by her daughter, Algeline Smith Crews. Manuscript Diary. The Huntington Library, San Marino, California.

Spencer, Lucinda Cox Brown Allen. "Pioneer of 1847." *Transactions of The Oregon Pioneer Association,* 1887, 74–78.

Stewart, Agnes. "Diary, 1853." Eugene, Ore.: Lane County Historical Society, 1959.

Stewart, Helen Marnie. "Diary 1853." Eugene, Ore.: Lane County Historical Society, 1961.

Stone, Elizabeth Hickok Robbins. *The Saga of "Auntie" Stone and Her Cabin.* Ed. Nolie Mumey. Boulder, Col.: 1964.

Tabor, Mrs. "Cabin Life in Colorado 1859–1860." Manuscript Diary. Bancroft Library, University of California, Berkeley.

Todd, Mary Ellen. Quoted in J. Faragher and C. Stansell, "Woman and Their Families on the Overland Trail to California and Oregon, 1842–1867." *Feminist Studies* 2 (1975): 150–65.

Tourtillott, Jane A. Gould. "Diary, 1862." Manuscript Diary. From the family of Jane Gould Tourtillott to the author. Photocopy, Bancroft Library, University of California, Berkeley.

Tuller, Miriam A. Thompson. "Crossing the Plains in 1845." *Transactions of The Oregon Pioneer Association,* 1895, 87–90.

Ward, Harriet Sherrill. "A Trip Across the Plains from Wisconsin to California, 1853." The Huntington Library, San Marino, Calif.

Warner, Mary Eliza. "Diary, 1864." Manuscript Diary. Bancroft Library, University of California, Berkeley.

Washburn, Catherine Amanda Stansbury. "Diary from Iowa to Oregon, 1853." Eugene, Ore.: Lane County Historical Society, 1967.

Waters, Lydia Milner. "Diary, 1855." *Quarterly of The Society of California Pioneers* 6 (1929): 59–79.

Welch, Nancy Dickerson. "Narrative, 1844." *Transactions of The Oregon Pioneer Association,* 1897, 97–103.

Whitman, Narcissa. "Diary." In Clifford Drury, *First White Women over the Rockies: Diaries, Letters and Biographical Sketches of the Six Women of the Oregon Mission Who Made the Overland Journey in 1836 and 1838,* 3 vols., pp. 40–59. Glendale, Calif.: A.H. Clark Co., 1963..

Williams, Velina Stearns. "Diary of a Trip Across the Plains, 1853." *Transactions of The Oregon Pioneer Association,* 1919, 178–226.

Wilson, Luzena Stanley. *Luzena Stanley Wilson, Forty-Niner: Memories Recalled for Her Daughter, Correnah Wilson Wright.* Mills College, Calif.: Eucalyptus Press, 1937.

Wilson, Susan. Narrative in Delilah L. Beasley, *The Negro Trail Blazers of California,* p. 122. (New York: Negro Universities Press, 1919, reprinted 1969).

Wood, Elizabeth. "Journal of a Trip to Oregon, 1851." *Oregon Historical Quarterly,* March 1926, 192–203.

Woodson, Rebecca Hildreth Nutting. "Diary, 1850." Manuscript Diary. Bancroft Library, University of California, Berkeley.

LETTERS

Mary E. Colby to her Brother and Sister, From Lebenon, Oregon Territory, February 8, 1849. From the Bennett Family papers, The Haverhill Public Library, Haverhill, Massachusetts.

Jane Jasper, Letters addressed "My Child," October 2, November 20, 1870. Manuscript Collection. Bancroft Library, University of California, Berkeley.

Abby Mansur, Manuscript letters written to her Sister, 1852–54, from Horseshoe Bar, Miner's Ravine, California. Beinecke Library, Yale University. Quoted in Christiane Fischer, *Let Them Speak For Themselves: Women in the American West, 1849–1900,* pp. 48–57. Hamden, Connecticut: Shoe String Press, 1977.

Mary Kincaid to Mamie Goodwater, February 28, 1896, Palmyra, Wisconsin. *To All Inquiring Friends: Letter, Diaries, and Essays in North Dakota,* Ed. Elizabeth Hampsten, Grand Forks: Department of English, University of North Dakota, 1979.

Rose William to Allettie Mosher, September 27, 1885. *To All Inquiring Friends: Letters, Diaries and Essays in North Dakota.* Edited by Elizabeth Hampsten. Grand Forks: Department of English, University of North Dakota, 1979.

Margaret Hereford Wilson to her Mother, Esther Sales, 1850. Manuscript Collection, The Huntington Library, San Marino, California.

Elizabeth Stewart Warner, Letter, 1856 or 1857, published with Diary, 1853, Agnes Stewart. Eugene, Ore.: Lane County Historical Society, 1959.

ACKNOWLEDGMENTS

I find I owe much to different people. Gerda Lerner, who saw the diaries when they were only scattered fragments, believed from the first that they could become the stuff of history. Her vision of what the book might become helped to give it form and bring it into being. Her gift was editing at its most creative.

The American Council of Learned Societies, which gave me a grant-in-aid during the summer of 1977, made it possible for me to read in the manuscript collections of the Bancroft Library, University of California, Berkeley, and the Huntington Library, San Marino, California.

Mrs. Gertrude T. Bradley, granddaughter of Jane Gould Tourtillott, has given permission to publish excerpts from that remarkable woman's diary, and has given me much useful information about Jane Tourtillott's life. The Haverhill Public Library, Haverhill, Massachusetts, led me to Mrs. Barbara Brasseur, who kindly gave permission to publish the letter of Mary E. Colby. My thanks, too, to Alice Kessler Harris who found the Colby letter in the course of her own research and sent it on to me.

Mrs. Virginia Rust, Associate Curator of Manuscripts of the Huntington Library, has been unfailingly generous through the years in helping me use the manuscripts of that fine collection. Richard Rudisill, Curator of Photographic History of the Museum of New Mexico, gave lavishly of his time to show me photographs.

Permission to publish excerpts from the letters and the diary of Mary Rockwood Powers has been granted by W. B. Thorsen, owner and first editor of the American Book Collector. The Powers diary is to be published by Ye Galleon Press, Fairfield, Washington, in 1981.

267

Permission to quote from the diaries of Algeline Ashley, Lucy Hall Bennett, Nancy Hembree Snow Bogart, Helen Carpenter, Angelina Smith Crews, Catherine Haun, Susan Parrish, Lydia Rudd, Harriet Sherril Ward, and from the letters of Jane Jasper and Margaret Hereford Wilson has been granted by the Huntington Library, San Marino, California.

Permission to quote from the diaries of Ellen Tompkins Adams, Catherine Bell, Lucinda Lee Dalton, Mary C. Fish, Mrs. Fowler, Abby E. Fulkerath, Maggie Hall, Mrs. M. S. Hockensmith, Martha Morrison Minto, Caroline Richardson, Mrs. Francis Sawyer, Mrs. Theodore Schultze, Mrs. Tabor, Maria Eliza Warner, Rebecca Hildreth Nutting Woodson is granted by the Bancroft Library, University of California, Berkeley.

Permission to quote from the diary of Esther Belle McMillan Hanna is granted by the Harvey W. Scott Memorial Library, Pacific University, Forest Grove, Oregon.

The Oregon Historical Society has given its permission to print excerpts from the manuscript diaries of Nancy A. Hunt, Catherine Sager Pringle, Harriet T. Clarke, and Jane Kellogg.

The Lane County Historical Society has given permission to quote from the diaries of Elizabeth Goltra, Charlotte Stearns Pengra, Agnes and Helen Marnie Stewart, Catherine Washburn, and from the undated letter of Elizabeth Stewart Warner.

The sources for the photographs in this book are listed below: p. ii, Courtesy Utah State Historical Society; p. 21, Courtesy Nebraska State Historical Society; p. 26, Courtesy Kansas State Historical Society; p. 29 top, Courtesy Western History Department, Denver Public Library; p. 29 bottom, Courtesy the Huntington Library; p. 33, Courtesy Society of California Pioneers; p. 34, Courtesy Oregon Historical Society; p.37, Courtesy Oregon Historical Society; p. 40, Courtesy Oregon Historical Society; p. 44, Courtesy Oregon Historical Society; p. 48, Courtesy Western History Department, Denver Public Library; p. 50, Courtesy *Oregon Historical Quarterly,* December 1925, p. 444; p. 52, Courtesy Oregon Historical Society; p. 63, Courtesy the Huntington Library; p. 65, Courtesy Montana Historical Society; p. 68, Courtesy Western Historical Collections, University of Colorado, Boulder; p. 70, Courtesy Arizona Historical Society; p. 79 top, Courtesy Oregon Historical Society; p. 79 bottom, Courtesy Western History Department, Denver Public Library; p. 86, Courtesy Special Collections, the Library, University of Oregon; p. 87, Courtesy Southern Oregon Historical Society; p. 88, Courtesy Western History Department, Denver Public Library; p. 90, Courtesy Southern Oregon Historical Society; p. 93, Courtesy Lane County Historical Society; p. 93,

Courtesy Lane County Historical Society; p. 97, Courtesy Lane County Historical Society; p. 103, Courtesy Nebraska State Historical Society; p. 107, Courtesy Utah State Historical Society; p. 110, Courtesy Oregon Historical Society; p. 121, Courtesy Society of California Pioneers; p. 126, Courtesy Huntington Library; p. 133 top, original in the collection of the late Mrs. Theodore J. Labhard, San Francisco, present location unknown. Copy print courtesy Richard Rudisill, Santa Fe; p. 133 bottom, Courtesy Richard Rudisill, Santa Fe; p. 134, Courtesy Nebraska State Historical Society; p. 137, Courtesy Southern Oregon Historical Society; p. 139, Courtesy Colorado Historical Society; p. 140–41, Courtesy Miriam Matthew, Los Angeles (two photographs); p. 142, Courtesy Oregon Historical Society; p. 146, Courtesy Oregon Historical Society; p. 149, Courtesy Special Collections, The Library, University of Oregon; p. 156, Courtesy California Historical Society; p. 162, Courtesy Lane County Historical Society, Eugene, Oregon; p. 184, Courtesy Huntington Library; p. 186, Courtesy Southern Oregon Historical Society; p. 200, Courtesy Oregon Historical Society; p. 216, Courtesy Mrs. Gertrude T. Bradley; p. 230, Courtesy Mrs. Gertrude T. Bradley; p. 246, Courtesy Southern Oregon Historical Society.

My thanks are also due to archivists I have never met, whose response to inquiries was both thoughtful and kind. In this regard I think of Richard Engeman of the Southern Oregon Historical Society. I also thank my students at the University of New Mexico, Tracey Emslie and Jessie Rinks, for the valuable family papers they shared with me.

Finally I account my gratitude to my husband and children who have lived with these diaries with good humor almost as long as I have. The manuscript itself was typed—and retyped—many times over by my mother. Her familiarity with the women of the trail is by now at least as great as my own. Her unflagging assistance showed me that there are frontiers of the spirit as large as the frontiers of the land.

When all is said and done, perhaps my greatest debt is to the overland women whose diaries I have lingered over these many years. To them and to their descendants, wherever this book may find them, I give my hearty thanks. I hope I have in small part restored these women who journeyed West to the history of their land.

INDEX

accidents, 13, 15, 39, 41–42, 49, 58, 135, 153, 176, 199, 209, 210, 220, 222, 223

Adams, Cecelia McMillen, 78, 81, 108, 112

Agatz, Cora Wilson, 140–44

"American Society for Encouraging the Settlement of the Oregon Territory," 19

aprons, 85, 88, 168, 193. *See also* clothing.

Ashley, Algeline, 114

Ballou, Mary, 136

Bell, Catherine and Charles, 128

Belshaw, Annie, 108

Belshaw, Candace, 109

Belshaw, George, 108–109

Belshaw, Gertrude Columbia, 16, 108

Belshaw, Maria Parsons, 109, 113

Bennett, Lucy Hall, 38

birth. *See* childbirth

birth control, 109–11

  abstinence, 109, 111

  diaphragms, 109–11

  women's desire for, 109

black families, 136, 138

  education, 138

  life in "New Country," 135–38

black women, 12, 136–38

  as free citizens, 136–38

  as slaves, 12, 136–38

  buying real estate, 138

  laundry work, 138

  in California, 136–38

  in mining camps, 136–38

  in Oregon, 136

bloomers, 98, 105, 128, 141. *See also* clothing.

Blue Mountains, 27, 46, 94–95, 194

Bogart, Nancy Hembree Snow, 43–45

Brown, Clara, 136–38, 155

Brown, John, 136

Brown, Lucinda Cox, 53–54

Buck, Mrs. W. W., 38

buffalo, 14, 42, 176–77

  as food, 176

  stampede, 176

buffalo "chips," 13, 36, 80, 176, 177, 182

burial on the road, 15, 41, 47, 51, 59–60, 108, 129, 130–31, 132, 181, 183, 190, 223, 224–25, 226–27

California, 19

  emigration to, 26–27

  mining in, 136

  slavery in, 136

  walking to, 190

  weather, 19

California Road, 24

canoes, 27, 36, 195, 196, 201

captivity accounts, 69

Carpenter, Helen M., 78, 125–27, 135–36

carriages, use of on journey, 104

Cascade Mountains, 95, 214

Catlin, George (painter), 105

Cayuse Indians, 41, 43, 213. *See also* Indians.

Cazneau, Jane, 30

census data, 109, 150–55

Chapin, Gusta Anderson, 154–55

Cheney, Roxana. *See* Foster, Roxana Cheney.

childbirth, 16, 35, 45, 82, 98–99, 108–109, 129, 152–53

  accounts of, 39, 45, 46, 51, 53, 57, 67, 69, 108–109, 113, 119, 120, 125, 127, 128, 129–30, 183, 216

  and secrecy, 108, 111, 199–201

  conditions on the road, 106, 111, 127

  death of mothers, 111, 153, 223

  taboos, 223

children, 27, 49, 66, 106

  accidents to, 13, 49, 135, 153, 176, 199, 209, 210, 222

  accounts of, 36, 41, 55, 56, 199, 219

  care of, 13, 41, 77, 82, 170–71, 225

  death of, 47, 49, 51, 58, 187

  illnesses of, 13, 82, 220

  lost, 13, 49, 199, 212

  older boys, 119

  orphans, 41

Chimney Rock, 102

division of wagon parties, 25, 174, 227
as survivors, 42
Emigrants Guide to Oregon ana California, 23, 46
emigration
composition of groups, 10
decision to emigrate, 10, 20–22, 28, 30, 35
reasons for, 22, 30
size of, 10, 23, 58, 130, 140, 144
emigration companies, 38
emotional instability on the trail, 25, 54, 88–89, 123–24, 125, 206
excretion, 98–99

families, 31, 42, 171–72
emigration of, 16, 31, 76–77
family life, 42, 43, 131, 149, 150, 158
family planning, 111, 151–52
grouping and regrouping, 89
the "happy death," 131
preservation of, by women, 15–16, 30, 51, 150, 155, 158
separation on the road, 96
size of, 48, 76, 109, 151–52
traveling with, 13, 31, 130, 171–72
fashions, 105–106, 125. *See also* clothing.
Findley, Caroline and James, 57–58
food, 42
baking, 64, 67, 77, 129, 130, 203, 219
berry picking, 53, 83, 192
cooking, 64, 67, 77, 129, 169, 171, 173, 203, 214, 221
from Indians, 53, 103, 154, 192, 199, 213, 221
taken on journey, 23
Fort Boise, 25, 27
Fort Bridger, 25
Fort Hall, 25, 31, 38, 42
Fort Independence. *See* Independence, Missouri.
Fort Kearney, 24
Fort Laramie, 24, 31, 59, 206
Foster, Roxana Cheney, 119, 148
Fourth of July celebrations, 99, 180–81, 192, 222
Fowler, Mrs., 135
Free Negro Admission Article (Oregon), 136

French, Barsina, 11, 144
friendships, accounts of women and, 28–30, 67, 180
Frink, Margaret S., 49, 60, 64, 136, 155
Frizzell, Lodisa, 72, 77, 113
Frost, Mary Perry, 122
Fulkerath, Abby E., 28

Geer, Elizabeth Smith, 54–57, 60
gold, 43, 56, 61, 62, 71
and cholera, 71
"gold fever," 30, 66, 166
gold rush, 56, 58–72, 119, 166
and women, 64, 155
Goltra, Elizabeth, 27
Goodwater, Mamie, 109
grave digging, 47–48, 60, 69, 189–90
gravesites, 71, 131, 182, 188–89, 190, 191
comparison of records, men's and women's, 112
marking, 131, 132, 135, 183, 221, 228
recording by women, 112–14, 115, 128–29, 220
Greeley, Horace, 20
guidebooks, 11, 20, 23, 38, 46

Hager family, 149
Hall, Maggie, 104, 119
Hanna, Esther, 35–36, 80, 104, 114, 115
"happy death," 131
Haun, Catherine, 60
diary excerpt, 165–85
health, as reason for emigration, 166
Helmick, Sarah and Henry, 49
Hines, Celinda, 102
"hired hands," 36, 138
Hixon, Adrietta, 25, 84, 108
Hockensmith, Mrs. M. S., 30
Hodder, Hallie Riley, 132–34
homes
leaving, 14, 28–30, 109, 132, 155
new, 123, 127, 147, 185, 197, 231
homesickness, 147, 169, 224, 228, 229
homesteading, 20, 154
horseback riding, 84, 85, 100, 104, 135, 183, 188, 220
hotels and lodgers, 61, 62, 64, 67, 71, 135
"housekeeping," 148, 180